About Island Press

Island Press is the only nonprofit organization in the United States whose principal purpose is the publication of books on environmental issues and natural resource management. We provide solutions-oriented information to professionals, public officials, business and community leaders, and concerned citizens who are shaping responses to environmental problems.

In 1999, Island Press celebrates its fifteenth anniversary as the leading provider of timely and practical books that take a multidisciplinary approach to critical environmental concerns. Our growing list of titles reflects our commitment to bringing the best of an expanding body of literature to the environmental community throughout North America and the world.

Support for Island Press is provided by The Jenifer Altman Foundation, The Bullitt Foundation, The Mary Flagler Cary Charitable Trust, The Nathan Cummings Foundation, The Geraldine R. Dodge Foundation, The Charles Engelhard Foundation, The Ford Foundation, The Vira I. Heinz Endowment, The W. Alton Jones Foundation, The John D. and Catherine T. MacArthur Foundation, The Andrew W. Mellon Foundation, The Charles Stewart Mott Foundation, The Curtis and Edith Munson Foundation, The National Fish and Wildlife Foundation, The National Science Foundation, The New-Land Foundation, The David and Lucile Packard Foundation, The Pew Charitable Trusts, The Surdna Foundation, The Winslow Foundation, and individual donors.

The Politics of Ecosystem Management

In the memory of Val and Irene Otteson and for Richard

For Margaret and Fred Moote and Joel Viers

The Politics of Ecosystem Management

Hanna J. Cortner • Margaret A. Moote

ISLAND PRESS

Washington, D.C.   Covelo, California

ISLAND PRESS is a trademark of The Center for Resource Economics.

Library of Congress Cataloging-in-Publication Data
Cortner, H. (Hanna)
   The politics of ecosystem management / Hanna J. Cortner and
Margaret A. Moote.
      p.   cm.
   ISBN 1–55963–671–8 (cloth). — ISBN 1–55963–672–6 (pbk.)
      1. Environmental management—Political aspects.   I. Moote,
   Margaret A.   II. Title.
      GE300.C66   1999   98–34883
      363.7′056—DC21   CIP

Printed on recycled, acid-free paper

Manufactured in the United States of America
10 9 8 7 6 5 4 3 2 1

Contents

Preface

As we enter a new century and a new millennium, it is appropriate to consider how our actions individually and collectively will be evaluated by our ancestors in another 100 years. Reflecting back, will they see us as leaders who strived to ensure that they would have a better world? Will they say we chose wisely or selfishly?

If it is to be the former, we believe that society and the professional resource community must own up to the negative as well as the positive consequences of land and water management. We must recognize that despite great strides in some countries and in some resource areas, on the whole our current policy path and traditional approaches to resource management are not ecologically sustainable.

We both have a long-standing interest in the politics of environmental and natural resource decision making. Hanna's particular interest in new ecological approaches to resource management that embrace the overriding goal of ecological sustainability emerged in the early 1990s with her involvement with the USDA Forest Service's New Perspectives program, as a participant in several agency-sponsored workshops. These workshops brought together members of the natural resource community to define, monitor, and evaluate that agency's attempts at integrating ecological sustainability into its management activities. Hanna's interest in new perspectives and ecosystem management grew through work initiated in 1991 on the Society of American Foresters' (SAF) Task Force on Sustaining Long-Term Forest Health and Productivity. Under the steady, guiding hand of Logan Norris that group took the bold, but highly controversial, step within the SAF of explicitly recommending that the professional society become an advocate promoting the understanding and adoption of ecosystem management.

Ann came to her work in community-based process through an interest in indigenous knowledge and new approaches to environmental and land-use planning that incorporate that knowledge. She began working on ecosystem

management as a graduate student at the University of Arizona, and continued as a research fellow at American Forests, participating in a project that
examined the challenges and opportunities for ecosystem management in
mixed-ownership landscapes. Returning to the University of Arizona as staff
in 1995, Ann focused her research on collaborative community-based
approaches to resource management.

We began our collaboration in 1991 with an exploration of the concept
of a paradigm shift in resource management. This collaboration subsequently
grew into a larger team project on the institutional barriers and incentives for
ecosystem management centered at the Water Resources Research Center at
the University of Arizona, where Hanna then served as director. Also central
to the team were Mary Wallace and Sabrina Burke. At the time, Mary was a
senior research specialist at the Water Center, and Sabrina a graduate student
in the School of Renewable Natural Resources. The team's work laid the basis
for this book as it probed the principal themes of ecosystem management,
contrasted the political theories guiding resource management under traditional and ecological approaches, explored the challenges of moving toward
more collaborative forms of public deliberation and intergovernmental coordination, and identified potential areas for research on the political–institutional aspects of ecosystem management.

We both have thus been involved in a number of efforts—jointly, sepa-
rately, and with others—to define, analyze, and advance the principles
embraced by the concept of ecosystem management. On the public record, we
are advocates for more ecological approaches to resource management, for policy changes that foster more open and collaborative decision-making processes, and for innovative ways to manage resources across mixed ownerships. In
this regard, our arguments are prescriptive and normative. We believe it is not
only the duty of scholars of public policy to describe and empirically explain
relationships, but also to promote the ideals of democratic governance and
citizenship. Engaging the civic community in normative discussions about the
current state of science and government, and about the desired future for these
institutions, is a role of the scientific community that needs to be nourished
and sustained. Nonetheless, as students of resource management, we have an
obligation to examine the arguments of critics of ecosystem management who
embrace alternate visions of the best way to ensure a good life and a healthy
planet for our descendants. We also need to be explicit about the social and
political challenges that turning the principles of ecosystem management into
practice will entail, and to warn of potential pitfalls along the way.

One of those pitfalls is assuming that science alone—more science, better
science, heeded science—is sufficient. Thus, we have expended considerable

effort in the past few years in making the argument that underlies this book, that is, ecosystem management is not just about the science, it is also about social and political change. Throughout, we have explored ecosystem management from the perspective that natural resource policies and management philosophies reflect the state of politics as much as they do current science. Natural resource and environmental management have never been based solely in science, or even in the best available science. It is impossible to separate values from science.

Ecosystem management is in large part a social movement that embraces a new philosophical basis for resource management. We therefore need to be explicit about the values and policy preferences that this new approach assumes. Whether society can move toward ecological sustainability will depend on the health of our governance processes and the political will to take the necessary steps to ensure the integrity and resilience of democratic ideals as well as critical ecological processes. Just as other natural resource and environmental policies evolve, so too will ecosystem management, and political considerations will play a large part in determining how it evolves.

In our explorations into the theory of ecosystem management and its political challenges, we have been assisted and influenced by the work of numerous collaborators and partners. We would like to thank the USDA Forest Service Pacific Northwest Research Station and Roger Clark for providing partial support for our initial work on institutional barriers and incentives for ecosystem management. Among the products of that support was a 1994 workshop focusing on preparation of a problem analysis to guide future research and study on the institutional dimensions of ecosystem management. Interactions with participants at that workshop, as well as with members of the SAF Task Force and the Summary Team of the 1995 Ecological Stewardship Conference, were instrumental in shaping our ideas about the origins and future potentials of ecosystem management. Partial financial support from the University of Arizona Agricultural Experiment Station and a sabbatical leave for Hanna granted by the University also assisted us along the way.

We have always enjoyed the interaction and support of a number of current and former colleagues at the University of Arizona and around the country, including Donna Chickering, Jeanne Clarke, Maia Enzer, Gerry Gray, Helen Ingram, Lynn Jungwirth, Dave King, Jonathan Kusel, Mitch McClaran, Al Sample, Denny Schweitzer, and Margaret Shannon. Sabrina Burke, who is now an AmeriCorps leader, made significant contributions to this book both as partner on our overall work in the institutional barriers and incentives project and in shaping our early conceptions of material that appears in chapters

3–5. Laura Tanzer, graduate student in the School of Renewable Natural Resources, assisted with bibliographic chores and figure 4.1. Thanks are also due to Ana Rodriguez who kept things moving smoothly administratively at the Water Center. Barbara Dean and Barbara Youngblood at Island Press have been supportive and forthcoming as our editors. Finally, we are indebted to Mary Wallace, currently a doctoral candidate in the University of Arizona's political science department, for the critical contributions she made as part of our research team, and particularly for her efforts as co-author on early versions of chapters 2–5. Mary's insights into social change and political theory helped us identify and refine many of the points in those chapters, and her ideas are reflected throughout the book. While the assistance and support from colleagues and friends were critical, we nonetheless accept full responsibility for any errors of omission or commission. If we generate further debate and discussion about the efficacy and feasibility of the political challenges of ecosystem management, we will have served our purpose well.

Hanna J. Cortner
Margaret A. Moote
Tucson, Arizona

Chapter 1

Politics and Natural Resources: Making the Link

Politics is often seen as a dirty word. We lament when issues become "politicized" or when "science gives way to politics." An old adage is "never discuss politics, religion, or sex." Yet, just as the biophysical world is the basic component of natural resources, politics is the "stuff" of people interacting with each other, their environment, and governmental institutions, all of which affect nature greatly. Resource management is, at heart, a very political process. All too often in the past we have tended to separate politics and resource management. Our theme is their interconnection. We believe natural resource management cannot be assessed from a solely biophysical perspective: to ignore sociopolitical influences is folly.

We are particularly interested in examining the interconnections between politics and new ecological approaches to resource management. While ecological approaches to natural resource management go by many names—ecological stewardship, integrated resource management, landscape ecology, watershed management—arguably the most commonly used term is *ecosystem management*, and it is the one used here. Our task is to place ecosystem management in a political context by asking whether, and if so how, ecosystem management could improve natural resource management by forging more effective political connections among humans, nature, science, and government.

In ecosystem management, objectives for land and water resources are related first and foremost to the integrity, vitality, and resilience of ecosystem structures and processes. Ecosystem management reflects growing public awareness and acceptance of environmental values, increasing emphasis of the

1

scientific community on ecological concerns such as biodiversity, and changing professional practices that view conditions of the land to be just as relevant as the quantities of outputs that can be produced.[1] Key to ecosystem management is the goal of ecological sustainability—protecting and restoring critical ecological components, functions, and structures in perpetuity so that future as well as current generations will have their needs met[2]—a concept that links politics and natural resources.

Although in recent years a number of books and articles have focused on the shift to ecosystem management, the political aspects of such a shift are often overlooked. Certainly, with few exceptions,[3] they are not examined in-depth. Questions of politics are often viewed as discrete issues, reflecting our historical tendency to separate humans from resources, the political from the technical, the social from the physical. It is an illusion, however, to see politics separate from ecosystem management; an inclusive, synergistic view is needed.

Government and Politics

In a day and age when citizens are increasingly questioning the role of government in any number of policy areas—welfare, health, and educational policy as well as in natural resources—it is instructive to ask the questions, "Why politics?" and "Why government?" To understand the need for government, we first turn to John Dewey's explanation in his classic work, *The Public and Its Problems*, and examine the relationship between the individual (private) and the collective (public) sphere. According to Dewey:

> We take then our point of departure from the objective fact that human acts have consequences upon others, that some of these consequences are perceived, and that their perception leads to subsequent effort to control action so as to secure some consequences and avoid others. Following this [clue], we are led to remark that the consequences are of two kinds, those which affect the persons directly engaged in a transaction, and those which affect others beyond those immediately concerned. In this distinction we find the germ of the distinction between the private and the public. When indirect consequences are recognized and there is effort to regulate them, something having the traits of a state comes into existence.[4]

Public problems arise when the consequences of people's actions are on such a scale that collective rather than individual action may be necessary to provide relief and repair. Government is that set of institutions established to allow collective action and make decisions binding on the whole of society. Inevitably, conflicts are generated as people explore the causes of public problems and organize to deal with them. Authoritative choices are made among values, determining who gets what, when, and how.[5] That is politics. It is "no more possible to 'take politics out of government' than it is to take emotion out of marriage."[6]

Changes in people, places, physical and social technologies, wishes and ideas, catastrophes, and personalities are the "raw material of politics" that give rise to public problems. To understand the ebb and flow of the functions of government, one must start "quite literally from the ground up; from the elements of place—soils, climate, location, for example, to the people who live there—their numbers and ages and knowledge, and the ways of physical and social technology by which, from the place, and in relationship with one another, they get their living."[7] The dynamics and politics of policy formation, administrative organization, and management result from such origins. As society is confronted with more and more changes and as public problems become more numerous, the sphere of government activity typically increases; individuals are, in effect, compelled to use government as an instrument of the shared public interest.

Philosophies of Democracy

Democratic government occurs when decisions are made directly by the people or through elected representatives and their agents in an open process of discussion and decision. Democracy can take several forms, and in a surprising trend, American citizens are returning to a debate about democracy that first took place in the decades following the revolutionary war. In public meetings and ad-hoc community forums around the country, citizens can be heard debating Jeffersonian versus Madisonian democracy.[8] Although Alexander Hamilton and John Adams, among others, were influential in the design of early government, it is the tension between the political thought of Thomas Jefferson and James Madison that has had the most profound effect on democracy in the United States. Madison and Jefferson had quite different views of democracy.

Madison's primary concern was "the mischief of factions," and the ability of one group of citizens to control government (the "tyranny of the majority") with no protections for the interests of minorities. Because the "latent causes of faction are . . . sown in the nature of man,"[9] direct democracy would not solve the problem; in a direct democracy there would be no controls preventing individuals without virtue to usurp control. Instead, Madison believed, a large republic with a system of constitutional checks and balances would serve to diffuse power among many parts so that no one part dominated the whole. Reflecting the Madisonian view of human nature, the Constitution divided power among three branches of government and between the national and state governments. Madison's influence on the Constitution is so significant that he is often called the "Father of the Constitution."[10]

For Thomas Jefferson, who was in Paris as U.S. minister to France at the time of the constitutional convention, the ultimate concern was that government be placed in the hands of the people: "I know of no safe depository of the ultimate powers of the society but the people themselves; and if we think them not enlightened enough to exercise their control with a wholesome discretion, the remedy is not to take it from them, but to inform their discretion by education."[11] Jefferson feared strong executive power, believed states should be the primary jurisdiction for domestic affairs, favored strict construction of the Constitution, and advocated the use of frequent constitutional amendment or entirely new constitutions to reflect the will of emergent majorities. He believed democratic ideals could best be realized by public participation in government. He was more tolerant of dissent than many of his contemporaries and supported the right of every citizen to be protected from government actions. During the debate over the ratification of the Constitution, he urged Madison to add a bill of rights.[12] While Madison's views framed the Constitution, Jefferson's beliefs in the value of people and their rights to participate fully in political decision making remain ideals toward which democratic governance continues to strive, particularly as our society faces the challenge of rejuvenating American democracy.

Political Health

Today, just as society's ability to achieve long-term resource sustainability is of concern, so is the health and resilience of current political processes. Writers increasingly discuss the "malaise" of the American political system, "degenerative democracy," the "death" of discourse, and the "erosion" of authority, language that evokes many of the same images people use when discussing ecosystem health.[13] Moreover, people are increasingly separating themselves from government. Polls track a significant decline in citizen trust in government. Where polls once showed that 75 percent of Americans trusted their government, today only 25 percent do so. Like the term *politics*, the term *government* is increasingly used in a pejorative sense. People have lost confidence in government.[14]

While many reasons are given for the overall malaise in politics, the policy prescriptions for remedying the situation generally fall into two major categories. The first perspective emphasizes declining levels of civic engagement and calls for rebuilding social capital. By analogy to physical and financial capital, social capital "refers to features of social organization such as networks, norms, and social trust that facilitate coordination and cooperation for mutual benefit."[15] Such social connections and associations are seen as requisite for either private or public problem solving.

In perhaps the most definitive assessment of American democracy ever written, the nineteenth-century French political observer Alexis de Tocqueville viewed America's tendency to work through associations of all types as one of the nation's peculiar strengths:

> The political associations which exist in the United States are only a single feature in the midst of the immense assemblage of associations in that country. Americans of all ages, all conditions, and all dispositions, constantly form associations. They have not only commercial and manufacturing companies, in which all take part, but associations of a thousand other kinds—religious, moral, serious, futile, extensive, or restricted, enormous or diminutive.[16]

Today, however, some observers are greatly concerned about declining levels of civic engagement.[17] According to one prominent social scientist:

> By almost every measure, Americans' direct engagement in politics and government has fallen steadily and sharply over the last generation, despite the fact that average levels of education—the best individual-level predictor of political participation—have risen sharply throughout this period. Every year over the last decade or two, millions more have withdrawn from the affairs of their communities.[18]

Since a strong reservoir of social capital is viewed as a precondition for the effective performance of political institutions, the remedy is to rebuild lost social capital. According to this perspective, action is generated from within the local community; it emphasizes strengthening the network of civic associations. The focus is on social and cultural factors.

The second perspective views the lack of civic engagement as a symptom, not the cause of the ills of current American democracy. It places renewed emphasis on governmental performance and strengthening of governmental structures. While noting that promising collaborative associations and public–private partnerships have indeed emerged, proponents of this perspective argue that only government has the capability to deal with the scope and magnitude of the truly critical and divisive problems confronting society today. Acknowledging the travails facing the modern state, proponents also see the need to reconceptualize the role of government and improve its ability to achieve agreement on the need for a sustainable future. According to this view, more attention needs to be given to improving statecraft (i.e., the art of governance) by reinvigorating existing governmental institutions and inventing new forms that can coordinate, mediate, and intervene on critical issues.[19] The focus is on structural factors.

The debate over structural versus social and cultural factors might simply be said to boil down to a question of whether to send in the community organizers or the constitutional lawyers. Without trying to play Solomon and splitting the baby, we view both approaches as necessary and more complementary than contradictory. Democracy is dependent on statecraft as well as individual and community responsibilities. The way society chooses to deal with its public problems (i.e., the politics it chooses) will necessarily shape how ecosystem management fares in the next century.

What Follows

Chapter 2 begins the task of making more explicit the link between politics and resource management by tracing the patterns of politics interwoven throughout the history of natural resource management in the United States. It begins with politics and resource management at the birth of the United States, and traces their history to the present. Policies put in place at the turn of the twentieth century overcame the earlier national propensity to view resources as unlimited and gave rise to the Progressive conservation movement. While the Progressive Era had many beneficial results for natural resources, it also left a politics of expertise, of maximum sustained yield, and of interest. These patterns of politics have prevailed even in recent years, when they have come increasingly under attack by those who raise significant questions about society's ability to achieve long-term resource sustainability. At the same time, threads of a more integrative, ecologically based approach to resource management can be found throughout history. We trace these roots of ecosystem management to the present.

Chapter 3 provides a more comprehensive overview of the theory of ecosystem management. It identifies the major themes that have emerged from the literature on ecosystem management, and uses the concept of "paradigm shift" (a revolution in the ideas, values, assumptions, and methodologies that guide scientific inquiry) to explore in greater detail how ecosystem management differs from traditional resource management. This chapter also outlines the major criticisms that have been targeted at ecosystem management and suggests that these criticisms are evidence that ecosystem management is currently in a "preparadigm" stage—not yet fully accepted either professionally or publicly.

While ecosystem management concepts and practices are increasingly being implemented and interwoven into planning, management, and science, there are, nonetheless, a number of fundamental political challenges to be confronted. Much of the politics of ecosystem management involves how those challenges are approached, by whom, and with what results. Chapters 4 and 5 begin the process of describing in more detail the political challenges confronting ecosystem management.

Chapter 4 examines more closely the potential inconsistencies and contradictions in the principles of ecosystem management introduced in chapter 3. Unlike many critics who see these inconsistencies as fundamental flaws, we view them as policy paradoxes that can be resolved, and if they are resolved, will improve efforts to implement ecosystem management. Three categories of paradoxes are examined: paradoxes of decision making, scale, and sustainability.

Chapter 5 presents a potentially larger hurdle to the acceptance of ecosystem management as a significant new paradigm for natural resource policy and management—the political theories that undergird traditional resource management in the United States. To understand these theories, we move our discussion to well before the formation of the American republic and examine how the ideas of the seventeenth- and eighteenth-century Enlightenment period affect how we think about nature and politics. Vestiges of Enlightenment thought, we argue, are the foundations for the ideas underlying our traditional patterns of politics and traditional resource management paradigm. Enlightenment ideas still define our relationships with nature, structure our scientific study of natural and social processes, and frame our laws and institutions. Alternative political principles inherent in ecosystem management are also identified in chapter 5, and we argue that these emerging principles must be institutionalized within our governance system if a significant paradigm shift is to occur in natural resource management.

Chapters 6 and 7 address the potential for resolving ecosystem management paradoxes and for institutionalizing alternative theoretical principles. Chapter 6 focuses on social capital and community associations. As noted above, some observers are concerned about declining levels of civic engagement and the loss of social capital. On the other hand, there is evidence that local citizens are increasingly organizing to have a greater voice in natural resource issues that affect their lives. This chapter examines the recent trend toward community-based conservation. It discusses the opportunities and barriers for achieving collaborative ecosystem management by building social capital and creating a more civic society that changes the ways humans relate with one another, with government, and with nature. Chapter 7 addresses the need to strengthen governmental institutions and policies to better connect people, government, and ecosystems. A number of possible ways to improve the art of statecraft and enhance the capability of government to apply ecosystem management principles are discussed, including reexamining laws, rethinking property rights and responsibilities, changing administrative organizations and processes, and aligning market operations with the goal of sustainability.

The concluding chapter, chapter 8, summarizes the social and political changes necessary to achieve actual policy performance and assesses, within a democratic context, the potential for making those changes. It argues that the extent to which we realize these changes will determine how effectively and rapidly ecosystem management will move toward ecological sustainability.

NOTES

Complete bibliographic information for all works mentioned in each of the chapter Notes can be found in the References section at the end of the book.

1. Grumbine, "What is ecosystem management?"; and Christensen et al., "The report of the Ecological Society of America Committee on the Scientific Basis for Ecosystem Management."

2. World Commission on Environment and Development, *Our Common Future*, p. 43. See also Christensen et al., "The report of the Ecological Society of America Committee on the Scientific Basis for Ecosystem Management"; U.S. Department of the Interior Bureau of Land Management, *Ecosystem Management in the BLM.*

3. See, for example, Gunderson et al., *Barriers and Bridges to the Renewal of Ecosystems and Institutions*; and Lee, *Compass and Gyroscope.*

4. Dewey, *The Public and Its Problems*, p. 12.

5. This definition of politics draws from both Lasswell, *Politics*; and Easton, *A Framework for Political Analysis.*

6. Wilson, *American Government*, p. 3.

7. Gaus, *Reflections on Public Administration*, pp. 8–9.

8. For example, "All Things Considered," National Public Radio, broadcast of October 16, 1996. See also, Ingram and Wallace, "An 'empire of liberty'"; and Goergen et al., "An old model for building consensus and a new role for foresters."

9. Federalist Paper #10. Federalist Paper # 51 also spells out Madison's philosophy on factions and the large republic as remedy.

10. Banning, "Madison, James." See also Meyers, *The Mind of the Founder.*

11. Jefferson in a letter to William Charles Jarvis, 1821, reproduced in Padover, *Thomas Jefferson on Democracy*, pp. 89–90.

12. Peterson, "Jefferson, Thomas." The story of President Jefferson's administration, however, is how he "escaped, evaded, or overcame the restraints of his own first principles in order to provide the strong leadership the country required," p. 1017.

13. See, for example, Lipset, "Malaise and resiliency in America;" Schneider and Ingram, *Policy Design for Democracy*; Sandel, *Democracy's Discontent*; and Collins and Skover, *The Death of Discourse*. We recognize the inadequacy of the health analogy as applied to ecosystems as well as to political systems. Nonetheless, it is a powerful metaphor that is currently shaping discussion in both politics and ecology.

14. Nye et al., *Why People Don't Trust Government*; Dionne, *Why Americans Hate Politics*; and Lipset and Schneider, *The Confidence Gap*.

15. Putnam, "Bowling alone," p. 67; and Putnam, "The strange disappearance of civic America."

16. de Tocqueville, *Democracy in America*, p. 114. Bellah et al., in *Habits of the Heart*, call *Democracy in America* "the most comprehensive and penetrating analysis of the relationship between character and society in America that has ever been written," p. vii.

17. One culpable villain is television. See Putnam's case against television in "Tuning in, tuning out." Also see Norris' rejoinder in "Does television erode social capital?"

18. Putnam, "Bowling alone," p. 68.

19. Caldwell, "The state as a work of art"; Lemann, "Kicking in groups;" and Tarrow, "Making social science work across space and time."

Chapter 2

The Evolution of Ecosystem Management

The United States has historically gone through at least two distinct periods in its attitudes and approaches to resource management. The first, predominant in the eighteenth and nineteenth centuries, was marked by unfettered exploitation of the nation's resources. The second, the Progressive Era of the late 1800s and early 1900s, reflected a significant shift in attitudes and continues to influence resource management today. As we shall see, while challenges to the management philosophy established during the Progressive Era have periodically been mounted, to date none has totally replaced the patterns of politics and professional approaches that emerged out of that era.[1] In this chapter we explore these two major periods, the patterns of politics that emerged during each, and their effects on the political and ecological landscape. This chapter also examines the changes in social values, scientific knowledge, and professional practice that may be propelling us toward another significant shift—a shift toward ecosystem management.

Wild and Free

The American ideal of a free and independent life developed early in United States history. The United States was a land of plenty, abounding in fertile grasslands, endless forests, and wild game. An eighteenth-century French naturalist reported that the most striking feature of the new American nation was "an almost universal forest," starting at the coast, "thickening and enlarging . . . to the heart of the country."[2] A seventeenth-century observer in New England wrote of the limitless flocks of passenger pigeons that blanketed the skies, "that to my thinking had neither beginning nor ending, length nor breadth, and so thick that I could see no Sun." Meriwether Lewis observed much the same thing as he descended the Ohio River in 1803 at the onset of his epic journey across the American continent.[3] Artist and naturalist George Catlin recorded grasses so tall riders were "obliged to stand erect in our stirrups, in order to look over its waving tops."[4] The federal government's main concern was to allocate goods and resources to private parties, making way for individuals to seek their own fortunes and ways of life. A nation was being built, and the land played an important cultural and economic role in fostering that development.

Government policies in the nineteenth century, such as the Homestead Acts and the Desert Land Act, encouraged western settlers to take advantage of the country's resource abundance and promoted an agricultural society. These policies were largely based on Jeffersonian concepts of democracy and eulogized "yeoman farmers"—individual farmers who cultivated their own small parcels of land. Settlers were beckoned with promises of free land and unrestrained opportunities for resource development. Converting the nation's vast expanse of land into small farms would avoid, it was believed, the European model of wealthy landlords and poor tenants. Instead, yeoman farmers improving their own land would create economic development. The nation's future would rest on a propertied class in a propertied nation. The frontier epitomized individualism, self-reliance, and independence, values that are still ingrained in mythic images of the American West and American society.[5]

As implemented, however, the settlement laws of the nineteenth-century society were, more often than not, the focus of unscrupulous land grabs, ensuring that speculators and corporations rather than hardy yeoman farmers reaped the benefits.[6] To encourage western expansion, railroad companies were given large land grants, totaling some 180 million acres of the public domain. As the nation experienced a period of tremendous growth and industrialization after the Civil War, railroad owners and other industrialists became extremely wealthy and ruthlessly powerful by exploiting resources and corrupting legislators. The wealth of these "robber barons," as they came to be known, concentrated political as well as economic power in the hands of a few.

Americans reveled in the seemingly infinite wealth of nature. As one noted ecological historian concluded: "The people of plenty were a people of waste."[7] They fished, hunted, and cleared land with abandon. Thomas Jefferson defended the often inefficient and wasteful practices of his fellow Virginia planters by declaring that the nation had "such quantities of land to waste as we please," plentiful enough to last "to the hundredth and thousandth generation."[8] As the nation grew, so did the impacts on the land. The expansion of the railroads linked the hinterlands to markets in growing urban centers eager for grain, lumber, and livestock, all of which were necessary for an expanding nation and growing economy;[9] the tall grass prairies of the Midwest were plowed to make way for cultivated grain; vast acreages in the Northeast and Great Lakes regions were deforested; and the Southwest became overrun with cattle and California and the Great Basin with sheep. Lands in the South were rapidly depleted by cotton and tobacco farming. Toward the end of the century, wild game hunting for commercial sale in markets became popular and wildlife populations were decimated. Buffalo hunters killed thousands of bison a day, often taking just tongues or hooves as trophies, and leaving the carcasses to rot. The passenger pigeons that once seemed limitless were killed by the millions.

Early conservation writers did warn of the dangers of resource waste, but they had little political impact at the time. Nonetheless, many of the themes of conservation that would later become policy in the Progressive Era are evident in nineteenth-century writings. In novels such as *The Pioneers*, *The Prairie*, and *The Deerslayer*, James Fenimore Cooper described the moral, spiritual, and aesthetic value of wilderness and deplored its thoughtless destruction. His frontier hero, Leatherstocking, condemns the exploiters with these words: "They scourge the very earth with their axes. Such hills and hunting grounds have I seen stripped of the gifts of the Lord, without remorse or shame!"[10] In 1832 George Catlin wrote of the overgrazing, overcutting, and general land misuse in the United States and proposed that some lands be removed from the public domain and be reserved as national parks. The writings of the Transcendentalists Ralph Waldo Emerson and Henry David Thoreau fostered a new appreciation by Americans of the unique heritage and benefits of forests and wilderness. Perhaps most significantly, in 1864 George Perkins Marsh published *Man and Nature*, which claimed humans were subverting the balance of nature to their own detriment.[11] So significant is the publication of his book, that Marsh, rather than later Progressive leaders, is considered the father of the modern conservation movement. Despite these early warnings, however, government policy did little to stand in the way of building a mighty industrial empire; "great waste [was] permitted for great accomplishment."[12]

Conservation and the Progressive Era

At the close of the nineteenth century, attitudes and policies toward natural resource use changed dramatically. Americans began to express their disgust with the robber barons and the widespread destruction of natural resources and implemented laws intended to restore democracy and conserve resources. At the turn of the century the Progressive Era was born, and with it the conservation movement. The nation began to deal with a variety of issues on a scale that had not been seen before. A changing economy, increased immigration, the growth of cities, labor–capital conflict, and the sociocultural tensions of a complex pluralistic polity led to increased demands for regulation.[13] The Progressives sought to curb the power of monopolies by regulating corporate practices and reducing control by party machines.[14] They supported women's suffrage, direct election of senators, primary elections, and other innovations in direct voter participation, such as the initiative, referendum, and recall. Whereas Madison and the other framers of the Constitution had believed that "liberty could best be preserved by distancing the people from the immediate operations of government, the Progressives saw no conflict between republican liberty and participatory democracy."[15]

The turn of the century conservationists epitomized the Progressive ideal. Along with many other policy areas, resource policy moved from fostering private entrepreneurship to supporting greater governmental regulation, establishing a collective rather than private purpose. Gifford Pinchot, a leader of the new conservationists and the first chief of the Forest Service, declared that the goal of resource management was to produce "the greatest good of the greatest number in the long run."[16]

The conservation movement spawned by the Progressive Era yielded impressive results throughout the twentieth century. Professional resource agencies were established to manage forest reserves, national parks, and public domain lands. The reclamation program that developed the water resources of the semi-arid and arid West made possible rich agricultural areas and great metropolitan areas. Controls were put on the harvesting of wildlife and fish resources and the grazing of livestock on public lands. Forests were regenerated. Schools were established to educate a cadre of professional resource managers and research scientists.

The approach to resource management Pinchot and the other leading conservationists took reflects an utilitarian philosophy. Resources are first and foremost to be used. Wrote Pinchot, "the first great fact about conservation is that it stands for development," and "the first duty of the human race on the material side is to control the use of the earth and all that therein is."[17] Nature was viewed as subservient to human wants and needs. Moreover, the duty to develop and use resources extended first to present generations. Under the utilitarian philosophy, neglecting the use and development of resources is considered as wasteful as their destruction. The interests of future generations would be served because in using resources to the fullest, the current generation did so without waste.[18]

A second view of nature, which became known as preservationism, also grew in popularity during the Progressive Era. John Muir, who worshiped nature as sacred and divine, is often identified as its major proponent.[19] According to preservationism, development is not the first and foremost use of resources, wilderness has an innate right to exist, and aesthetics are considered as important as human use. The disagreements between Muir and Pinchot over the grazing of sheep in the national forests and a dam in Yosemite's Hetch-Hetchy Valley have often been used as a convenient marker to distinguish the split in the early conservation movement between utilitarian and preservationist schools of thought.

Over the years, efforts to preserve wildlands from development resulted in the establishment and expansion of the nation's wilderness system, and the continued elevation of the importance of aesthetic and recreational uses.[20] Despite the gains made by the preservationists, however, the dominant philosophy and approaches guiding resource management for most of the twentieth century remained those of the utilitarian conservationists.[21] They institutionalized a set of values and fostered a set of political relationships that, while innovative for their time, may not be either ecologically or politically sustainable from today's vantage point. The legacy of the last 100 years of resource management is a politics of expertise, of maximum sustained yield, and of interest.

The Politics of Expertise

The Progressive conservationists were concerned about the waste, destruction, and inefficiency they saw in the use of natural resources. Using the latest scientific research, they sought to eliminate wasteful use by efficiently managing resources. Conflicts between competing claimants to resources were to be resolved by experts through the "scientific calculation of material benefits rather than through political struggle."[22] Rational, neutral, fact-based science was advanced as the appropriate basis for agency administration, as well as a way to solve social problems. This coincided with the promotion of positivistic thought throughout the sciences, in which empirical measurements were the mark of "good science." The Progressives assumed that their commitment to efficiency in conservation would spill over into other areas of social life, guaranteeing American advantage in the commercial struggle among nations and ensuring a more democratic society.[23] So central was the Progressive's belief in the salutary effects of efficiency that one leading commentator has termed this commitment the "gospel of efficiency." Conservationists "envisaged ... a political system guided by the ideal of efficiency and dominated by technicians who could best determine how to achieve it."[24]

Despite their overall political support for more participatory democracy, the Progressives advocated a civil service independent of political control or influence, free to determine the most efficient means to implement policy decisions. "Administration," wrote Woodrow Wilson, "lies outside the proper sphere of politics.... Administrative questions are not political questions.... Politics is thus the special province of the statesman, administration of the technical official."[25] Wilson and other Progressives criticized the Constitution for weakening the executive branch and allowing special interests to prevail in the legislative branch. They sought to reestablish the Constitution on a more scientific basis, one in which administrators would be neutral conduits for executive leadership. It followed then that "since natural resource matters were basically technical in nature ... technicians, rather than legislators, should deal with them."[26] Professionalism became epitomized by the neutral expert who based decisions solely on empirical measurements and methods and who was in no way tainted by political ideology. The belief that fundamental allocation decisions regarding resource use should be entrusted to experts (i.e., to themselves) permeated agencies and professional schools, and still does to this day.

The reliance on expert opinion has come to have profound consequences for the role of the public in political matters. Experts render judgment, eclipsing the role of the citizen. Under the claim of professionalism and objectivity, experts convey an image that they are not involved in politics or decisions involving values, all the while making decisions reflecting their own professional values and definitions of the public interest.[27] The public has become an object to be studied, managed, and converted to the experts' position. As a result, experts often discount public opinion, assuming that

> public opinion is of good quality when it agrees with their own views and of poor quality when it does not. The logic is this: they, the experts, are well informed; the public is poorly informed. Give the public more information, and it will agree with them. But what if even after being better informed, the public still does not agree? Rarely do the experts conclude that the public has a different point of view equally worthy of consideration.[28]

Ironically, the Progressive proponents of greater participatory politics created a governance structure that discourages public input to decision making.[29]

The Politics of Maximum Sustained Yield

The primary goal of resource management—sustained yield—evolved from the utilitarian values of the Progressive Era. Intuitively, sustained yield is a logical and laudable goal: no more is taken than can be replenished. As it has come to be implemented, however, the concept of sustained yield has been modified to mean taking the maximum supply a system can withstand (i.e., the furthest point to which production can be pushed without impairment of the resource's ability to reproduce).[30] One of our colleagues calls this "managing at the edge of harm."

As practiced, *sustained yield* means providing a continuous supply of market-oriented goods: in forest management the timber cut; in range management the stocking rate; in water management the acre-foot. In the late 1930s and early 1940s, sustained-yield forestry also came to embrace the goal of community stability, that is, harvesting timber at a rate that would sustain mill operations and thus provide economic stability for timber dependent communities.[31]

The sustained-yield approach became incorporated into the statutes of agencies. The statutory mandates of both the Forest Service (the Multiple-Use–Sustained-Yield Act and the National Forest Management Act) and the Bureau of Land Management (the Federal Land Policy and Management Act), for example, specifically direct these agencies to employ a multiple-use–sustained-yield approach to resource management. More often than not, however, these agencies adjusted the multiple-use concept to correspond to their primary resource production objective: timber in the case of the Forest Service and grazing in terms of the Bureau of Land Management. Although sustained yield is not specifically mentioned in the legislative mandate of agencies such as the National Park Service or the Bureau of Reclamation, they too have traditionally managed for maximum sustained yield of a single resource: visitor use in the case of the parks, and water supply in the case of water resources.[32]

With the advent of the environmental movement in the late 1960s and 1970s, resource management agencies and legislation started to respond to changing social values concerning the environment. In the 1970s, agencies began to give amenity resources more consideration. Nevertheless, public demands for habitat protection, recreation, and pollution control continued to be mainly viewed as constraints to output maximization rather than the goal of natural resource management. While analytical tools became more sophisticated, allowing trade-offs between development and environment to be more visibly displayed, these tools still reflected a bias toward maximum sustained yield. Linear programming models developed to balance multiple uses were unable to maximize more than one use at a time, and so maximized a single use while treating all other uses as constraints to management for that use. They also ignored or "guesstimated" values for uses that could not be quantified in monetary terms.[33] Furthermore, the models could only accommodate a limited number of "multiple uses." An eminent forest ecologist recalls that

> we did not even consider biological diversity—only game fish and wildlife.... Furthermore—and, perhaps, most important—*multiple use* emphasized outputs of goods and services as the objective of management rather than the stewardship of the ecosystem. It was output oriented rather than sustainability oriented.[34]

Another forestry analyst notes that at best, the agencies achieved "multiple use by adjacency: in a given forest, timber was harvested in one place, recreation services provided somewhere else, and 'multiple use' was claimed overall."[35] Almost four decades after the Multiple-Use–Sustained-Yield Act was passed, the concept of multiple-use–sustained-yield "still awaits becoming a definable system of land management."[36]

The Politics of Interest

Over the years, the resource agencies that formed during and following the Progressive Era developed close political connections with the beneficiaries of their programs. Scholars and journalists wrote of agencies "captured" by vested interests. Grazers, for example, dominated the Bureau of Land Management, timber companies and loggers the Forest Service, and local water users the Bureau of Reclamation and Army Corps of Engineers.[37] The larger public interest was subjugated by a politics of interest that concentrated power in economic beneficiaries who sought the maximum yield of specific resource outputs and dollars.

The environmental laws enacted during the 1970s began to break down the power the traditional interests exerted on resource policy. These laws required the explicit consideration of environmental values during decision making and placed greater emphasis on citizen review and involvement. The elaborate administrative frameworks and publicly-open planning and environmental assessment processes established by these laws made it more difficult for development interests to influence management. The preponderance of federal legislative activity tended to centralize decision making in Washington, assuring the primacy of "national interests" defined by national interest groups. Washington-based agency leadership and Washington-based interest groups took center stage. Decisions with local impacts often became separated from local interests, history, and culture.[38]

The great majority of environmental groups adjusted to the dominance of expertise and interest group-driven politics by joining rather than attempting to change the political process.[39] They hired their own scientific experts and established themselves as legitimate participants in scientific debate at the national level. Although environmental groups secured a place at the negotiating table and are now powerful organizations, critics note "the interest group identity for mainstream environmentalism seems more entrenched than ever."[40] Through lobbying, lawsuits, and appeals, these groups have strengthened the role of environmental values in governmental decision making, but they have done little to build a sense of public responsibility in public affairs.

Furthermore, resource agencies often promote divisiveness and polarization of interests by asserting authority rather than sharing power.[41] Rather than eliciting public participation from as representative a sample of the public as possible, traditional agency procedures tend to foster participation by organized interest groups while limiting participation by the general public.[42] Participation is narrowed into a set of techniques designed to secure administrative compliance with statutory and regulatory requirements. Citizens are encouraged to use formal means of communicating with the agency, even though they consistently prefer methods that involve two-way communication and shared decision making.[43] Methods such as formal hearing periods do not address effectively public concerns because they do not provide an adequate forum for representing public interests; they exclude the general public in favor of polarized interest groups; and they do not allow for constructive information exchange between the public and agency professionals.[44] When the public is viewed only as a set of interest-holding individuals, public participation becomes merely a means to gather data for an information base. Individuals and interest groups are not encouraged to interact with the agency or with one another in forums where they can learn about themselves and about one another. Rather than leading to public learning, current participation techniques often lead to political alienation.[45] This lack of dialogue increases controversy over resource management decisions, because it forces interested parties to take extreme stands in order to be heard.[46] Citizens also become more likely to use other forums, such as the courtroom, to affect agency decisions and policies. In such venues, issues are cast in narrow legal terms and decisions declare winners and losers, further polarizing the interests. Rather than realizing the harmonious balancing of factional concerns envisioned by Madison, the emergence of competing groups has created an often dysfunctional system of interest group acrimony and gridlock.[47]

The Roots of Ecosystem Management

By the late 1980s, the focus of resource management had begun to shift from sustained yield to sustainability. Whereas sustained yield focuses on outputs and views resource conditions as constraints on maximum production, sustainability makes resource conditions the goal and a precondition for meeting human needs over time. Outputs, then, are interest on the resource capital.[48] Leading resource management professionals began to ask whether the multiple-use–sustained-yield concept, *as implemented*, had outlived its usefulness. Three increasingly integrated themes began to emerge: a concern for the health of ecosystems; a preference for both landscape-scale and decentralized management; and a new kind of public participation integrating civic discourse into decision making.

By the early 1990s, these refrains had melded into the philosophy of ecosystem management. Reports by the National Research Council, the Ecological Society of America, and the Society of American Foresters all called for applying new ecological approaches to the study and management of resources.[49] By 1994, eighteen federal agencies had adopted some form of ecosystem management as a guiding policy.[50] State and local resource agencies began implementing ecosystem management projects and landscape level studies as well.[51]

Ecosystem management, however, is not just a product of the 1990s. Its roots go back to changes in social values, scientific knowledge, and professional and administrative practice that have occurred in spite of the dominance of Progressive Era ideas, laws, institutions, and political relationships that are the legacy of the past 100 years. Just as the seeds for the Progressive conservation movement can be found in ideas advanced by the conservation writers of the nineteenth century, the precursors of ecosystem management can be traced to ideas and events that developed in an earlier time.

Changing Societal Values

In the United States, conservation leaders from George Perkins Marsh to John Muir and Aldo Leopold were early proponents of many of the themes that characterize ecosystem management today. During the 1930s, for example, Aldo Leopold championed ecological integrity and a changed human relationship to land and nature, elaborating both a land ethic and a Golden Rule of Ecology. His famous land ethic calls for enlarging the

> boundaries of the community to include soils, waters, plants, and animals, or collectively: the land. . . . In short, a land ethic changes the role of *Homo sapiens* from conqueror of the land-community to plain member and citizen of it.

Leopold's Golden Rule of Ecology asserts that "a thing is right when it tends to preserve the integrity, stability, and beauty of the biotic community. It is wrong when it tends otherwise."[52]

During the decades that followed Leopold's writings, several scholars wrote texts and articles that attempted to bring ecosystem concepts into natural resource management,[53] but it was not until more recently that such concepts began to take firmer root in national policy, finding fertile ground prepared by the burgeoning environmental movement. In what one environmental historian has called "the gospel of ecology,"[54] environmentalists utilized the term *ecosystem* as an emblem of their earth-connectedness and holism.[55] To a large extent, ecosystem management may rightfully be viewed as rooted in environmentalism and the evolving socio-political values captured by that movement.[56]

Some observers consider Rachel Carson the mother of the environmental movement. Her 1962 book on the dangers of pesticides, *Silent Spring*, was the first to raise significantly public consciousness about the damages that indiscriminate use of human technologies inflicted on natural environments.[57] Heightened public concerns about pesticides and pollution of air and water were made graphic by images of the burning Cuyahoga River, oil-soaked birds on the beaches of Santa Barbara, and smog-filled air in Birmingham, Alabama. These and similar catastrophes eroded the American devotion to technology and growth, which began to be usurped by a belief that there were environmental limits to growth.[58] On April 22, 1970, the first Earth Day was held, drawing an estimated 20 million Americans to public celebrations and demonstrations and firmly establishing environmental quality as a national concern. Support for environmental values would continue to grow. Studies of public attitudes would consistently identify a shift from traditional values embracing materialism, efficiency, wealth, and hierarchical power to environmental values emphasizing living in harmony with nature, quality of life, and limits to economic growth.[59] Today, most Americans strongly support environmental values and consider themselves environmentalists.[60]

A flurry of federal environmental and natural resource management legislation in the late 1960s and throughout the 1970s institutionalized the public's embrace of environmental values. Public desire to protect the nation's natural resource heritage was reflected in new laws, including, for example, the Wilderness Act of 1964, the Wild and Scenic Rivers Act of 1968, the National Environmental Policy Act of 1969, the Clean Air Act of 1970, the Federal Water Pollution Control Act Amendments of 1972 (Clean Water Act), and the Endangered Species Act of 1973. Much of this federal legislation was enacted in response to complaints by the general public—and particularly national environmental groups—that agencies were more amenable to commodity than environmental values and oblivious to the popular "limits to growth" and "balance of nature" concepts.

Public support for environmental programs and values remained high in the 1980s during the conservative administrations of Presidents Ronald Reagan and George Bush.[61] A major goal of both the Reagan and Bush administrations was to reduce the size and scope of the federal government, and this was reflected in their environmental and natural resource management policies. Although for the most part the Reagan and Bush policies did not support environmentalist values, some of the policy initiatives of the 1980s, such as improved accounting procedures to weed out below-cost timber sales and the inclusion of cost-sharing requirements for financing federal water projects, utilized concerns about the size of the federal budget to reduce environmental impacts and achieve environmental goals.[62] An emphasis on market approaches to resource conservation and privatization married environmental protection to the need for financial economy and political decentralization.[63] It became increasingly recognized that to conserve financial resources, the nation must manage its land and water resources with extensive cooperation among public agencies and, to the extent possible, with private individuals and organizations. Reliance on decentralized decision making and collaborative partnerships began to be woven into the philosophy of resource management.[64]

By the late 1980s, the Reagan–Bush administrations' critique of big Washington government and the need to decentralize decision making to those communities closest to the resource also began to resonate more broadly: with local economies and communities hit hard by federal laws and decisions that favored resource protection over extraction; with scientists who saw the need to better link human wants and needs to an understanding of the dynamics of ecosystem processes; and with agency visionaries who realized that the problems they experienced in fulfilling their mandated public involvement requirements could never be corrected unless they dispersed and shared power. The result was a shift in public sentiment; rather than favoring centralized protection of environmental quality and natural resources, support grew for decentralized approaches that assumed local communities could in some ways be better equipped to steward natural resources. Collaborative ventures began emerging among industry, environmental interests, agencies, and local citizens to address natural resource and environmental issues. Increasingly, these efforts focused on integrated planning and management of ecosystems or watersheds.[65]

Growing Scientific Knowledge

Ecosystem science, with its emphasis on holistic understanding of the interconnections among all components of nature, is a second root of ecosystem management. The ecosystem concept developed out of the science of ecology, but ecosystem science has since broadened to include several other sciences, including the social sciences.

Ecosystem ecology was born in 1935, when British ecologist Arthur Tansley defined an ecosystem as "the whole *system* (in the sense of physics) including not only the organism-complex, but also the whole complex of physical factors forming what we call the environment of the biome—the habitat factors in the widest sense."[66] Tansley's definition was greatly influenced by the then currently popular systems theory, which looked at any system, be it sociological, chemical, or physical, as a whole made up of patterns of structure and behavior. Tansley and other early ecosystem ecologists applied the physical concept of equilibrium to the organization and maintenance of ecosystems.[67]

A major shift in ecosystem ecology was initiated by the Hubbard Brook studies in the 1960s and 1970s, which set several precedents in ecosystem research. Where previous ecosystem ecologists had focused on energy flow through the ecosystem, the multidisciplinary Hubbard Brook scientists focused on flow of matter, particularly water and nutrients. They also offered a means of bounding terrestrial ecosystems in terms of hydrologic watershed boundaries, which permitted applied research.[68] Building on background meteorologic and hydrologic data from the USDA Forest Service, this team began exploring streamwater chemistry and the details of the input–output relations of a small watershed within the Hubbard Brook Experimental Forest. Researchers, looking at the ecosystem as a unit, manipulated the whole ecosystem to study its construction, function, and responses to disturbance and stress. One of the advantages of the Hubbard Brook site was that it provided several similar watersheds, which allowed some to be used as controls for experiments conducted on adjacent watersheds. Over 150 scientists took part in studies of the Hubbard Brook ecosystem in the 1960s and 1970s, producing over 450 research articles. The Hubbard Brook studies were the basis for future ecosystem research design and provided extensive empirical data for use in resource management.[69]

In the 1970s, as research into ecological systems expanded, ecosystem ecologists realized they did not have the necessary expertise in disciplines like chemistry, geology, and hydrology to study fully ecosystem functions. Furthermore, they realized that population dynamics, genetics, and other sciences previously dismissed as "reductionist" provided critical information for analysis of ecosystem function. Ecosystem ecologists began collaborating with scientists from other disciplines in studies they called "ecosystem science."[70]

As social values and law—and therefore political interests and government funding—placed greater emphasis on ecological impacts, scientific research

began to pay more attention to the impacts of environmental change and to
the societal and ecological benefits of noncommodity and amenity resources.
A more diverse cadre of scientific disciplines were integrated into the evolving discipline of ecosystem science.[71] In 1985, an eminent ecologist wrote:

> Until recently ecology was generally considered to be a subdivision
> of biology dealing with the relationships of organisms with the
> environment. Then, during the environmental awareness decade,
> 1968 to 1981, a school of ecosystem ecology emerged that con-
> siders ecology to be not just a subdivision of biology, but a new
> discipline that integrates biological, physical and social science
> aspects of man-in-nature interdependence.[72]

Other "trans-disciplinary" or "synthesis" disciplines, such as conservation
biology and ecological economics, emerged in the 1980s. Both conservation
biology and ecological economics are avowedly normative and committed
to the goal of ecological sustainability. Conservation biologists, for example,
clearly believe that preserving biological diversity should be pursued as a
policy.[73]

Conservation biology arose because none of the traditional applied disciplines (e.g., agriculture, forestry, wildlife management, fisheries biology) could
comprehensively address threats to biological diversity. "Conservation biology has two goals: first, to investigate human impacts on biological diversity
and, second, to develop practical approaches to prevent the extinction of
species. . . ."[74] It bridges the biological sciences and the more applied natural
resource disciplines, providing a theoretical approach to the protection of biological diversity while also attempting to provide answers to specific questions
that arise in the field. Conservation biology is more normative than most natural sciences. It also differs from traditional natural resource management "by
having the long-term preservation of the entire biological community as its
primary consideration, with economic factors often being only a secondary
consideration."[75]

Ecological economics, another synthesis discipline, seeks to bridge the disciplines of ecology and economics, based on a belief that traditional ecology
has tended to overlook human dimensions and that traditional economics is
built on the ideal and possibilities of unrestrained economic growth.[76]
Conventional ecology is criticized because it rarely studies humans, often
focusing instead on pristine ecosystems. Conventional economics is criticized
because it reduces human motivations to individual self-interest, determines
value through exchange and prices, and ignores many items that cannot be cap-

tured through market exchanges (externalities): "Economics too often trivializes the most important questions in social and political life, including the intrinsic value of healthy ecosystems."[77] Ecological economists advocate a better understanding of human–nature interconnections and an expansion of the traditional economic emphasis on efficiency to include considerations such as intergenerational equity, communalism, and improved tools for incorporating ecological costs into economic accounting.[78] Unrestrained economic growth is rejected as unattainable. Accordingly, the "limiting factor in development is no longer manmade capital but remaining natural capital."[79]

In the 1990s, large-scale disturbances, such as those associated with the eruption of Mount St. Helens and the Yellowstone fires, provided laboratories for study of ecosystem dynamics and pointed to the role that disturbances and biological legacies play in recovery processes.[80] They also made dramatically clear the inadequacy of legal boundaries for delineating management districts. Many ecosystem scientists and resource managers began collaborating in cooperative ventures, studying and managing resources across a patchwork of jurisdictions and ownership patterns. Science and policy became linked in places such as the Northern Lands, the Greater Yellowstone Ecosystem, and the Great Lakes Ecosystem. Resource managers were no longer excluded from the realm of ecosystem science.[81]

Although there continues to be debate over the definitions of *ecosystem* and *ecosystem ecology*,[82] ecologists increasingly are embracing the integrated and comprehensive nature of ecosystem science as critical to ecosystem management at the landscape scale. As an eminent Hubbard Book ecologist put it, "unless we stop addressing such complex problems in a fragmented way, management actions will be piecemeal and often ineffectual."[83] Ecosystem science provides tools for understanding the interconnections within and between landscapes.

Evolving Resource Management Experience

Professional experience and learning based on efforts to implement new resource management programs is a third root of ecosystem management. To be sure, management perspectives evolve in response to shifts in societal values and scientific knowledge. But because they are often the ones testing new technologies and implementing complex and sometimes ambiguous legislation, managers themselves play a central role developing planning and decision-making models that take a whole systems approach to resource management.

In the 1980s, resource management agencies began managing more explicitly for ecological values. Ecological conditions prompted discussion about deficiencies in the current system of laws and management that guided resource management and the viability of multiple-use–sustained-yield as it was currently being implemented. Foresters, for instance, began to doubt whether they could both manage trees as a crop and adequately meet other social goals, such as maintaining water quality and endangered species populations.[84]

In the 1980s, natural resource management agencies began changing their management priorities to reflect these ideas. The Forest Service's New Perspectives program fostered local projects that attempted to take an ecosystem approach to land management, and promoted new partnerships among managers, researchers, educators, and citizens to develop and carry out those projects. In the early 1990s, largely on the basis of its experience with New Perspectives, the agency committed itself to an ecological approach to management of national forests and grasslands.[85] The Bureau of Land Management made protection and acquisition of riparian areas and fish and wildlife habitats a priority.[86] The National Park Service reinterpreted its mandate and broadened its perspective beyond the preservation of individual scenic resources to the management of natural and historic resources as part of the entire ecosystem and social system in which they are found.[87] The Park Service also began to expand its system of "partnership parks" or "living landscapes" that included private lands managed by the agency. The Army Corps of Engineers and the Bureau of Reclamation increased spending on environmental restoration, mitigation, and enhancement, and became more involved in fixing environmental problems created by their own projects. The Environmental Protection Agency established a Community-Based Environmental Protection program and a new Office of Sustainable Ecosystems and Communities.

Changes in management philosophy and technology began to encourage more adaptive and collaborative resource management planning. Following the lead of corporate management,[88] resource professionals began examining their role as "leaders" in modern society. New leadership concepts addressed the chaotic, constantly changing, and increasingly conflictual environment in which resource managers operate by advising them to develop strong personal ethics and communication skills, embrace change by being flexible and open to new ideas, and share responsibility with others. Under the new leadership model, leaders are also "followers" or "servants" of the public interest, sharing decision making with the public. Thus, responsibility for problem solving belongs to the group and not to a single leader.[89] Embracing these new concepts, resource professionals began labeling the traditional leadership model as "authoritarian" and "hierarchical," with managers acting like "benevolent monarchs."[90] Resource managers began reaching out to other disciplines and to the general populace for ideas on improving management. Leadership became increasingly linked with the need and passion for a land ethic, the reason of good science, and a connection to the evolving social values of the larger society.[91]

Advances and experience with information technologies, such as remote sensing and geographic information systems, as well as the explosion of personal computing capabilities and electronic communication opportunities, made it possible to gather and portray ecological data at a variety of scales and quickly simulate the results of different management options. Multiple constituencies could now participate more effectively in analysis and decision making. These information technologies made scientific information more accessible throughout and between agencies, and to the public. By increasing access to agency planning, these communication tools allow parties to learn about issues, participate in discussions about them, and collaborate in implementing and monitoring management prescriptions.

Environmental and resource management professionals also began reexamining their traditional ethics in the late 1980s and early 1990s. For example, in 1989, members of the Society of American Foresters began to debate whether they should add preservation of ecological integrity to their codes of ethics, and in 1992 added a land ethic canon.[92] Concern for the environmental consequences of industrial activities also swayed private sector policies. As a business strategy to attract investors and increase competitiveness, industry began to embrace "green production," which uses a total systems concept to minimize emissions, effluent, and use of virgin materials.[93] One major forest products association, the American Forest and Paper Association, took a bold new step by approving a set of sustainable forestry principles and implementation guidelines to which members are expected to adhere.[94] Environmental labeling and third-party certification that production processes adhere to certain environmental standards emerged in several manufacturing sectors.[95]

Specters of the Past

History has left its mark on modern natural resource management policy and practices, often in ways that our predecessors would never have predicted. Early federal land policy envisioned a nation peopled with yeoman farmers, who would ensure a prosperous future for the nation, but instead the land disposal policies of the nineteenth century facilitated unscrupulous land grabbing by large wealthy interests. Vestiges of the "wild and free" frontier mentality can still be seen in laws like the General Mining Act of 1872, which allows mining companies to obtain federal lands at a fraction of their current value. One scholar refers to the outdated laws, policies and ideas that still guide management today as the "Lords of Yesterday."[96]

The Progressive Era also left a strong imprint on resource management. Progressive Era initiatives left an invaluable legacy of resource conservation and political reform, but also created institutions that now appear to impede rather than further effective natural resource management. The conservation movement created professional, scientifically-based resource management disciplines dedicated to reversing the previous century's practices of resource abuse and waste, but also resulted in aloof and sometimes elitist natural resource managers and agencies. The laudable conservationist concept of sustained yield became institutionalized as a politics of maximum sustained yield. Policy and agency budgets came to stress commodity production, even as the environmental decade demanded more attention to the environmental consequences of such production. Progressive Era concepts of pluralist governance gave the public more access to government decision making, eventually becoming institutionalized in laws like the Administrative Procedure Act, the National Environmental Policy Act, the National Forest Management Act, and the Federal Land Policy and Management Act. As implemented, however, public involvement policies have resulted in a politics of interest, creating an adversarial style of public involvement in resource management dominated by national interest groups.

Increasingly, however, Americans have been challenging prevailing natural resource management policies. Hostile standoffs between the public and agencies across the country indicate that the values some people place on natural resources are in conflict with the institutions that direct resource management. People are demanding that resource management ensure ecological sustainability *and* that the needs and concerns of the citizenry be met by involving them directly in the decision-making process. As a society, Americans' vision of what forest, rangeland, and riparian ecosystems are, and ought to be, as well as how people should use them, appear to be undergoing a fundamental shift. The convergence of changing social values, growing scientific knowledge, and evolving professional and managerial experiences around concepts of integration and ecological sustainability signals a potential revolution in natural resource management. Chapter 3 describes the evolving ecosystem management concept—the presumed outcome of that revolution—and the likelihood that revolution will occur.

NOTES

1. Klyza, *Who Controls Public Lands?*

2. C. Volney, quoted in Perlin, *A Forest Journey*, p. 324.

3. Cronon, *Changes in the Land*, p. 23; and Ambrose, *Undaunted Courage*, p. 112.

4. George Catlin quoted in Cronon, *Nature's Metropolis*, p. 213.

5. White, *It's Your Misfortune and None of My Own*, pp. 57, 138; and Hofstadter, *The American Political Tradition*. Also see Ingram and Wallace, "An 'empire of liberty.'"

6. White, *It's Your Misfortune and None of My Own*; and Dana and Fairfax, *Forest and Range Policy*.

7. Cronon, *Changes in the Land*, p. 170.

8. Jefferson as cited in Ambrose, *Undaunted Courage*, p. 33; and Jefferson in his First Inaugural Address as cited in Hofstadter, *The American Political Tradition*, p. 31.

9. See Cronon's *Nature's Metropolis* for a discussion of the impact of railroad expansion on the nation's urban development as well as on its wildland resources.

10. Cooper, quoted in Primack, *Essentials of Conservation Biology*, p. 13.

11. Catlin, "An artist proposes a national park"; and Marsh, *Man and Nature*. For a description of the contributions of Thoreau and Emerson and other early nineteenth-century writers to the development of conservation thought see Payne, *Voices in the Wilderness*.

12. Hofstadter, *The American Political Tradition*, p. 165.

13. Keller, *Parties, Congress, and Public Policy*.

14. Curbing monopolies, according to Pinchot in *Breaking New Ground*, was the third great principle of conservation. On the Progressives' administrative reform attempts see Knott and Miller, *Reforming Bureaucracy*.

15. Diggins, "Progressive constitutional thought," p. 1482.

16. This philosophy was stated in a letter sent from Secretary of Agriculture James Wilson to Gifford Pinchot upon the transfer of the forest reserves from the Department of the Interior to Agriculture via the Transfer Act of 1905. Pinchot actually drafted the letter, but credits his friend and the "scientific brains" of the conservation movement, WJ McGee, with defining the new policy. See Pinchot, *Breaking New Ground*, pp. 261, 325–326.

17. Pinchot, *The Fight for Conservation*, p. 42; and Pinchot, *Breaking New Ground*, p. 505. The fledgling Forest Service's Use Book, precursor to the modern agency manual, stated that the "prime object of the forest reserves is use." Cited in Pinchot, *Breaking New Ground*, p. 273.

18. Pinchot, *The Fight for Conservation*, pp. 42–50.

19. John Muir is often cited as the father of the wilderness movement. The outspoken supporter of preservation founded the Sierra Club in 1892. For biographies of Muir see Wolfe, *Son of the Wilderness*; and Fox, *The American Conservation Movement*.

20. The first primitive area was set aside in 1924 through the efforts of Aldo Leopold. The Wilderness Act of 1964 established the National Wilderness System. On the evolution of wilderness and aesthetic concepts in American culture and politics see Nash, *Wilderness and the American Mind*; Allin, *The Politics of Wilderness Preservation*; and Hays, *Beauty, Health, and Permanence*.

21. Klyza, *Who Controls Public Lands?*; and Wilkinson, *Crossing the Next Meridian*.

22. Hays, *Conservation and the Gospel of Efficiency*, p. 249. The Progressives embraced the "scientific management" movement, inspired by the writings of mechanical engineer Frederick Winslow Taylor, who stressed finding the most efficient method for getting the job done. Taylor's principal method of discovering the one best way was the time and motion study. See Knott and Miller, *Reforming Bureaucracy*. In terms of the Forest Service, Hirt calls the resultant reliance on expert opinion and technology the "conspiracy of optimism." Hirt, *A Conspiracy of Optimism*. For other discussions of the main articles of faith in forest management see Duerr and Duerr, "The role of faith in forest resource management"; and Behan, "The myth of the omnipotent forester."

23. Pinchot, *The Fight for Conservation*.

24. Hays, *Conservation and the Gospel of Efficiency*, p. 3.

25. Wilson, "The study of administration," p. 210; and Mahoney, "Wilson, Woodrow."

26. Hays, *Conservation and the Gospel of Efficiency*, p. 3.

27. Henning, "Natural resources administration and the public interest"; and Behan, "The myth of the omnipotent forester."

28. Yankelovich, *Coming to Public Judgment*, p. 17.

29. Ingram and Wallace, "An 'empire of liberty'"; and Dewey, *The Public and Its Problems*. Rather than render judgment, Dewey believed experts should assist the public as teacher and interpreter. For applications of Dewey's philosophy concerning the role of the expert to today's resource situations see Shannon, "Community governance"; and Lee, *Compass and Gyroscope*. But note that Dewey and other Progressives "all also agreed that standing in the way of federal regulatory policies was a debilitating Jeffersonian heritage that made private rights anterior to public responsibilities, a destructive individualism that frustrated the ideals of political authority and civic duty." Many were "convinced that both the Constitution and Republic could be preserved from the corruptions of business interests only by augmenting the authority of an efficient and enlightened state." Diggins, "Progressive constitutional thought," p. 1482.

30. Pinchot, in *Breaking New Ground*, p. 32, wrote that "The purpose of Forestry, then, is to make the forest produce the largest amount of whatever crop or service will be most useful, and keep on producing it for generation after generation of men and trees." On the evolution of sustained yield see Parry et al., "Changing conceptions of sustained-yield policy on the national forests"; Hagenstein, "Some history of multiple use/sustained yield concepts"; Leshy, "Is the multiple use/sustained yield management philosophy still applicable today?"; and Behan, "The irony of the multiple use/sustained yield concept." Also see Dove, *Multiple Use, Sustained Yield, and Other Philosophies of Federal Land Management*.

31. The thinking and activism of lumberman David T. Mason were influential in redefining and expanding the sustained-yield concept to embrace the goal of community stability. See Loehr, *Forests for the Future*.

32. See Frome, *Regreening the National Parks*; and Everhart, *The National Park Service*, for examples of sustained-yield management in the Park Service. In the case of water resources see Liebman, *The Water Resources Council*; Holmes, *A History of Federal Water Resources Programs and Policies, 1800–1960*; Holmes, *A History of Federal Water Resources Programs and Policies, 1961–1970*; and Jaffe, "Benefit-cost analysis and multi-objective evaluations of federal water projects," p. 70.

33. Kimmins, "Modeling the sustainability of forest production and yield for a changing and uncertain future"; Kessler et al., "New perspectives for sustainable natural resources management." For critiques of quantitative tools see Brewer, "Some costs and consequences of large-scale social systems modeling"; Cortner and Schweitzer, "Institutional limits and legal implications of quantitative models in forest planning"; Mitroff, "The myth of objectivity or why science needs a new psychology of science"; and Parker et al., "Use and misuse of complex models."

34. Franklin, "Ecosystem management."

35. Behan, "Multiresource forest management," p. 13.

36. Wolf, "The concept of multiple use," p. 78.

37. See generally Klyza, *Who Controls Public Lands?*; Wilkinson, *Crossing the Next Meridian*; and Clarke and McCool, *Staking Out the Terrain*. On grazing, in particular, see Foss, *Politics and Grass*. On timber see Clary, *Timber and the Forest Service*, and Hirt, *A Conspiracy of Optimism*. On water see Reisner, *Cadillac Desert*; Gottlieb, *A Life of its Own*; Miller, "Recent trends in federal water resources management"; Maass, *Muddy Waters*; and Ferejohn, *Pork Barrel Politics*.

38. During the 1980s, for example, environmental group membership doubled. See Hendee and Pitstick, "The growth of environmental and conservation-related organizations." Reapportionment during the 1960s also gave urban areas increasing political power. The environmental movement was largely urban-based and not reluctant to press Washington to exert its influence over decisions affecting resource management in distant rural areas.

39. Discussion in this paragraph is adapted from Ingram and Wallace, "An 'empire of liberty,'" p. 103.

40. Gottlieb, *Forcing the Spring*, p. 317. See also Sale, "Schism in environmentalism," for a discussion of the divisions within the environmental movement. Some segments of the movement argue that mainstream environmental groups are too "establishment," too anthropocentric, too willing to compromise, and too coopted by Washington politics.

41. Sirmon et al., "Communities of interests and open decisionmaking."

42. Facaros, "Public involvement in national forest planning"; and Shannon, "Public participation in the RPA process."

43. Force and Williams, "A profile of national forest planning participants."

44. Moote et al., "Theory in practice"; Advisory Commission on Intergovernmental Relations, Citizen Participation in the American Federal System; Blahna and Yonts-Shepard, "Public involvement in resource planning"; Facaros, "Public involvement in national forest planning"; Feller, "Grazing management on the public lands"; Fortmann and Lewis, "Public involvement in natural resource management"; Shannon, "Public participation in the RPA process"; Shannon, "Building public decisions"; Wondolleck, "The importance of process in resolving environmental disputes"; and Wondolleck, *Public Lands Conflict and Resolution*.

45. Cortner and Shannon, "Embedding public participation in its political context."

46. Sirmon et al., "Communities of interests and open decisionmaking"; Moote et al., "Theory in practice"; and Blahna and Yonts-Shepard, "Public involvement in resource planning."

47. See Cawley and Freemuth, "A critique of the multiple use framework in public lands decisionmaking." Lowi, in *The End of Liberalism*, critiques the assumption that bar-

gaining among competing groups is self-correcting and discusses the negative consequences of a politics built around interest groups.

48. Alston, "Are sustained yield and sustainable forests equivalent?"; Brooks and
Grant, "New approaches to forest management"; and Bailey, "Good forest management
for the future."

49. The National Research Council's (NRC) *Forestry Research* report called for a new
environmental research paradigm, which would include "an understanding of the fundamental structures, processes, and relationships within forests" to allow management on the
scale of landscapes and regions, p. 12. The NRC report also recommended collaboration
among forest managers and user groups. The Ecological Society of America's 1991 report
on its sustainable biosphere initiative, which has been described as a "call-to-arms" for all
ecologists, stressed the critical need to manage for ecosystem sustainability. See
Lubchenco et al., "The sustainable biosphere initiative." In 1993, a Society of American
Foresters' task force released its report, *Task Force Report on Sustaining Long-Term Forest Health
and Productivity*, which stated that natural resource management should "maintain the
structural and functional integrity of the forest as an ecosystem," p. xiii. The report concluded that traditional sustained-yield management as implemented does not ensure that
the integrity of the ecosystem is maintained or that it adequately meets the desires of people for more attention to noncommodity values. The report proved to be highly controversial within the professional society.

50. Morrissey et al., *Ecosystem Management*. The twenty-first annual report of the
Council on Environmental Quality, released in 1990 under the Bush administration,
advocated taking an ecosystem approach to planning under the National Environmental
Policy Act and other environmental laws. Council on Environmental Quality, *Twenty-First
Annual Report of the Council on Environmental Quality*. In 1993, the Clinton Administration's
National Performance Review released its environmental report, *Reinventing Environmental
Management*, which recommended cross-agency ecosystem planning and management under
all federal programs affecting ecosystems. This administration also established the
President's Council on Sustainable Development (PCSD), which released its *Sustainable
America* report in 1996.

51. In 1995, the Council of State Governments surveyed states about their ecosystem
management activities. See Brown and Marshall, "Ecosystem management in state governments." Ecosystem management is not just a western-state phenomenon. The state of
Pennsylvania, for example, where over 70 percent of land is in private ownership, has
adopted ecosystem management as policy for managing state-owned forests and for guiding assistance programs that deal with private forest resources. See Pennsylvania Bureau of
Forestry, *Penn's Woods*, pp. 8–10.

52. Leopold, *A Sand County Almanac and Sketches Here and There*, p. 204, pp. 224–225. For
a biography of Leopold, see Meine, *Aldo Leopold*.

53. Salwasser, "Ecosystem management"; Slocombe, "Environmental planning,
ecosystem science, and ecosystem approaches for integrating environment and development"; and Francis, "Ecosystem management," provide historical examples of attempts to
develop and apply ecological approaches in the natural resource management disciplines
as well as in a number of social science and humanities disciplines. In 1970, Lynton
Caldwell, who is also known as the principal intellectual architect of NEPA's environ-

mental impact statement requirement, specifically advocated the use of the ecosystem as a criterion for public land policy. Caldwell, "The ecosystem as a criterion for public land policy."

54. Nash, *American Environmentalism*, pp. 187–189.

55. Golley, *A History of the Ecosystem Concept in Ecology*, p. 3.

56. Paehlke, *Environmentalism and the Future of Progressive Politics*; Cortner and Moote, "Sustainability and ecosystem management."

57. Carson, *Silent Spring*.

58. See Meadows et al., *The Limits to Growth*.

59. A summation of American values in the area of the environment and natural resources is contained in Milbrath's work, *Environmentalists*, which examines the shift from the Dominant Social Paradigm to the New Environmental Paradigm. See also Dunlap and Van Liere, "The 'new environmental paradigm'"; Dunlap, "Polls, pollution, and politics revisited"; Dunlap and Mertig, *American Environmentalism*; and Inglehart, *The Silent Revolution*.

60. Bosso, "Seizing back the day"; Ladd and Bowman, "Public opinion on the environment"; and Kempton et al., *Environmental Values in American Culture*. Deason points out that public support for environmental values is worldwide. Deason, "Changing world attitudes on environmental values and sustainability."

61. Dunlap and Mertig, *American Environmentalism*.

62. Implementation of the sweeping environmental and natural resource legislation of the late 1960s and 1970s was also beginning to take an economic toll on the federal budget. "In the United States, we spend over $100 billion per year on pollution abatement and control." Long and Arnold, *The Power of Environmental Partnerships*, p. 4.

63. Anderson and Leal, *Free Market Environmentalism*; Hess, *Visions Upon the Land*; and O'Toole, *Reforming the Forest Service*.

64. For example, an amendment to the Endangered Species Act in 1982 facilitated the development of cooperative private–public conservation plans that take an ecosystem approach to species conservation.

65. Caldwell, *Perspectives on Ecosystem Management for the Great Lakes*; Adams and Atkinson, *Watershed Resources*; Sample et al., *Building Partnerships for Ecosystem Management on Mixed Ownership Landscapes*; and Natural Resources Law Center, *The Watershed Source Book*.

66. Tansley as quoted in McIntosh, *The Background of Ecology*, p. 193. See also Golley, *A History of the Ecosystem Concept in Ecology*; and Hagen, *An Entangled Bank*, for discussion of the history of ecosystem science.

67. Golley, *A History of the Ecosystem Concept in Ecology*, pp. 33–34.

68. Golley, *A History of the Ecosystem Concept in Ecology*, p. 145.

69. McIntosh, *The Background of Ecology*, citing Bormann and Likens, *Pattern and Processes in a Forested Ecosystem*; and Golley, *A History of the Ecosystem Concept in Ecology*.

70. McIntosh, *The Background of Ecology*, pp. 202–203.

71. The new ecosystem science went well beyond systems analysis. "It is more empirical and experimental and much less involved in abstract generalization and mathematical formulation" than systems ecology. Systems ecology, based in the laws of thermodynamics, is heavily dependent on computer simulation models to track complex interrelation-

ships among ecosystem components. See McIntosh, *The Background of Ecology*, pp. 207, 210–213.

72. Eugene Odum, cited in McIntosh, *The Background of Ecology*, p. 202.

73. Meffe and Viederman, "Combining science and policy in conservation biology"; Soulé, "What is conservation biology?"; and Primack, *Essentials of Conservation Biology*. See also Soulé, *Conservation Biology*; Meffe and Carroll, *Principles of Conservation Biology*; and Knight and George, "New approaches, new tools."

74. Primack, *Essentials of Conservation Biology*, p. 5. "Conservation biology should be considered a crisis discipline," p. 7.

75. Primack, *Essentials of Conservation Biology*, p. 7.

76. Costanza et al., "Goals, agenda, and policy recommendations for ecological economics"; Costanza, *Ecological Economics*; Folke, "Ecologists and economists can find common ground." While ecological economics criticizes traditional economics because it is too utilitarian, Sagoff contends that ecological economics is also based on utilitarian logic. Sagoff, "Carrying capacity and ecological economics."

77. Bradley and Lewis, "Ecological economics," pp. 31–32.

78. Page, "Sustainability and the problem of valuation"; Clark, "Rethinking ecological and economic education"; Rylander, "Accounting for nature"; Norgaard and Howarth, "Sustainability and discounting the future"; Daly, "Sustainable growth"; and Daily, *Nature's Services*.

79. Costanza et al., "Goals, agenda, and policy recommendations for ecological economics," p. 8.

80. See Franklin, "Biological legacies"; Maser et al., "Dead and down woody material"; Swanson and Berg, "The ecological roots of new approaches to forestry"; Perry and Amaranthus, "Disturbance, recovery, and stability"; and Ehrenfeld, "Ecosystem health and ecological theories," pp. 137–139 regarding recognition that disturbance is an integral, perhaps essential, feature of ecological communities.

81. See, for example, Harper et al., *The Northern Forest Lands Study of New England and New York*; Clark and Minta, *Greater Yellowstone's Future*; Clark et al., "Policy and programs for ecosystem management in the Greater Yellowstone ecosystem"; Dworsky, "Ecosystem management"; Francis and Regier, "Barriers and bridges to the Great Lakes Basin ecosystem"; and Johnson et al., *Bioregional Assessments*.

82. Some ecologists do not distinguish between ecology and ecosystem science; both are "the study of the relationships among ecological entities, e.g., individual organisms, populations, and systems, and their environments." Likens, *The Ecosystem Approach*, p. 8.

83. Likens, *The Ecosystem Approach*, p. 137.

84. Gordon, "From vision to policy"; and Behan, "The obsolete paradigm of professional forestry." In the fall of 1989, the forest supervisors from the northern region of the Forest Service sent Forest Service Chief Dale Robertson a letter that said, "We are not meeting the quality land management expectations of our public and our employees." Memorandum from the Region One Forest Supervisors to Chief Dale Robertson, "An Open Letter to the Chief from the Region One Forest Supervisors," November 1989. In the summer of 1990, supervisors of other regions followed suit. The reports and recommendations to the director of the National Park Service from the agency's 75th anniver-

sary meeting in Vail, Colorado, also expressed concern that the ability of the agency to meet "the most fundamental aspects of its mission has been compromised." Steering Committee of the 75th Anniversary Symposium, "National parks for the 21st century," p. 437.

85. Kessler and Salwasser, in "Natural resource agencies," note that "For now, it is important to understand that New Perspectives was an internal, grassroots process for change," p. 175. For a policy evaluation of the New Perspectives program, see Shands et al., *From New Perspectives to Ecosystem Management*. The Forest Service's announcement in June 1992 that it would henceforth be taking an ecological approach to management of the national forests and grasslands was somewhat overshadowed by the announcement in the same memo that it would be reducing clear-cutting as a standard timber practice. See Robertson, "Ecosystem management of the national forests and grasslands," Attachment 2.

86. U.S. Department of the Interior Bureau of Land Management, *Riparian-Wetland Initiative for the 1990s*; and U.S. Department of the Interior Bureau of Land Management, *Fish & Wildlife 2000*.

87. Commission on Research and Resource Management Policy in the National Park System, *National Parks*. The first recommendation was that the National Park Service develop and use the concept of ecosystem management. The agency's Vail agenda also recommended that parks be managed under "ecological principles." See Steering Committee of the 75th Anniversary Symposium, "National parks for the 21st century," p. 440. See also Halvorson and Davis, *Science and Ecosystem Management in the National Parks*.

88. See, for example, Kouzes and Posner, *The Leadership Challenge*.

89. Berry and Gordon, *Environmental Leadership*; Kouzes and Posner, *The Leadership Challenge*; Block, *Stewardship*; Sirmon et al., "Communities of interests and open decisionmaking"; Heifetz and Sinder, "Political leadership"; and Shannon, "Building trust."

90. Sirmon et al., "Communities of interests and open decisionmaking."

91. Cornett, "Birch seeds, leadership, and a relationship with the land."

92. Smyth, "Foresters and the land"; Craig et al., "Land ethic canon proposal"; and Coufal, "The land ethic question." See also Irland, "Developing ethical reflection"; and Reeves et al., *Ethical Questions for Resource Managers*.

93. See Hart, "How green production might sustain the world"; Bhat, *The Green Corporation*; and Press and Mazmanian, "The greening of industry."

94. American Forest and Paper Association, *Sustainable Forestry Principles and Implementation Guidelines*; and Wallinger, "A commitment to the future."

95. Dudley et al., "A framework for environmental labeling."

96. Wilkinson, *Crossing the Next Meridian*.

Chapter 3

A Paradigm Shift?

In many ways, ecosystem management is dramatically different from traditional, sustained-yield resource management, with its focus on utilitarian values. (See table 3.1 for comparison.) Traditional resource management is pragmatic, seeing in nature a collection of resources that can be manipulated and harvested, with humans in control. Ecosystem management, on the other hand, views nature with some reverence and respect for the awesome complexity with which its components are interwoven. Protection of ecosystem attributes and functions, particularly biodiversity, is critical. Ecosystem management involves preserving intrinsic values or natural conditions of the ecosystem; commodities are secondary by-products, much like interest on capital. Unlike traditional resource management, you do not begin by enumerating outputs. The first priority is conserving ecological sustainability; levels of commodity and amenity outputs are adjusted to meet that goal. Science is viewed as highly uncertain, evolving, and multidisciplinary, with no claim on truth or best answers. Ecosystem management is necessarily flexible and adaptive, no longer rigidly following centralized protocols. Furthermore, where decision making was the sole province of resource management professionals, under ecosystem management it is a public, politicized, shared-ownership endeavor, where different interests and values are openly addressed. Some have suggested that these differences amount to no less than a radical revision of professional perspectives, values, and management practices[1]—in other words, a paradigm shift.

Paradigms and Paradigm Shifts

A *paradigm* is a framework of understanding or perspective shared by members of a profession or discipline. In his classic work, *The Structure of Scientific*

Table 3.1 Traditional Resource Management versus Ecosystem Management

	Traditional Management	Ecosystem Management
Nature	A collection of resources to be dominated and mastered.	Complex, ever-changing, interrelated systems. No domination required.
Ethics	Compartmentalized; interrelationships marginal.	Holistic; interrelationships important.
Science and Models	Deterministic, linear, static, approaching steady-state equilibrium.	Stochastic, nonlinear, dynamic: variable-rate dynamics with temporary equilibria upset periodically by chaotic moments that set the stage for the next temporary equilibrium.
	Robust, well-defined theory; discrete data and highly predictable outcomes.	Embryonic, beginnings of theory, theory and practice intertwined, interrelated data, and unreliable outcomes. "Expect to be surprised."
	Maps, linear optimization, monetized cost-benefit analysis; quantitative.	Geographic Information Systems (GIS), relational databases, nonlinear simulation (time and space dependent), quantitative and qualitative evaluation for social, economic, and political aspects.
Management and Organization	Centralized; rigid, little focus on incentives or innovation.	Decentralized, interrelated teams; adaptive; flexible; much focus on incentives and innovation and shared learning.
	Hierarchical, top-down bureaucracies.	Adaptive, bottoms-up, open, cooperative.
Planning	Comprehensive, rational.	Interrelated, chaotic, looking for order in chaos. Imaginative.
Decision making	Rigid, chain of command, authoritarian: heavy reliance on experts/professionals' opinions.	Deliberated: all stakeholders' opinions count.
	Science provides "the answer."	Science provides information. Science alone cannot provide answers.
		Adapted to context of problem, interrelated to other problems; considers externalities.
Participation	Influence, money.	Discursive, deliberative.
Leadership	Authoritarian: leaders designated.	Situational: leaders arise from the community when needed.

Source: Adapted from Iverson, An ecosystems approach to management.

Revolutions, Thomas Kuhn describes the dominant paradigm within a science discipline as the set of values, theories, methodologies, tools, and techniques that is sanctioned and utilized by the professional community. The accepted paradigm structures the questions deemed worthy of scientific attention and defines the processes by which those questions are examined. Because the paradigm is widely accepted, it results in consistent actions. However, this unquestioned acceptance can also lead scientists to prematurely reject new information that contradicts the accepted paradigm.[2]

Although Kuhn explicitly applied his theory to the natural sciences, it has since been widely adopted by other disciplines, including the social sciences and the humanities. From the broader perspective of the social sciences, a paradigm is

> a world view, a general perspective, a way of breaking down the complexity of the real world. As such, paradigms are deeply embedded in the socialization of adherents and practitioners telling them what is important, what is legitimate, what is reasonable. Paradigms are normative; they tell the practitioner what to do without the necessity of long existential or epistemological considerations.[3]

According to this broader view, a paradigm is "a view of the world—a *Weltanschauung*—that reflects our most basic beliefs and assumptions about the human condition."[4] Again the normative—even sanctified—nature of the paradigm typically causes its adherents to reject or discount new information or values that do not fit within it.[5]

A paradigm *shift* occurs only when a significant body of knowledge or information accumulates that is contradictory to, or unexplained by, the accepted paradigm. When a critical mass of contradictory information has accumulated, a "revolution" occurs within the discipline. The established paradigm is rejected, new schools of thought proliferate, and from them a new paradigm emerges that accounts for deviations from the old paradigm. Paradigm shifts are dramatic events, as the accepted world view within a discipline is shattered and a new one adopted. According to Kuhn, more than just the discipline is affected: the way in which its practitioners perceive the universe will undergo a fundamental change after a paradigm shift.[6]

In terms of attitudes toward the environment and natural resources, a transition from viewing nature as a set of resources to be managed for human use to a belief that maintaining ecological sustainability is paramount could be viewed as a paradigm shift. Yet as the following sections show, even as the emerging theory of ecosystem management is becoming more clearly delineated, increasingly it is criticized.

Definitions of Ecosystem Management

As ecosystem management has become more widely endorsed, fairly consistent definitions of the term have emerged (see box 3.1). Most proponents of ecosystem management agree that its ultimate purpose is sustainability, both ecological and socioeconomic. The overall goal of ecosystem management is sustaining ecological attributes and functions into perpetuity, thereby ensuring that future societies enjoy the same ecosystem values that we do today.[7]

Proponents of ecosystem management consider social and ecological sustainability interdependent, in that the sustainability of human communities depends on the sustainability of the ecosystems in which they live. Many ecological scientists further maintain that just as the future of human populations depends on maintenance of ecological sustainability, ecological sustainability depends on human behavior. Human beings are considered integral parts of the ecosystems that they inhabit and use, because humans are both affected by, and affect, ecosystem functions.[8]

Principles of Ecosystem Management

As the ecosystem management concept has been debated and honed by researchers, resource managers, scholars, and citizens, four basic themes have emerged to characterize it: (1) socially defined goals and objectives; (2) holistic, integrated science; (3) adaptable institutions; and (4) collaborative decision making. These broad themes, or principles of ecosystem management, reflect the overall goal of ecological and socioeconomic sustainability and are accepted by most ecosystem management scholars and practitioners. As becomes clear in the discussion that follows, these principles of ecosystem management are not discrete—there is considerable overlap among them.

Socially Defined Goals and Objectives

Although it can be argued that the goals and objectives of resource management have always been socially defined, ecosystem management makes this explicit. This reflects a recognition that many scientific concepts, including the definition of an ecosystem and criteria for a healthy ecosystem, are essentially value judgments.[9] For example, successional theory, which dominated the field of ecology for years, places a bias on climax communities as being the optimal and best ecological condition, thus placing less value on systems in

Box 3.1: Definitions of *Ecosystem Management*

"Ecosystem management involves regulating internal ecosystem structure and function, plus inputs and outputs, to achieve socially desirable conditions."

—Darryll Johnson and James Agee,
National Park Service scientists, 1988.[1]

"Ecosystem management focuses on the conditions of the [ecosystem], with the goals of maintaining soil productivity, gene conservation, biodiversity, landscape patterns, and the array of ecological processes."

—Society of American Foresters Task Force
on Long-Term Forest Health and Productivity, 1992.[2]

"The primary goal of ecosystem management is to conserve, restore, and maintain the ecological integrity, productivity, and biological diversity of public lands. . . . The overriding objective of ecosystem management is to ensure the ecological sustainability of the land."

—Bureau of Land Management, 1994.[3]

"The approach is characterized by synthesis or integrated knowledge, a holistic perspective interrelating systems at different levels of integration, and actions that are ecological, anticipatory, and ethical in respect to other systems of Nature."

—George Francis, professor of environment
and resource studies, 1993.[4]

"Ecosystem management integrates scientific knowledge of ecological relationships within a complex sociopolitical and values framework toward the general goal of protecting native ecosystem integrity over the long term."

—Ed Grumbine, conservation biologist, 1994.[5]

"The goal of the ecosystem approach is to restore and sustain the health, productivity, and biological diversity of ecosystems and the overall quality of life through a natural resource management approach that is fully integrated with social and economic goals."

—Interagency Ecosystem Management Task Force, 1995.[6]

"Ecosystem management is management driven by explicit goals, executed by policies, protocols, and practices, and made adaptable by monitoring and research based on our best understanding of the ecological interactions and processes necessary to sustain ecosystem composition, structure, and function. . . . Sustainability must be the primary objective, and levels of commodity and amenity provisions adjusted to meet that goal."

—Ecological Society of America, 1996.[7]

1. Johnson and Agee, "Introduction to ecosystem management," p. 7.
2. Society of American Foresters, *Task Force Report on Sustaining Long-Term Forest Health and Productivity*, p. xv.
3. U.S. Department of the Interior Bureau of Land Management, *Ecosystem Management in the BLM*, pp. 2, 3.
4. Francis, "Ecosystem management," p. 331.
5. Grumbine, "What is ecosystem management?," p. 31.
6. Interagency Ecosystem Management Task Force, *The Ecosystem Approach*, p. 3.
7. Christensen et al., "The report of the Ecological Society of America Committee on the Scientific Basis for Ecosystem Management," pp. 665, 682.

earlier stages. Similarly, the recent popularity of returning ecosystems to "pre-European settlement conditions" is based in social values more than evolutionary ecology.[10] Desired ecological conditions, including "ecological sustainability," are socially defined concepts, as are desired ecosystem outputs, such as biodiversity, recreational opportunities, and forage. In fact, it is *necessary* that society define its goals, if ecosystem management is to be effective. Management prescriptions will depend on what society wants from a specific ecosystem.[11]

Ecosystem management theorists warn, however, that humans are dependent on the ecosystems in which they live, and therefore societies need to protect crucial ecological processes for their very survival. According to ecosystem management theory, unless humans decide to maintain healthy ecosystems and adjust their behavior accordingly, ecological sustainability will not be attained. Moreover, intergenerational equity, the obligation of current generations to future generations, requires that critical ecological services be sustained.[12] Thus, while ecosystem management explicitly recognizes that social goals and objectives play a central role in framing management direction, it also presumes that humans will decide to make protection of ecological processes their overriding social objective.

Holistic, Integrated Science

In ecosystem management, there are no externalities.[13] (Externalities are environmental effects that are not factored into economic analysis and decision making.) Instead, downstream and long-term effects of changes in any ecosystem component are taken into account. Ecosystems are recognized as open, changing, complex systems made up of social, political, economic, biological, and physical components. The ecosystem management concept is synthetic, opposing "the classical idea that the world can be analyzed as separate, independent parts,"[14] and focusing instead on processes—the interrelationships among ecosystem components. Taking an "ecosystem perspective" means looking at ecological, social, and economic processes and recognizing "that a process may be the result of many interactions and that an action can cause numerous interactions to reverberate throughout a system."[15]

Science for ecosystem management takes a broad perspective, recognizing the interconnectedness of ecosystem variables across large spatial and long temporal ranges. For instance, research in conservation biology and landscape ecology has redefined the scale of management for biodiversity from hundreds to thousands of acres, by showing that parks and other nature preserves are too small and fragmented—isolated "islands" of wilderness within a sea of land developed for agricultural and urban uses—to support large megafauna and allow genetic exchange.[16] Ecologists now speak of the need to take entire bioregions into account when managing to sustain the biological diversity considered critical to ecological sustainability. Similarly, ecosystem managers must understand long-term ecological change (on the order of centuries) to be able to predict ecological behavior and ensure delivery of desired products.[17]

Yet managing for sustainability will also require an understanding of some very small-scale ecosystem functions. Regardless of the specific outcomes desired, biodiversity and ecosystem structures and processes, such as nutrient cycling and resilience from disturbance, must be maintained to ensure future desired uses of the ecosystem are not compromised.[18] In terms of the biological sciences alone, "Ecosystem management depends on research performed at all levels of organization, from investigations of the morphology, physiology, and behavior of individual organisms, through studies of the structure and dynamics of populations and communities, to analysis of patterns and processes at the level of ecosystems and landscapes."[19] Ecosystem management will rely on information from a similar cross section of physical and social sciences. For instance, social needs and institutions and the dynamics within and among them will have to be understood, from the level of local communities to the national and even global levels. Ultimately, variables occurring on many different scales and at vastly varying rates must be addressed.

The range and breadth of factors that contribute to ecosystem functioning indicate a need for an interdisciplinary approach to research and management that fully integrates an ecosystem's social and physical components. Natural scientists, for instance, need to recognize the importance of context and incorporate qualitative data as well as quantitative data into their research. To effectively manage for ecological sustainability, the complexities of social and political interactions with an ecosystem must be understood. Scientists and managers from several different disciplines need to work together to understand, to the best of their abilities, all of the factors influencing, and influenced by, all of the component parts and functions of an ecosystem.

Adaptable Institutions

The complex and dynamic nature of ecological and social systems means there can be no explicit guidelines or management prescriptions for ecosystem management; uncertainty will always be inherent to it.[20] In order to operate under such conditions of uncertainty, ecosystem management institutions themselves must be "characterized by an emphasis on the interrelatedness, hierarchical complexity, dynamism, openness, and creativity of systems to be managed."[21] In other words, institutions such as organizations, laws, policies, and management practices need to be flexible, in order that they may rapidly adapt to changes in social values, ecological conditions, political pressures, available data, and knowledge.[22] Considerable emphasis is put on the value of decentralized decision-making arrangements to avoid the rigidities of highly centralized institutional arrangements with inflexible prescriptions.

In order to adjust management prescriptions as new information becomes available, adaptable institutions treat management as a learning process in which decisions are continuously revisited and revised, never final. This implies that resource managers, instead of simply following rulebooks and standardized procedures, have the capacity to identify and adapt to new knowledge, including changing public attitudes, and learn lessons from new research and on-the-ground management experiences.[23] Well-developed learning capacities are thus another key component of ecosystem management.

Adaptive management has been offered as one way to address the staggering information requirements of ecosystem management while allowing management to move forward in the face of uncertainty. In essence, adaptive management involves repeatedly monitoring the outcomes of alternative management practices, either in the field or through simulation modeling, and making adjustments based on what is learned. Adaptive management utilizes scientists, resource managers, policy makers, interest groups, and citizens to collectively identify management problems and to set initial management goals. The proposed means of achieving these goals, such as management prescriptions, are treated as working hypotheses. The importance of hypothesis testing through experimentation lies in its ability to rapidly produce information that can be used to review and revise management decisions. By treating their management prescriptions as research hypotheses, resource managers can continuously monitor and modify decisions and practices as needed.[24] The iterative nature of hypothesis testing offers continual refinement of social understandings of ecological responses to management.[25]

Collaborative Decision Making

Ecosystem management means management across ecological, political, generational, and ownership boundaries. Clearly, when management units are defined ecologically rather than politically, greater coordination among local landowners and between private landowners and natural resource management agencies is required. Management decisions must be made collectively by all parties because in most cases no single entity has jurisdiction over all aspects of an ecosystem. Combined with the need for interdisciplinary science discussed previously, this suggests that ecosystem management requires the acquiescence, if not active support, of a broad cross section of society. The need to integrate the knowledge and values of a broad array of organizations and individuals implies a need to blend organizational and community (i.e., public and private) planning through collaboration among resource owners, managers, and users. From a purely practical standpoint, if any ecosystem residents or users consider their needs unmet by an ecosystem management plan, they are liable to resist or block its implementation.

Collaborative decision making is also important for reasons of equity. Ecosystem management requires a delicate balancing of complex social values and legal mandates with the need to maintain ecological sustainability. Ultimately, in a democratic society, the public must decide what value to place on each issue surrounding an ecological approach. Recognizing the diversity of opinion among social values and concerns, ecosystem management proponents advocate open communication and collaborative decision making, including, but not exclusive to, technical experts. As one scholar puts it:

> This promising paradigm can only be instituted as a general guide to management if conservation biologists, restorationists, and environmental managers reduce their isolation and participate in a public dialogue. Likewise, philosophers, anthropologists, humanists, economists and citizens must join the search for appropriate public values.[26]

Thus, under ecosystem management, the roles of scientists and managers are redefined from expert to educator, public relations specialist, technical advisor, or some combination of these. Correspondingly, the role of the citizen also includes resource management, for under ecosystem management, all citizens take responsibility for achieving ecological sustainability.

Criticisms of Ecosystem Management

Along with fledgling efforts to implement ecosystem management have come questions of its feasibility and criticisms from those who find it untenable on moral, philosophical, legal, and logical grounds.

It's Fuzzy, Ambiguous, and Untested

Among researchers, there is little consensus on new terminology, conceptual categories, and classifications for use in discussing ecosystem management. While many agree that it is important to maintain ecological sustainability, integrity, productivity, and biological diversity, there is no agreement on what this means exactly in terms of management outcomes. A prominent forest ecologist, for example, advocates (I) "preventing the degradation of the productive capacity of our lands and waters—no *net loss* of productivity; and (2) preventing accelerated loss of genetic diversity (including species), recognizing that evolutionary processes will result in changes—no *accelerated* loss of genetic potential."[27] Another leading scientist, a conservation biologist, goes further, requiring that ecosystem management "maintain viable populations of *all* native species in situ [and] represent, within protected areas, *all* native ecosystem types *across their natural range of variation*."[28] Without clear conceptions of the desired future condition of the ecosystem or the management objectives to be achieved, ecosystem management is said to be too susceptible to subjective judgment, bias, and personal policy preferences.[29] Because there are no agreed-on definitions for terms such as *sustainability, ecosystem integrity,* or *ecosystem health,* critics argue ecosystem management lacks a scientific basis. Other terms, like *ecosystem management* and *watershed management,* are often used interchangeably, sometimes resulting in confusion.[30] Thus, it is not surprising that ecosystem management has been criticized as an ambiguous, "fuzzy" concept, providing a muddled basis for policy and with limited ability to provide operational directives. Absent performance standards to determine when policy or management goals have been achieved, ecosystem management is not considered operationally useful.[31]

Moreover, critics claim that ecosystem management is the creation of individuals sitting behind computers rather than those engaged in practical field operations. Consequently, it is argued, many of the concepts of ecosystem management have not been adequately tested, and knowledge based on years of professional experience is being prematurely and cavalierly discarded.[32]

Finally, critics object to the ecosystem being the focus for analysis, arguing that since an ecosystem can be anything one defines it to be, it is unsuitable for spatially-based decisions and not useful as either a biological or a policy concept.[33] Ecosystems are also criticized because their boundaries cannot be matched to existing institutional jurisdictions. For some, the fact that an ecosystem can be defined at different scales makes it impractical as a management unit. Some consider the watershed a more tenable unit of analysis because it is geographically recognizable and its boundaries can be used as a basis for organizing community participation and governance institutions.[34]

It's Legally and Politically Untenable

Other critics consider the legal and political barriers to ecosystem management to be insurmountable. While planning on an ecosystem basis has been upheld by at least one court, it is argued that ecosystem management nonetheless has no explicit basis in existing law.[35] Moreover, some legislation, such as the Sherman Anti-Trust Act, which would likely interpret cooperation on the level envisioned by ecosystem management to be a form of collusion among industrial landowners, is seen as inimical to ecosystem management.[36] Considerable opposition rests on the claim that ecosystem-scale management will result in unwarranted intrusions on the rights of private property owners. Supreme Court cases such as *Lucas v. South Carolina Coastal Commission* and *Dolan v. City of Tigard*, which upheld the rights of property owners over the right of the state to regulate for environmental protection, are thus seen to cast doubt on the constitutionality of ecosystem management.[37]

With no identifiable constituency, ecosystem management is further said to be resting on politically shaky ground. Whereas organized groups who benefitted from the agencies' outputs could be counted on historically to support agency budget requests, such constituencies are expected to show little inclination to support ecosystem management politically.[38] Moreover, the collaborative nature of decision making called for in ecosystem management is seen to bear little resemblance to American representative democracy, in which elected officials and powerful interests make decisions for the majority.[39] The emphasis on the collective is also argued to devalue the individual and individual freedoms.[40]

Finally, critics argue, asking for a fundamental reframing of how humans work with nature is infeasible and defies common sense.[41] Worldwide, nations are organized around the concept of developing resources, maximizing economic returns, and increasing human consumption. In their official capacities, nations exhibit a lack of commitment to the principles that define ecological perspectives. Unless nations reconfigure their priorities, the sovereign claims of nations to pursue their economic destinies by turning nature into exploitable resources—claims that severely limit ecosystem management—are likely to be honored.[42]

It's Old Wine in New Bottles

Ecosystem management is perceived by some as an attempt by natural resource experts to recapture the ground they have lost since extensive public participation was institutionalized in the 1970s. From this perspective, the central role of science in ecosystem management is seen as a way to put scientists back in the pivotal decision-making role, reasserting the primacy of technocratic utilitarianism.[43] Critics challenge that only scientists will be able to determine how ecosystems function and assess actual and desired ecosystem conditions; only scientists will be able to determine the criteria of sustainability; and ultimately, only scientists will remain involved.[44] According to these critics, ecosystem management is nothing new; it's just a strategy for shoring up the politics of expertise extant in the traditional paradigm. The name *ecosystem management* itself has also been criticized because, it is argued, including *management* as a descriptor implies nothing new or different from past practices.[45] Yet others say it is a way to disguise destructive practices with new environmental labeling and that it may even preclude setting aside wilderness "cores," a central concept in conservation biology.[46]

Ironically, those explicitly advocating that professional experts do indeed need to recapture lost ground are also among the most vocal critics of ecosystem management. In the case of forestry, for example, the argument is made that instead of shifting to ecosystem management, "U.S. forest management must be given back to trained and experienced foresters; they are best qualified to scientifically manage our most important renewable natural resource."[47] According to a recent president of the Society of American Foresters,

> the profession must focus on the establishment, protection, growth, and harvesting of commercial crops of timber. This does not mean that other products and benefits should be ignored. It simply means that timber comes first. It keeps us in line with the natural order of things.[48]

Closely aligned with this position is the argument that ecosystem management is simply a new device for environmentalists to attack the essence of professional resource management with "pseudoscience" and emotionalism.

It's a Form of Cooptation

All sides of the debate over ecosystem management distrust one another. Agencies, environmental interest groups, and commodity interest groups have been fighting one another for decades in courts, through the media, and on the ground and are highly suspicious of calls to lay down their lawsuits and cooperate. Ecosystem management is thus seen as an implausible lifeboat that agencies have assembled to rescue themselves from the state of perpetual conflict in which they find themselves.[49]

Some critics consider ecosystem management an environmentalist plot to turn all public lands into nature preserves and expand environmental regulation of private land. They are concerned that ecosystem management is a disguise for efforts to give preservation primacy and that it signals the end of production or output-oriented management.[50] In 1994, the conservative Cato Institute likened ecosystem management to "a federal land grab" and labeled it a "train wreck in the making."[51] Ecosystem management is seen as a form of political correctness to shield agencies from having to deal head-on with a public that wants to consume high, but produce low.[52] At the other end of the spectrum are those who consider ecosystem management a kind of industrial imperialism, a classic case of cooptation of the resource management agencies and environmental interests by commodity groups, and an empty promise that we can have our cake (ecological sustainability) and eat it too (development).

In a related criticism, representatives of national environmental interests charge that the site-specific nature of ecosystem management translates to "anything goes." They further claim the emphasis on involvement by "communities of place" or "resource dependent communities" typically translates to increased influence by commodity interests, to the detriment of national environmental interests. In 1996, an official of the Sierra Club warned, "Industry thinks its odds are better in these forums. . . . It believes it can dominate them over time and relieve itself of the burden of tough national rules. It has ways to generate pressures in communities where it is strong, which it doesn't have at the national level."[53] Industry's support of collaborative forums is seen as a strategy to use vague concepts such as community and lifestyle to preserve the status quo of industrial subsidies and privilege.[54] Rural community groups retort that neglecting to involve local communities in identification of conditions and trends and in decision making "perpetuates the opportunity for interest groups to create narrow definitions of community well-being or economic health."[55]

It's Contradictory

Proponents of ecosystem management increasingly recognize that there is no formula or set of prescriptions for adopting an ecosystem approach. The site-specific characteristics of ground-level management are seen as critical elements that respect variations in biophysical, social, and economic characteristics of different geographic areas. Each ecosystem has unique problems that reflect its own conditions. The hydrologic conditions of the eastern United States, for example, differ from those of the arid and semi-arid West; the old-growth forests of the Northwest involve different social and ecological relationships than the pine forests of the Southeast. Nonetheless, ecosystem management will necessarily require more widespread agreement about the central principles and performance standards that undergird this management philosophy.

In this search for more explicit parameters, however, contradictions in the central tenets of ecosystem management become apparent. Calls for better use of ecosystem science in decision making, for example, elicit cries of "biological imperialism," reflecting the concern that basing decisions on ecological requirements in effect runs roughshod over the principle that humans and their wants and needs are also a part of ecosystems. Further, the need to address resource management on broad temporal and spatial scales and to integrate data collection and monitoring may conflict with the concept that ecosystem management needs to be tailored to local ecological, social, economic, and political conditions. Finally, while ecosystem management calls for more attention to social goals and objectives, it assumes that humans won't choose to sustain higher levels of outputs at the expense of sustaining ecological services. It appears to preclude the goal, "we should use as much as we can get now," and the alternative moral position that the current generation does not have a specific obligation to future generations.[56]

A Revolution in Natural Resource Management?

With an overriding goal of ecological sustainability—to be achieved using socially defined goals and objectives, holistic and integrated science, collaborative decision making, and adaptable institutions—ecosystem management is a marked departure from multiple-use–sustained-yield. Indeed, ecosystem management differs from traditional resource management so much that several observers have called it a new resource management paradigm.

Yet others question whether ecosystem management is much different than resource management as practiced today. Resource management, it is argued, has always been about sustainability, and the job of the future is simply to "refine the ecologically based management principals of our early professional history so we can continually improve our stewardship of the land."[57] Undeniably some of the "new" ecosystem management concepts have been around for quite a long time, and some of the "old" sustained-yield premises are quite current.

The view that ecosystem management is business as usual stems in part from a common use of the term *ecosystem management*, favored by most natural resource management agencies, in which the primary goal is sustaining all *desired human uses* of ecosystems. Thus, ecosystem management becomes "a resource management system designed to maintain or enhance ecosystem health and productivity while producing essential commodities and other values to meet human needs and desires within the limits of socially, biologically, and economically acceptable risk."[58] The focus is still on products; sustaining ecosystems is viewed as a constraint to management, rather than its primary goal. We view this "sustain-all-uses" approach to ecosystem management as an attempt to fit the principles of ecosystem management into the prevailing multiple-use–sustained-yield paradigm, with ecological sustainability taking its place as another in a growing litany of multiple uses. Thus, according to one proponent: "the incremental fitting of multiple uses into ecosystems according to their ability to support the uses—the traditional approach to forest management—is the way an ecosystem management approach must be carried out."[59] This adaption of the ecosystem management concept represents a significant incremental change to sustained-yield natural resource management, but it is not a paradigm shift.

It would be premature to declare ecosystem management, as it has been laid out here, the new resource management paradigm, for there is still no consensus on the way in which the natural resource management community sees the world. The numerous criticisms of ecosystem management and attempts to mold it to fit the prevailing natural resource management paradigm suggest it may be in what Kuhn called a "preparadigm stage." In the preparadigm stage of a scientific revolution, the traditional paradigm is under significant and increasing attack, but no new paradigm has been universally accepted by the professional community. While substantial information has been accumulated regarding ecological processes and the political dysfunction of the traditional paradigm, the values, theories, methodologies, and tools of the old paradigm have not yet been discarded.

Clearly, there are a number of major philosophical and institutional hurdles to be addressed and overcome before ecosystem management can be fully accepted and implemented as a new paradigm. Adopting the ecosystem management paradigm would mean rejecting traditional resource management policies and practices in favor of policies and practices selected primarily for the purpose of sustaining ecosystem health. These new policies and practices may well require strict limits on the social and economic uses of resources and sacrifices of short-term socioeconomic gains.[60] There are more than semantic changes that have to be made before ecosystem management—managing for ecological sustainability—can be realized on the ground in more than a few experimental plots.

Initial studies have suggested that implementing ecosystem management will require extensive social and political changes, ranging from redefinition of the values that define relationships among humans and nature, professions and citizens, and government and citizens to the creation, reform, or even dismantling of traditional resource management institutions, such as agencies and laws.[61] The following chapters examine the policy and potential problems posed by a shift to ecosystem management and the philosophical, social, and governance changes that may be required to resolve them.

NOTES

1. See, for example, Marsh, "Conservation planning under the ESA"; Brooks and Grant, "New approaches to forest management"; Kessler et al., "New perspectives for sustainable natural resources management"; Knight and Bates, *A New Century for Natural Resources Management*; and Norton, "A new paradigm for environmental management."

2. Kuhn, *The Structure of Scientific Revolutions*.

3. Patton, *Alternative Evaluation Research Paradigm*, p. 5, cited in Lincoln, "Introduction," p. 29.

4. Lincoln, "Introduction," p. 29.

5. Patton, *Alternative Evaluation Research Paradigm*, cited in Lincoln, "Introduction," p. 29.

6. Kuhn, *The Structure of Scientific Revolutions*.

7. Christensen et al., "The report of the Ecological Society of America Committee on the Scientific Basis for Ecosystem Management," p. 668; Franklin, "The fundamentals of ecosystem management with applications in the Pacific Northwest"; More, "Forestry's fuzzy concepts"; Pastor, "Ecosystem management, ecological risk, and public policy," p. 286; and World Commission on Environment and Development, *Our Common Future*. For further discussion of the general themes of sustainability, see Social Science Research Group, *Principles of Sustainability*. That report distilled six common themes from the literature on sustainability: (1) maintain ecological functions, conditions, and/or biodiversity; (2) evaluate and adapt social processes and governance functions; (3) adapt to change; (4) integrate ecological, cultural, and economic systems; (5) ensure intergenerational equity; and (6) accept ambiguity of the concept of sustainability.

8. Gordon, "Ecosystem management"; Christensen et al., "The report of the Ecological Society of America Committee on the Scientific Basis for Ecosystem Management"; Grumbine, "What is ecosystem management?"; and Costanza et al., "Goals, agenda, and policy recommendations for ecological economics."

9. Caldwell, "Implementing an ecosystems approach"; Kennedy and Thomas, "Managing natural resources as social value"; Norton, "A new paradigm for environmental management"; and Bird, "The social construction of nature."

10. Westoby et al., "Opportunistic management for rangelands not at equilibrium"; Floyd and Frost, "Measuring management objectives with condition classes"; Smith, "An evaluation of the range condition concept"; and Sedjo, "Toward an operational approach to public forest management," p. 26.

11. Christensen et al., "The report of the Ecological Society of America Committee on the Scientific Basis for Ecosystem Management"; and Norton, "A new paradigm for environmental management."

12. Christensen et al., "The report of the Ecological Society of America Committee on the Scientific Basis for Ecosystem Management." On intergenerational equity see Weiss, "Our rights and obligations to future generations for the environment."

13. Gordon, "Ecosystem management," p. 18.

14. Thomas et al., "The ecosystems approach," p. 41.

15. Golley, *A History of the Ecosystem Concept in Ecology*, p. 166.

16. Noss, "A regional approach to maintain diversity"; Noss and Harris, "Nodes, networks, and mums"; Newmark, "Legal and biotic boundaries of Western North American national parks"; Soulé, *Conservation Biology*; Franklin, "Preserving biodiversity"; Agee and Johnson, *Ecosystem Management for Parks and Wilderness*; and Grumbine, "Viable populations, reserve size, and federal lands management."

17. Franklin, "Ecosystem management."

18. "Detailed knowledge of why things occur as they do is ... the only path to the prediction of ecosystem behavior and output." Gordon, "Ecosystem management," p. 243. See also Franklin, "Ecosystem management."

19. Christensen et al., "The report of the Ecological Society of America Committee on the Scientific Basis for Ecosystem Management," p. 669.

20. Yaffee, "Ecosystem management in practice"; and Pastor, "Ecosystem management, ecological risk, and public policy."

21. Norton, "A new paradigm for environmental management," p. 37.

22. McLain, "Toward more effective ecological learning"; and Franklin, "Ecosystem management."

23. Christensen et al., "The report of the Ecological Society of America Committee on the Scientific Basis for Ecosystem Management," p. 666; and Breckenridge, "Reweaving the landscape," p. 372.

24. Holling, *Adaptive Environmental Assessment and Management*; McLain, "Toward more effective ecological learning"; and Franklin, "Ecosystem management." A purely quantitative approach to adaptive management has some limitations: "It incorrectly assumes that decision-making is a rational process that is both logical and objective; it overemphasizes the production and use of scientific knowledge while devaluing the importance of other kinds of knowledge; it devalues objectives that cannot be stated in quantitative terms; ... [and] it places a premium on scientific information." McLain, "Toward more effective ecological learning," executive summary. Therefore, where an entire ecosystem, including its related social systems, is involved, "given the improbability of quantifying many key human concerns, values and impacts ... the [adaptive management] model is more apt to be conceptual than quantitative." Geisler, "Rethinking SIA," p. 333.

25. McLain and Lee, "Adaptive management"; Breckenridge, "Reweaving the landscape"; and Lee, *Compass and Gyroscope*. According to Norton, "in management, innovation and adaptation are preferable to fixed principles and ... experimentation is essential." Norton, "A new paradigm for environmental management," p. 37.

26. Norton, "A new paradigm for environmental management," pp. 37–38. See also Shannon, "Foresters as strategic thinkers, facilitators, and citizens."

27. Franklin, "Ecosystem management," emphasis added.

28. Grumbine, "What is ecosystem management?," p. 31, emphasis added.

29. Lackey, "Radically contested assertions in ecosystem management."

30. Brown and Marshall, "Ecosystem management in state governments."

31. Fitzsimmons, "Sound policy or smoke and mirrors"; Lackey, "Ecosystem management"; Quarles, "The failure of federal land planning"; O'Keefe, "Holistic (new) forestry"; Sedjo, "Toward an operational approach to public forest management"; and MacCleery and Le Master, "Producing and consuming natural resources within an

ecosystem management framework." On the need to define sustainability in terms of time frames of concern and the relative priority of the costs and benefits see Lackey, "Seven pillars of ecosystem management." On the other hand, it is argued that because sustainability is dependent on social definition, which changes over time, there can be no objective definition of sustainability. Social Science Research Group, *Principles of Sustainability*. See also Gale and Cordray, "What should forests sustain?"; Orians, "Ecological concepts of sustainability"; and Shearman, "The meaning and ethics of sustainability."

32. Hunt, "Forest management abandoned" (letter to the editor); and Atkinson, "Silvicultural correctness."

33. Fitzsimmons, "Sound policy or smoke and mirrors."

34. Odum, for example, notes the utility of watersheds for ecological planning. Odum, *Fundamentals of Ecology*. The Tennessee Valley Authority is an early U.S. example of the use of the watershed as a basis for planning and management of both physical and human resources. For comparative discussion of both the watershed and ecoregion as analytical frameworks, see Omernik and Bailey, "Distinguishing between watersheds and ecoregions."

35. Flick and King, "Ecosystem management as American law"; and Quarles, "The failure of federal land planning."

36. Smith, "Antitrust and ecosystem management"; and Meidinger, "Organizational and legal challenges for ecosystem management."

37. *Lucas v. South Carolina Coastal Council*, 505 U.S. 1003 (1992); and *Dolan v. City of Tigard*, 129 L Ed 2d 304 (1994).

38. Sedjo, "Toward an operational approach to public forest management."

39. Moote and McClaran, "Implications of participatory democracy for public land planning."

40. Lee, *Broken Trust, Broken Land*.

41. Glenn, "Ecosystem management."

42. Ward, "Sovereignty and ecosystem management." On environmentalism as a structural characteristic affecting the response of nation-states to environmental policies, see Dietz and Kalof, "Environmentalism among nation-states."

43. Cawley and Freemuth, "A critique of the multiple use framework in public lands decisionmaking"; Freemuth, "The emergence of ecosystem management"; and Lawrence and Murphy, "New perspectives or old priorities?" Fairfax, "Remarks made at the symposium, Creating a New Forestry for the 21st Century"; and Slocombe, "Implementing ecosystem-based management." Shepard in "Seeing the forest for the trees" and Cortner and Moote in "Sustainability and ecosystem management" made early arguments that ecosystem management will not succeed if it rests on the assumption that the policy failures in resource management can be technically fixed.

44. Klyza, *Who Controls Public Lands?*; and Cooperrider, "Science as a model for ecosystem management."

45. Czech, "Ecosystem management is no paradigm shift."

46. See Roberts, "The federal chain-saw massacre"; and Bass, "On wilderness and Wallace Stegner."

47. Maxey, "Foresters," p. 44.

48. Barton, "Telling our story," p. 3.

49. Jones et al., "Ecosystem management"; See also Webster and Chappelle, "The curious state of forestry in the United States."

50. Statement of Dr. Alan A. Lucier, program director, Forest Environmental Studies, National Council of the Paper Industry for Air and Stream Improvement, Inc. Hearing on Ecosystem Management for the Committee on Agriculture, Nutrition and Forestry, Subcommittee on Agricultural Research, Conservation, Forestry and General Legislation, United States Senate, November 9, 1993; and Flick and King, "Ecosystem management as American law."

51. Fitzsimmons, "Federal ecosystem management."

52. Webster and Chappelle, "The curious state of forestry in the United States."

53. McCloskey, "The skeptic." See also Coggins, "Of Californicators, quislings and crazies."

54. Coggins, "Of Californicators, quislings, and crazies."

55. Lead Partnership Group, "Social and economic monitoring in rural communities," pp. 37–38.

56. See D'Amato, "Do we owe a duty to future generations to preserve the global environment?"

57. Banzhaf, "The videoconference," p. 3. See also Wenger, "What is ecosystem management?"

58. American Forest and Paper Association, *Ecosystem Management*, p. 1.

59. Fedkiw, "The Forest Service's pathway toward ecosystem management," p. 34. Ecosystem management is defined as "another stage in the agencies' evolving efforts to satisfy their obligation to stakeholders" in Haynes et al., *A Framework for Ecosystem Management in the Interior Columbia Basin and Portions of the Klamath and Great Basins*, p. 4. See also Hensen and Montrey, *Ecology Based Multiple-Use Management Strategy*. For discussion of this approach see Lackey, "Seven pillars of ecosystem management"; and Lackey, "Ecosystem management."

60. Wood, "Ecosystem management"; Franklin, "Ecosystem management"; Christensen et al., "The report of the Ecological Society of America Committee on the Scientific Basis for Ecosystem Management"; and Stanley, "Ecosystem management and the arrogance of humanism."

61. Interagency Ecosystem Management Task Force, *The Ecosystem Approach*; Cortner and Moote, "Trends and issues in land and water resources"; Cortner et al., *Institutional Barriers and Incentives for Ecosystem Management*; and U.S. General Accounting Office, *Ecosystem Management*.

Chapter 4

Policy Paradoxes

Since ancient times, paradoxes have puzzled and challenged humans with their apparent contradictions. In science and philosophy, the challenges posed by paradoxes have played an important role, often stimulating revolutionary developments in science, mathematics, and logic. Albert Einstein, for example, explored the paradoxes that resulted from the scientific premise that time was absolute. His early twentieth-century work on the theory of relativity introduced new concepts that revolutionized scientific ideas about the relationship of space and time. However, Einstein's theory of relativity is inconsistent with another cornerstone of modern physics—quantum mechanics. Modern day physicist Stephen Hawking, the greatest theoretical physicist since Einstein, is examining the apparent paradox of relativity and quantum mechanics, devoting a major portion of his life's work searching for a new theory that will incorporate them both.[1]

Natural resource management, too, is full of unresolved paradoxes. Many resource management policies contain competing goals that are rarely confronted, such as the National Park Service mandate to manage for both use and preservation. Too often, one goal is forsaken for another (e.g., economic development is undertaken at the expense of ecological sustainability). As discussed in chapter 3, ecosystem management is similarly fraught with contradictions. For many, these contradictions are further evidence of fatal flaws in a nebulous, unworkable, and undesirable approach to resource management. From another perspective, however, accepting and addressing contradictions is the key to understanding the challenges that efforts to implement ecosystem management will inevitably face and to identifying innovative solutions.

The Nature of Paradoxes

A paradox may be defined as something with seemingly contradictory qualities that are both true.[2] Paradoxes can be characterized as seeking disparate,
even contradictory elements simultaneously. With regard to social problems,
paradoxes arise when a problem embodies dissimilar goals that are equally vital
to problem resolution. Paradoxes have puzzled and stimulated humans and
challenged their reasoning since ancient times; the contradictions they contain
provoke human thought. The desire to solve problems with seemingly irreconcilable elements is part of human nature, and philosophers and others have
long realized the importance of paradoxes in understanding political life.
From a policy perspective,

> paradoxes are nothing but trouble. They violate the most elemen-
> tary principle of logic: something cannot be two different things
> at once. Two contradictory interpretations cannot both be true. A
> paradox is just such an impossible situation, and political life is
> full of them.[3]

Approaches to paradoxes vary: "Faced with a contradiction that seems fundamentally irreconcilable, one can ignore it or deny it, worship it or try to
remove it."[4] There are two quite distinct ways to view paradoxes. A common
construction of paradoxes comes in the form of a trade-off. A *trade-off* is a
statement that acknowledges competition between two ideas, goals, or objectives. Ideas are set in a context of competition when the relationship between
them is regarded as *A* versus *B*. Constructing paradoxes in this manner sets
goals as competing and mutually exclusive. Solving the problem (paradox)
leads to the dominance of one idea, goal, or set of interests over the other.
Therefore, the resolution of the paradox is a zero-sum relationship—for one
goal to be achieved the other is not and it takes a secondary position to the
first. In these cases, the problem remains essentially unresolved.

There is, however, another way to construct paradoxes—one that improves
problem-solving capabilities. Instead of seeing paradoxes as trade-offs, they
can be viewed as tensions to be balanced. The difference between these two
views of paradoxes is profound. Key assumptions underlying the idea of a
trade-off are that various goals are not attainable at the same time, and that
often one goal must be given up for another. *Tension*, on the other hand, is
defined as a balance maintained between opposing forces or elements. When
we view paradoxes as involving tensions, we can conceive of seemingly contradictory goals being reconciled and simultaneously achieved. In short, tensions
are resolvable; trade-offs are not.

To resolve paradoxes we must face them head-on. Often we have thwarted our own efforts by attempting to achieve conflicting goals without acknowledging and reconciling the discord between them. The alternative is to carefully examine the paradox and to transfigure two seemingly irreconcilable goals into a double concerto,[5] as an orchestra creates harmony through the simultaneous playing of contrasting compositions.

Paradoxes of Ecosystem Management

Ecosystem management brings its own set of specific contradictions as well as highlights long-standing political contradictions that are characteristic of American government. It is not surprising, then, that ecosystem management entails some of the same paradoxes that traditional natural resource management encounters. In some cases, ecosystem management accentuates those paradoxes; in other cases, it emphasizes a different balance between goals (e.g., as between economic development and ecological sustainability). To examine in more detail the mix and nature of the paradoxes that confront and challenge ecosystem management, we distinguish three categories: paradoxes of decision making, of scale, and of sustainability.

Paradoxes of Decision Making

A democratic society places considerable emphasis on making public agents both accountable for the decisions they make and responsive to public wishes. Certain behaviors are prescribed, others are proscribed, often in elaborate and detailed manuals. At the same time the public worries about red tape and automaton bureaucrats. Several paradoxes that challenge ecosystem management concern how to balance the principles of adaptive management and collaboration with the need for decision making that is politically responsive and publicly accountable.

Flexibility and Consistency

Ecosystem management requires planning and management procedures flexible enough to allow for rapid adjustments in response to change or new knowledge. On the other hand, like all management policies, ecosystem management also requires some degree of uniformity among management goals, and consistent measures by which goal attainment and employee performance can be evaluated. Overly prescriptive laws, regulations, and agency procedures are often seen as impediments to ecosystem management. Yet those laws, regulations, standards, and procedures were designed to address valid public concerns, such as open access to meetings, protection and recovery of threatened and endangered species, and assurance that the nation's waters are being made swimmable and drinkable. Many are prescriptive precisely because the intent is to circumscribe managerial discretion and flexibility. Dismantling some of these standards and prescriptions might permit "better" management in some cases, by allowing the development of more innovative or site-specific management prescriptions than the law currently allows. Yet flexibility to the extreme can also lead to arbitrary and capricious decision making, and decision making that is not responsive to legislative intent. Ecosystem management must be both flexible *and* consistent.

Inclusiveness and Accountability

A related paradox concerns reconciling open or consensual decision making (especially in a rapidly changing sociopolitical context) with the need to establish management goals, and ultimately standards of accountability.[6] An open, collaborative process involving all stakeholders can slow decision making and diffuse authority, thereby reducing accountability. Collaborative decision making is affected by many variables, including the number of participants included, how the goals are described, the nature of the conflict, and the values at stake. Consensual agreement in particular may become difficult as the number of participants increases.[7] The power of one individual to veto an otherwise essentially unanimous process is also a consideration; decision making by consensus paradoxically concentrates power in the individual. If the definition of legitimacy under ecosystem management is the openness and inclusiveness of the decision-making process, where does the authority to make decisions lie, and is it readily apparent? Who is accountable both legally and morally for the results of the decision, all or only some of the participants?

A good example of the tension between inclusiveness and accountability is found in the Federal Advisory Committee Act (FACA). Along with the Government in Sunshine Act, the Freedom of Information Act, and the Administrative Procedure Act, FACA is one of the pillars of the open-government laws.[8] These laws ensure public access to agency records and decision-making processes, and are often called sunshine laws to emphasize the legal intent to move agency activity from behind closed doors to the full light of public scrutiny. FACA, which was enacted in 1972, was originally designed to make government decision making less susceptible to control by special interests who could enhance their access and influence through the nonpublicly visible work of advisory committees. Under FACA, all advisory committees must have fairly balanced membership and follow formal administrative procedures, such as publishing notice of meetings in the Federal Register, taking detailed minutes of meetings, and opening all meetings to the public.

As implemented, however, FACA may be a deterrent to federal agency efforts to meet the collaborative decision-making principle of ecosystem management. Informal, collaborative, place-based groups often do not conform to FACA's requirements. Confusion over its legal restrictions has led to considerable "FACA phobia" among federal agency employees, with the result that many refuse to participate in public forums that do not meet the strictures of FACA advisory committees.[9] A 1995 amendment exempted intergovernmental partnerships from the act's procedural provisions, but did not address agency collaboration with nongovernmental agencies. However, any efforts to amend or reinterpret FACA to permit more agency participation in such groups or to facilitate private–public partnerships will need to be carefully crafted so as to not undermine the law's original intent by once again shielding agency interactions with interested stakeholders from broader public scrutiny.

Expert and Open Decision Making

Ecosystem management emphasizes both collaborative decision making and the importance of using integrative, holistic science. It will require a much more active role for citizens than has been true of past resource planning and management efforts. Yet at the same time, the strong role envisioned for science can have the effect of delegating decision-making authority to experts, limiting the role of citizens. Thus, a paradox that is heightened under ecosystem management involves balancing the values of expertise and scientific knowledge with social consensus and civic discourse. For example, a key question posed by analysts with the 1994 Forest Ecosystem Management Assessment Team (FEMAT)—which was responsible for developing President Clinton's plan for management of old-growth forests in the Northwest and is often cited as one of the first large-scale applications of ecosystem analysis and planning—was, "How can society balance the politics of expertise with the politics of inclusion?"[10] Ironically, the FEMAT team itself was not inclusive and has been characterized as exclusive and technocratic.[11]

As shown in chapter 2, since the beginning of the conservation movement in the late 1880s, resource management has traditionally tipped the scales in favor of scientific efficiency and the politics of expertise. Yet, public distrust of scientists and professional experts in agencies has continually increased over the last few decades. Science cannot decide what are essentially value questions, and scientists do not know enough to make such decisions. Moreover, limiting decision making to a narrow group of experts can limit the alternatives eventually offered as solutions.[12] Certainly the concept and language of *science-based* decision making reinforces the perception that science alone decides and heightens the paradox of expert versus open decision making.

Perhaps this paradox can be more effectively addressed if it is posed somewhat differently: how to balance the values of expertise and scientific knowledge, that is, *science-informed* decision making with social consensus and civic discourse.

Bureaucracy and Responsiveness

A related paradox concerns the nature of bureaucracies themselves. Civil service reforms in the late nineteenth century, responding to the extensive corruption and graft of that time, were based on the premise that democracy requires a strong, impartial civil service, protected from the whims of day-to-day politics. But civil service bureaucrats are still responsible to their bosses: the president, Congress, and the public. As one scholar notes:

> On the one hand, we confer on them tenure in their positions so that they will be guided by rigorous criteria of professional judgement, integrity, decency, impartiality, and the public interest in the performance of their duties, and not by every passing political wind or request for special favors. On the other hand, we tell them they are agents of the elected government and should comply with the directives of their political superiors.[13]

At the same time, bureaucrats must be professional experts who are "above politics," they must, paradoxically, be politically responsive.

A strong bureaucracy can provide citizens with information, knowledge about laws, and other tools to empower them. The German sociologist Max Weber (1864–1920) was the first to undertake a methodological study of bureaucracy and remains one of the most influential writers on the modern state. Weber observed that

> bureaucracy inevitably accompanies modern *mass democracy* in contrast to the democratic self-government of small homogeneous units.... Bureaucratic organization has usually come into power on the basis of a leveling of economic and social differences.... Bureaucracy is *the* means of carrying 'community action' over into rationally ordered 'societal action.'... More and more the material fate of the masses depends on the steady and correct functioning of the increasingly bureaucratic organization....[14]

Yet Weber also saw bureaucracy as a threat to basic democratic liberties. He believed that elected leaders would inevitably lose control over the modern bureaucracy. The key factor was not the size of bureaucracy, but the control of information. "Bureaucracy naturally welcomes a poorly informed and hence a powerless parliament—at least in so far as ignorance somehow agrees with the bureaucracy's interests."[15]

Weber's descriptions of the development, growth, and characteristics of bureaucracies are eerily applicable to modern administrative organizations. As American bureaucracy has grown, so have the pathologies associated with such large, complex organizations, including red tape, conflict, duplication, imperialism, and waste.[16] Layer upon layer of bureaucracy have been added to government, to the extent that accountability and administration become much harder to pinpoint. Agencies have developed specialized information and jargon that increase their remoteness from ordinary people.[17] Because control over the bureaucracy is divided among different branches of government that do not always sing with the same voice, bureaucrats can play one boss off against another and the public. Being accountable to so many makes it easier to be accountable to no one. As previously noted, even the public participation processes established by agencies have served in many cases to discourage, not encourage, public involvement.[18] Thus, there is an apparent contradiction between the democratic principles of open, responsive decision making and modern bureaucratic politics that tends to exclude the public from decision making.

Conflict and Collaboration

Another apparent paradox occurs between collaboration and conflict. Although at first sight these two goals appear contradictory, on closer examination they are interdependent. Some even argue that conflict is necessary to achieve collaboration, because it permits all concerns to be aired and ideally addressed. While involving all interests in policy making is sure to engender increased conflict, *not* involving them virtually begs opposition later on. Paradoxically, then, "conflict can be indispensable as an integrating mechanism" for ecosystem management: "political conflict can provide ways to recognize [and correct for] errors, complementing and reinforcing the self-conscious learning of adaptive management."[19] To realize these benefits of conflict, however, society must set parameters or guidelines for working with it, which requires collaboration. Efforts to balance conflict and collaboration can be seen in the recent surge of interest in conflict resolution and community-building.[20]

Paradoxes of Scale

The spatial scale of ecosystem management is both large and small. Ecosystems should be managed on a landscape scale, including all natural resources and social institutions, and their interconnections, in a combined effort to achieve sustainability. Yet ecosystem management also calls for small-scale management, adapting management prescriptions to local conditions. Other paradoxes of scale arise in management agencies. While managers grapple with the need to collect, analyze, and apply more information, they are also being told to decentralize, reduce staff, and work with smaller budgets. Similarly, agencies are being asked to manage on an ecological time frame with budgets and policy directives that are still structured on short-term political schedules.

Centralization and Decentralization

Historically in the United States, many decisions about resources have been centralized at the federal level. At the same time, local jurisdictions have maintained considerable autonomy. This split in authority is an intentional function of our federalist system of government. Centralizing authority often translates to large hierarchical institutions that are inflexible, slow to adapt to change, and insensitive to the impacts of governmental action on the lives of those affected. Inevitably, decisions made at the system or national level may appear unjust or illogical from the local perspective. Yet when local preferences are allowed to predominate, congruity at the system level is reduced and "there may be losses to the whole—losses that result in barely perceptible overall erosion or in a shifting of damage from one place to another."[21] For example, on the one hand, allowing regional or local development of best management practices for pollution control may result in practices that protect an ecosystem better than do state or national standards. On the other hand, removing standards could also permit local communities to choose to apply *no* best management practices, or practices that are less appropriate than the standards.

Some contend the only way to deal with the global problems the world faces is to centralize authority. Proponents of this view argue that the human threat to ecosystem health is so great—as evidenced by exponential rates of human population growth and consumption levels—that only more centralized governmental authority and power will be able to protect and manage ecosystems for the future.[22] There is a high level of distrust of local communities, and fear that for them the pressures to succumb to the lure of short-term economic gains are just too powerful.

Others argue that a more decentralized approach to resource administration is needed so that people closest to the problems can take responsibility, and management can be tailored to local ecosystem conditions.[23] This assumes that when local communities are empowered to assert leadership they will choose to be good ecosystems stewards, and will do so more effectively than distant and remote bureaucracies. Ecosystem management thus involves "a paradox of scale; small-scale institutions are required to effectively regulate large-scale ecological processes."[24] Add other observers: "*Act locally but think globally* is not merely a cliché. And it is harder to do than many people think."[25]

The decentralization–centralization paradox is not new to resource management. Planners and managers have always struggled with the ongoing conflict between local and national interests. Most often, however, this paradox has been viewed in terms of trade-offs. A more fruitful perspective would be to view decentralization and centralization as tensions to be balanced: "both are important to the search for sustainability: task-based learning is important to carry out projects in cost-effective ways; system knowledge is essential to improving strategies in light of experience."[26] Synergistically, better management may result when planners and managers try to link national-level perspectives with decentralized action.

Managing More with Less

Ecosystem management requires understanding and tracking vast amounts of information, from ecological structures, processes, and stressors to ecological indicators and social values. As noted in chapter 3, there are no externalities in ecosystem management. Society needs to consider all the effects of its management decisions: on downstream ecosystems, global economies, and local communities, to name a few. This requires an extremely broad geographic focus. Understanding the potential effects of decisions also requires information on the detailed aspects of ecosystem functions at site-specific locations. Yet the late twentieth century has been an era of government downsizing. Resource management agency budgets and staff have been drastically reduced. Rather than expending resources to know all there is to know about relatively small management areas, as in the past, resources are likely to be expended achieving a more sweeping, holistic view of the interrelationships of spatially larger landscapes (i.e., knowing a little about a lot rather than a lot about a little). Clearly, some ingenuity will be required to balance more in-depth and larger-scale management with fewer government resources.

Ecological and Human Time Frames

Another paradox of scale relates to time. Government time lines often do not match the temporal scales of research and management called for under an ecosystem approach. While it may take decades to obtain results from ecosystem experiments, government policies often change with elections.[27] Moreover, the politician's need to curry favor for the next election rewards decisions that deliver immediate benefits to constituents and campaign contributors, even if they entail long-term ecological costs. In other instances, government policy schedules—particularly the schedules by which agency budget requests are cycled to the president and Congress—do not respond well to ecosystem management's need for immediate response or adaptation in the face of rapidly changing conditions.

Paradoxes of Sustainability

Ecosystem management itself can be viewed as a paradox. At its heart, ecosystem management is proposed as a means to reconcile a central social paradox concerning goals of economic development and ecological sustainability.[28] Our society values the goals of ecological protection and economic development; they are both valid goals. However, as a whole, contemporary society has yet to find a means of balancing those goals. As ecosystem managers address the tensions between economic development and ecological sustainability, they will encounter several paradoxes.

Sustainable Development

Most contemporary discussions of sustainability refer back to the definition of *sustainable development* offered in the 1987 report by the World Commission on Environment and Development. That study, which is commonly known as the Brundtland Report, defined *sustainable development* as activity "that meets the needs of the present without compromising the ability of future generations to meet their own needs."[29] For sustainable development, an intergenerational obligation, rather than maximization of short-term gain, is paramount. However, sustainable development has also been called an oxymoron by those who consider development and sustainability to be mutually exclusive concepts.[30] Similarly, the presumption that humans can manage for ecological integrity has been deemed not just paradoxical, but arrogant.[31] To reach and sustain an acceptable standard of living for all humans will require increased production of goods and services, particularly as the human population continues to increase. Figure 4.1 illustrates the dramatic increase in population growth that is projected for the next 50 years. The goal becomes harder when the economic standard of living is based on the wealth and consumption rates of people in the most developed countries. The U.S., for example, which has 5 percent of the world's population, uses 40 percent of the world's natural resources. Thus, we face a paradox of sustaining ecological productivity while meeting ever-increasing rates of resource consumption for an expanding population.

Warnings about the impact of population growth on human natural

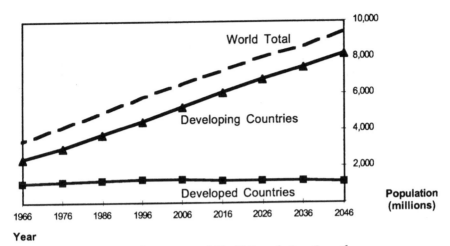

Figure 4.1 Projected World Population Growth
Source: Population Division, Department of Economic and
Social Affairs, United Nations, NYC; Brown, Lester R., Christopher Flavin,
and Hilary French, *State of the World.*

resources occurred as early as two centuries ago when Thomas R. Malthus
wrote *An Essay on the Principle of Population.* Malthus argued that unless birth rates
were checked, famine and hunger would be inevitable; the world's natural
resources could not feed a larger population. He also argued, however, that
there were "natural" checks on population—factors affecting mortality, such
as nutrition, disease, work conditions, environment, and war; and factors
affecting fertility, such as sexual practices and controls.[32] Malthus's theories
stirred up a controversy that has yet to abate. Publication in 1968 of *The
Population Bomb*, which linked unrestrained population growth, food shortages,
and pollution impacts, coincided with the emergence of the environmental
movement and sparked the modern public debate over population and the
environment.[33] *The Limits to Growth*, the widely publicized 1972 report of the
Club of Rome, also warned that there weren't enough critical resources for
continued growth in industrialization, consumption, and population.[34]

While some perceive the population demands placed on the world's
resources as overwhelming, others take a more positive view. They argue that
the assumption that resources are limited implies a zero-sum game, that is, one
person consumes more, thus another must consume less. Accordingly, "a
closed-world, zero-sum vision also points thinking toward *conservation* rather
than *creation of resources.*"[35] An alternative view is that depletion of some
resources leads to the discovery of others, thus opening the way to new and

better technology and a higher standard of living for all. Raising the global standard of living is seen as necessary to reverse environmental degradation, since people living at subsistence level cannot afford to preserve ecosystems.[36] Also widely advanced is the argument that wealthier people will become convinced to have fewer children; as the population projections in figure 4.1 illustrate, birth rates in developed countries are likely to remain stable.

Although continued population growth and higher economic standards seem to conflict with a goal of ecological sustainability, some analysts believe that with improved technology, natural resource consumption will be reduced to the point where it will be negligible, permitting continued use of ecosystem products without negatively impacting ecological integrity. This is countered by others who maintain that while in theory technological advances may allow for increased economic growth without impacting ecological integrity, it seems unlikely that technology will develop at the rate that global human population is exploding.[37] Without evidence of a vastly improved and constantly improving technology, the tension between maintaining ecological functions and demographic and economic growth remains one of the most challenging paradoxes of ecosystem management.

Managing for Both Ecosystem Use and Preservation

Ecosystem management paradoxically advocates preserving ecosystems, or some aspects of ecosystems, from human use, even while acknowledging a human need—and right—to use them. The tension between preserving ecosystem values and also providing opportunities for ecosystem use can be seen in the hostile standoffs between land managers "protecting" public lands and special interests desiring greater access to "our" public resources. It is evident in the polarized stances of environmentalists, who lobby for more wilderness designations, and the growing "Wise Use" movement, which advocates human use and development of publicly-owned resources.

This paradox may stem in part from the unique sense of individual ownership Americans feel for their public lands, a sentiment summed up in the popular Woody Guthrie song lyric, "this land is your land; this land is my land." In a country where individual property ownership is one of the most vigilantly held values, Americans perceive individual rights in a collective resource. This results in an array of special interests trying to cordon off resources or parcels of public land for specific uses. Yet it is in close examination of the concepts of property ownership, land tenure, and usufruct that resolution to this paradox may lie. Just as private property rights have long been redefined by regulations to protect the common interest, the concept of public property is evolving to include a wide variety of semi-private entitlements (e.g., national parks and conservation preserves on state or private land). While it is often believed that the lines between private and public property are absolute (just like societal notions of time before Einstein's work on relativity), in fact the line is increasingly blurred, opening up the possibilities of new management models that create more private rights to public property and not just more public regulation of private property.[38]

In the 1930s, Aldo Leopold identified another classic paradox of humans preserving nature. Leopold wrote, "but all conservation of wildness is self-defeating, for to cherish we must see and fondle, and when enough have seen and fondled, there is no wilderness left to cherish."[39] More recently it has been observed that the more we destroy nature, the more we may find we need it: "It is one of the most profound and subtle of the contradictions at the heart of overdeveloped societies that the more crowded, affluent, and technologically sophisticated we become, the more we become aware of our need for wilderness, and the scarcer wilderness becomes for each of us."[40] As special areas are identified and protected, the "irony of victory" often occurs:[41] we destroy what we most want to protect.

Planning for Uncertainty

Finally, there is a paradox between the goal of sustainability and the uncertainty inherent in ecosystem management. Planning for sustainability means taking into account all of the potential products, both commodity and noncommodity, that may be required of that ecosystem in the future, as well as all of the potential impacts that management decisions may have on any aspect of the system.[42] However, current systems theory tells us that ecosystems—including human social systems—are constantly changing in ways that we frequently cannot predict. Under ecosystem management, therefore, we are asked to develop management plans that ensure the continued stability and productivity of complex systems that will never be completely understood. In essence, we are asked to determine the "how" for a constantly changing "what." The tension here is between the traditional concept of planning for a definite goal or state and the reality that ecosystems are too variable for us to be able to plan with any certainty.

Resolving the Tensions

Ecosystem management is paradoxical, but paradoxes are inherent to natural resource management and to governance. They are a fact of political and social life. It is critical to address these paradoxes, but not by forcing trade-offs between conflicting options. It is the difficult process of confronting the tensions in paradoxes that encourages innovation.

This chapter summarized three categories of paradoxes. Paradoxes of decision making occur between the goals of flexibility and consistency, inclusiveness and accountability, expert and open decision making, bureaucracy and responsiveness, and conflict and collaboration. Paradoxes of scale include tensions between centralization and decentralization, managing more with less, and managing on both ecological and human time frames. Paradoxes of sustainability include sustainable development, planning for uncertainty, and the dual goals of ecosystem use and preservation. Resolving these will require major revisions of social beliefs, values, norms, and governance practices. Paradoxes of sustainability are the most intractable paradoxes of ecosystem management, and the ones most likely to require revolutionary changes in the basic philosophical values of American society. It is to these changes we now turn our attention.

NOTES

1. Hawking, *A Brief History of Time.*
2. Quine, "Paradox," p. 84.
3. Stone, *Policy Paradox and Political Reason,* p. I.
4. Rapaport, "Escape from paradox," p. 50; and Quine, "Paradox," p. 84.
5. Hesse, *Magister Ludi (The Glass Bead Game),* p. 94. See also Worster, *Rivers of Empire,* p. 80.
6. Agee and Johnson, "A direction for ecosystem management."
7. Dryzek, *Rational Ecology.*
8. Nuszkiewicz, "Twenty years of the Federal Advisory Committee Act," p. 966.
9. Court rulings have interpreted FACA to prohibit agencies from taking any advice from groups that include individuals who are not federal government employees and that are not constituted as formal advisory committees under the act. For example, the Northwest Forest Resource Council brought suit against the Federal Ecosystem Management Assessment Team (FEMAT) that had been established to present to President Clinton a plan for resolving the spotted owl/old-growth forest controversy in the Pacific Northwest. The Council claimed, and the court concurred, that the assessment team, which was composed of agency and nonagency scientists and whose work excluded observation of day-to-day operations, constituted an advisory committee in violation of the act.
10. Forest Ecosystem Management Assessment Team (FEMAT). *Forest Ecosystem Management* p. VIII-9. See also Manring, "Reconciling science and politics in Forest Service decision making."
11. Johnson et al., "Developing a forest plan for federal forests of the Pacific Northwest," p. 53.

12. Lackey, "Ecological risk assessment"; Cooperrider, "Science as a model for ecosystem management"; and Shannon and Antypas, "Civic science is democracy in action."

13. Kaufman, "The paradox of excellence," p. 12.

14. Weber, *Wirtschaft und Gesellschaft*, quoted in Gerth and Mills, *From Max Weber*, pp. 224, 228, 229, emphasis in original. According to Weber, bureaucracy is characterized by a certain rigidity. There is a hierarchical structure of authority, with "fixed and official jurisdictional areas, which are generally ordered by rules, that is, by laws or administrative regulations." Official assignments and promotions are based on "thorough and expert training." Positions are highly specialized to maximize efficiency, and standard rules of operation ensure consistency and preclude emotional reasoning. Bureaucratic officials are characterized by complete loyalty to the organization, in return for which they receive social standing, a salary, and job security. Bureaucracy, Weber wrote, offers stringent standards, precision, reliability, and efficiency, pp. 196, 198. See also Pinchot and Pinchot, *The End of Bureaucracy and the Rise of the Intelligent Organization*.

15. Weber, *Wirtschaft und Gesellschaft*, quoted in Gerth and Mills, *From Max Weber*, p. 234.

16. Wilson, *American Government*, p. 280.

17. Schneider and Ingram, *Policy Design for Democracy*, p. 154.

18. Held, *Models of Democracy*; Kathlene and Martin, "Enhancing citizen participation"; and Pateman, *Participation and Democratic Theory*.

19. Lee, *Compass and Gyroscope*, p. 87.

20. See, for example: Yaffe and Wondolleck, "Building bridges across agency boundaries," and Maser, *Resolving Environmental Conflict*.

21. Lee, *Compass and Gyroscope*, p. 113.

22. Ophuls, "Reversal is the law of the Tao."

23. Behan, "A plea for constituency-based management"; and Rodman, "Paradigm change in political science."

24. Lee and Stankey, "Evaluating institutional arrangements for regulating large watersheds and river basins," p. 30. On decentralization–centralization, see Press, *Democratic Dilemmas in the Age of Ecology*.

25. Salwasser et al., "An ecosystem perspective on sustainable forestry and new directions for the U.S. National Forest System," p. 65, emphasis in original.

26. Lee, *Compass and Gyroscope*, p. 114.

27. Volkman and Lee, "The owl and the Minerva," p. 49.

28. Caldwell et al., "Making ecosystem policy"; and Schlager and Friemund, "Institutional and legal barriers to ecosystem management."

29. World Commission on Environment and Development, *Our Common Future*, p. 43.

30. Maser, "Do we owe anything to the future?"

31. Maser, "Do we owe anything to the future?"

32. Malthus, *An Essay on the Principle of Population*.

33. Ehrlich, *The Population Bomb*. See also Brown, *State of the World 1991*; and Ehrlich et al., *The Stork and the Plow*. Six years after publication of *The Population Bomb*, the first official International Conference on Population and Development took place in Bucharest in

1974. This conference has been repeated each decade, the most recent having occurred in Cairo, Egypt in 1994, two years after the Earth Summit in Rio de Janeiro. In Cairo it was apparent that deep divisions surrounded the issue of abortion and the consumption patterns of industrialized countries.

34. Meadows et al., *The Limits to Growth*.

35. Simon, *Population Matters*, p. 7, emphasis in the original. See also Simon, *The Ultimate Resource*.

36. Fri, "Sustainable development." According to Fri, the Brundtland report equates the absence of economic development with environmental degradation and considers human population growth inevitable.

37. Salwasser et al., "An ecosystem perspective on sustainable forestry and new directions for the U.S. National Forest System," pp. 50, 62.

38. Geisler, "Cultural factors in public land policy," p. 10; Geisler and Kittel, "Who owns the ecosystem?"; and Reidel and Richardson, "A public/private cooperative paradigm for federal land management."

39. Leopold, *A Sand County Almanac and Sketches Here and There*, p. 101.

40. Rodman, "The liberation of nature," p. 113.

41. Nash, *Wilderness and the American Mind*, pp. 263–264.

42. Ultimately, ecosystem management strives "to avoid near-term resource management decisions that may overly restrict or foreclose future management options." Sample et al., "Introduction," p. 6.

Chapter 5

Philosophical Underpinnings

In a statement given to Congress, legal counsel for a major industrial association criticized ecosystem management by quoting a statement by the chief of the Forest Service and then inserting his own parenthetical comments: "New efforts by scientists, philosophers, technologists, leaders, and managers can be targeted at the sharpening of evolving [ecosystem] concepts and practices. [*Did you catch that? 'Philosophers' right after scientists and before 'leaders and managers.'*]"[1] The lawyer's outrage reflects the perspective of many in the natural resource professions, both proponents and opponents of ecosystem management. Yet, as this chapter will show, philosophers do indeed have a critical role to play in shaping the formulation and implementation of ecosystem management.[2]

All natural resource policies and practices embody key philosophical principles. Whether implicit or explicit, these principles underlie our ideas, actions, and institutions. Examining the principles shows that different philosophies yield very different answers to important questions about governance in general and natural resource policy in particular. These questions include: What is the view of society toward nature? What is the role of government in the management of natural resources? What is the role of the market? What is the role of citizens in forming natural resource policy? Answers to questions such as these reflect assumptions about what makes a good society and good government[3] and form the basis upon which natural resource policies are made.

Analysis of philosophical questions can improve our understanding of current problems, and can assist in evaluating policies and framing new political theory and policy alternatives. The examination of philosophical principles is especially important in the case of ecosystem management, because many of the above questions are answered in a fundamentally different way for ecosystem management than for the traditional natural resource management paradigm. Ecosystem management calls for a shift in the way humans approach the natural world and requires an explicit examination of our patterns of politics and methods of scientific inquiry. Philosophy is the realm in which we can begin to address many of the paradoxes described in the previous chapter. If ecosystem management is to truly emerge as a new paradigm, we must indeed look to philosophers as well as to scientists, leaders, and managers.

In the past, discussions about attitudes toward natural resources in the United States have been largely framed by opposing the philosophies of John Muir against those of Gifford Pinchot, or setting a preservationist view against an utilitarian perspective.[4] In reality, however, the roots of the discussion about the relationship between humans and nature run much deeper and are found in the wider context of Western political thought. Moreover, the definition of the relationship between humans and the natural world has important implications beyond whether nature is to be preserved or utilized. The way in which a society defines the human–nature relationship is reflected in its methods of governance, scientific inquiry, interactions among humans, and, ultimately, natural resource policies.[5]

The roots of discussion about human–nature relationships indeed go back as far as Greek and Roman and medieval times.[6] However, the traditional paradigm of natural resource management—characterized as it is by the politics of expertise, maximum sustained yield, and interest—can primarily be traced to philosophical principles that crystallized during the era of the Enlightenment in the seventeenth and eighteenth centuries. In this chapter, we examine the mark that the Enlightenment Era has left on American political thought and the traditional paradigm of resource management and show how ecosystem management rests on alternative theoretical principles. Significant differences can be found along four dimensions: the relationship between humans and nature, the concept of rationality, the role and structure of science, and the social relations among humans.

Enlightenment Thought

Enlightenment thought includes a large and diverse body of literature, including the writings of John Locke, René Descartes, Immanuel Kant, Georg W. F. Hegel, and David Hume. Enlightenment thought encompasses several generations with branches in various European countries and, eventually, North America.[7] Political theorists, even those who rarely agree, concede Enlightenment thought has had a profound effect on the Western world, but most particularly the United States.[8] The American constitutional system, for example, was modeled to a large degree on the political theory of John Locke. Locke's defense of the English Glorious Revolution of 1688 in *Two Treatises of Civil Government* became the dominant source of political theory relied on by Madison and the other framers during the formative years of the American Republic. "Locke was indeed the prime source of founding principles: Locke construed by Madison in the light of American experience and usage."[9]

The Enlightenment marked a new era for human civilization. The principles of Enlightenment thought largely shape how we view the modern world; they continue to influence writers and thinkers as well as the form of societal structures and the conduct of scientific inquiry. Undeniably, Enlightenment writers are a diverse lot.

> Some parties give primacy to rights and others to utility; some think they can support a correspondence theory of truth and others adopt a more pragmatic theory; some think there is no God and others think that a God with a limited earthly presence is necessary to the integrity of reason, morality and politics; some incline toward the market and others toward the state; some favor democracy and others a bureaucratic politics; some celebrate individual freedom and others believe that freedom can exist only in community.[10]

Yet while profound differences exist among Enlightenment writers, as a whole they share similar beliefs in the power of reason, the rejection of superstition and authority, and the supremacy of the individual, as well as a firm belief in human progress.

Part of the allure of Enlightenment thought, an allure that continues today, has always been its promises. Enlightenment thought views knowledge as a liberating force to help move people toward human liberty, equality, and progress. In contrast to medieval times,

> In the century of Enlightenment, educated Europeans awoke to a new sense of life. They experienced an expansive sense of power over nature and themselves: the pitiless cycles of epidemics, famines, risky life and early death, devastating war and uneasy peace—the treadmill of human existence—seemed to be yielding at last to the application of critical intelligence.[11]

To achieve this liberation, Enlightenment thought sought to intensify the "'light' of reason, first lit in Greece, which had been 'rekindled' in the fourteenth century after almost a millennium of darkness."[12] The Enlightenment

Era promised that reason would triumph over superstition, authorities would be subject to reasoned criticism, and that human liberty, equality, knowledge, and progress would prevail. Reason and science would give birth to justice, peace, and democracy.[13]

Enlightenment thought is also centered on the individual. By contrast, in the Greek world, the social and political community, and political institutions in particular, were considered essential in helping form good citizens.[14] Enlightenment thought, on the other hand, places high priority on the principles of individualism. Individual reason, conscience, and feeling predominate in both private and public life. As Kant so concisely said: "the maxim of always thinking for oneself is enlightenment."[15]

For Enlightenment writers, the individual, armed with reason, could stand against any authority—whether it be the church or the monarchy. The Enlightenment meant it would no longer be necessary to rely on persons and institutions who claimed privileged access to the good life. The unique and universal features of human reason and experience would make the good life attainable by all.[16] This promise held out the hope of loosening the societal strictures present in the seventeenth and eighteenth centuries. It was believed that through the pursuit of truth and knowledge, humans would realize progress in the social world.

Without doubt, much of the progress we enjoy today in social equality and in the quality of political life was initiated by Enlightenment thought. For example, the rejection of dogma, superstition, and the arbitrary use of authority is an enduring contribution to Western political systems. The principles of popular government, political equality and individual rights—principles embodied in the U.S. Constitution—are largely the heritage of this era. The power of science and technology to improve our lives cannot also be denied.

However, many prominent Enlightenment promises failed to bear fruit. In the twentieth century, critics, particularly those labeled the critical theorists, saw a darker side of the Enlightenment and began to question its basic tenets.[17] Strongly influenced by the horrors of Nazi Germany, the critical theorists began to question how something like the holocaust could happen in the midst of a society strongly influenced by the Enlightenment. To seek answers they began to examine the basic tenets of Enlightenment thought.

A central argument of the critical theorists is that the very ideals of the Enlightenment—reason and science—have at times been destructive. For many of these theorists, the culmination of Enlightenment thought can be seen most clearly in the relationship between humans and nature in contemporary society. In particular, it is argued that humans have sought to dominate and master nature, which in turn has negatively shaped social relations and the formation and conduct of scientific inquiry.[18] Four profoundly negative and interrelated effects of Enlightenment thought on modern society are discussed below, including: (1) an emphasis on human mastery over nature; (2) a narrow conception of reason; (3) science defined as positivism; and (4) domination of humans over humans.

Human Mastery over Nature

A key criticism of Enlightenment thought offered by the critical theorists is that it has resulted in an attitude of domination and mastery toward nature that has had far reaching consequences for modern society. The attitude of humans is one of acquiring absolute mastery over nature, of "converting the cosmos into one immense hunting ground."[19] Building upon the political theory of Locke, land is seen as inert until human labor converts it into something that can be made one's own (i.e., private property). When nature is viewed in these terms, knowledge, especially in relation to the natural world, becomes a tool of domination, not liberation. Nature itself becomes an instrument because "what men want to learn from nature is how to use it in order wholly to dominate it and other men. That is the only aim."[20]

Further, according to the critical theorists, humans view the world in terms of predictable relationships, and the quantification of these relationships is prerequisite for dominating nature. The result is a nature devoid of meaning apart from provision of commodities and other measurable items. While some small areas of nature have been protected, society, in general, treats nature as an instrument of destructive productivity.[21] Nature is transformed into natural resources for either production or as an object of scientific inquiry.

A Narrow Conception of Reason

A second criticism of Enlightenment Era thought is that the concept of reason changed, taking on a very narrow character. By comparison, Greek philosophers such as Aristotle had a much richer connotation of reason: it was a companion to wisdom and an integral part of the way to achieve true happiness. During the Enlightenment, the critical theorists argue, the concept of reason changed substantially and became a mere instrument in social life. Reason was reduced to a narrow conception of rationality—instrumental rationality. Instrumental rationality is defined as "the selection of efficacious means to previously given ends."[22] Under instrumental rationality, little importance is attached to the larger question of whether the ends themselves are reasonable. Efficiency becomes the basic value; there is no normative foundation on which to act.[23] It is this type of rationality that underlies much of modern society.

The consequence for society of this narrow type of reason, according to the critics, is that concepts such as justice and equality lose their intellectual roots. There is no way to link these concepts to any objective reality. Values and ethics become situational, changing to fit the circumstance. The consequence for nature is that it is increasingly conceived as an object for total exploitation, as a tool to be used by humans without reasoned purpose and with no limits.[24] Larger questions concerning attitudes toward efficiency and growth, which are necessary to begin addressing the paradoxes of sustainability, are rarely, if ever, asked. Because it does not allow an examination of larger issues, instrumental rationality is labeled "antidemocratic" and "repressive."[25]

Science as Positivism

The critical theorists argue that Enlightenment thought, with its emphasis on instrumental and technological rationality and the domination of nature, has profoundly influenced scientific inquiry. Modern science has essentially become the handmaiden for the mastery of nature. The type of knowledge that the "Enlightenment has in mind is the form of knowledge which copes most proficiently with the facts and supports the individual most effectively in the mastery of nature."[26] Other types of knowledge that do not conform, such as folk knowledge or oral histories, are excluded—whatever does not conform to the rules of computation and utility is discounted.[27] The quantitative replaces the qualitative.

The type of science produced is essentially positivism. Knowledge that can be quantified, verified by empirical methods, and reduced to unified laws is prized. This conception of science has profound impacts on language and culture as well. Attention is focused on recording data. Scientific terms become impenetrable; jargon creates an exclusive culture of science.[28] That scientific facts are social constructions, and that negotiation is fundamental to fact construction, are often overlooked.[29] Further, science is often controlled and defined by technological questions.[30] The emphasis on quantifiable science characterizes both the natural and social sciences. The quantitative methodologies of the natural sciences increasingly have become the model for scientific endeavor in the social sciences, and thus forms of social knowledge and social critique not amenable to quantification often are excluded as inconsequential.[31]

Domination of Humans over Humans

In their most controversial thesis, the critical theorists argue that treating nature as an object of domination, reducing reason to instrumental rationality, and limiting science to that which can be quantified ultimately lead to domination in the social world—of humans over humans. Such repression of others becomes embedded in social institutions and influences how humans treat each other and regard themselves. The most profound enigma of Thomas Jefferson, for example, who has been called both the American architect of freedom and the American spirit, was his acquiescence to the institution of slavery. British philosopher Edmund Burke offered an explanation of why the Virginians of the Enlightenment could both expound on human liberty yet still be slave owners. "Where there is a vast multitude of slaves as in Virginia," he observed, "those who are free are by far the most proud and jealous of their freedom. . . . To the masters of slaves, the haughtiness of domination combines with the spirit of freedom, fortifies it, and renders it invincible."[32] The social contract that binds all people together in a vision of broadly shared prosperity and freedom becomes broken. Humans renounce important aspects of their being, including appreciation of emotions, instincts, aesthetics, and other expressive actions. The price is self-repression and the repression of others. Thus, there is a link between social control, economic issues, and technology. In the name of economic and technological progress, technical rationality is linked to social control; the individual is devalued in relation to economic powers, powers that continue to press for even greater control of nature.[33]

In sum, Enlightenment critics argue that knowledge, conceived of as a liberating force by Enlightenment thought, has often been used instead as a tool to dominate nature and as a way for humans to dominate humans. They argue that positivism not only has served as a tool for the mastery of nature, but has also limited the nature of scientific inquiry to preconceived categories and principles. One critic writes, "Nature was not simply disenchanted by the Enlightenment—it was killed."[34]

Enlightenment Thought and the American Experience

American culture and society have been strongly influenced and defined by Enlightenment thought. The Old World may have imagined and invented Enlightenment thought, but it was the New World in America that most fully realized it. The founders embraced Enlightenment principles, wrote them into law, then embedded them in the nation's new institutions.

While our basic constitutional principles owe much to the positive influences of Enlightenment thought, the dark side of the Enlightenment is also evident in the United States. The American frontier of the New World, with its seemingly unlimited resources and freedom from societal strictures, was a perfect testing ground for Enlightenment thought. And in fact, from water to range lands to forest lands, many policies governing resource allocation and management in the United States today reflect the attitudes toward nature, reason, and science that developed out of the Enlightenment and transformed the frontier.

Western water development provides a classic example of the desire to master nature, although much the same story could be told about forests, minerals, and range.[35] The arid nature of the West left settlers with two options—either adapt to it or try to engineer it out of existence.[36] For much of the last century, the latter option—to engineer aridity out of existence—has been chosen. This attitude and spirit are reflected in the fate of U.S. Western river basins. Western writer and environmentalist Wallace Stegner decries this drive to master nature as a force that

> has so dammed, diverted, used, and reused the Colorado River that its saline waters now never reach the Gulf of California, but die in sand miles from the sea; that has set the Columbia, a far mightier river, to tamely turning turbines; that has reduced the Missouri, the greatest river on the continent, to a string of ponds; that has recklessly pumped down the water table of every western valley.[37]

In the process of developing water sources, little room was left for environmental or amenity values. For example, riparian vegetation was considered a competitor to useable water supplies and best eliminated. Beneficial use meant water removed from a stream and put to consumptive use; to not use water meant waste. In the words of the Bureau of Reclamation, for example, it turned "a natural menace"—the Colorado River—into a "natural resource ... to be utilized to the very drop."[38] Wetlands were perceived as swamps, a haven for pests, and best drained, filled, and turned into cultivated fields or paved for industrial development.

With the advent of the environmental movement, environmental considerations began to play a more important role in water resources decision making. Water resource agencies by law and political necessity are now focusing on correcting the environmental problems their own projects caused. However, many laws and policies, and the attitudes of some Western water officials, still reflect the classical conception of how water resources should be controlled. In spite of some progress, the movement to reform Western water is still young and reform has often been marginal.[39]

Reflecting the frontier mystique, most natural resource policies traditionally have emphasized the ascendancy of the rational, rugged individual over the community as a whole.[40] Instrumental rationality, particularly when defined in economic terms, dominates resource decision making; it is the language of economics and its measure of efficiency to which administrators most often turn in order to talk rationality.[41] As a result, most resource policies emphasize means over ends, production over stewardship, and outputs over ecological conditions. Likewise, rational planning is often used as a justification for distributing resources to the privileged, which exacerbates rather than narrows economic and social differences.[42] Native American and Hispanic people have seen their traditional access to resources ignored or denied, while Asian and African American perspectives are often simply precluded. Issues such as racism and income inequality frequently are met with denial, resignation, or silence.[43]

Finally, science defined as positivism also profoundly shapes resource management in the United States. There is an aura of "objectivity" around positive science that masks the values the scientist or analyst bring to any inquiry, including the fact that even deciding what to investigate has normative assumptions.[44] Positivist science fosters the politics of expertise, with its reliance on expert opinion and technology to solve problems. This reliance on experts has significant consequences for the role of the public in decisions about resources; democratic processes are ignored in favor of scientific decision making.

Decision making by experts and instrumental rationality, coupled with a desire to master nature, profoundly shape policy. Natural resource institutions, in particular, are utilitarian in focus and solicitous of turf. Many citizens feel increasingly alienated from political arenas in which they wield little or no power. While we undoubtedly made considerable progress in conservation and preservation efforts during the twentieth century, much of our present natural resource policy can also be said to reflect the darker side of Enlightenment thought.

Emerging Theoretical Principles

The principles of ecosystem management (socially-defined goals and objectives; holistic, integrated science; collaborative decision making; and adaptable institutions) indicate that changes will be required in the way scientists, managers, and the public participate in decisions about resources. It will be difficult to implement ecosystem management, however, if American society and resource institutions remain wedded to vestiges of Enlightenment thought without a critical exploration of both its negative and positive aspects. The development of new philosophical principles that retain the best of

Enlightenment thought but discard its dark side will be needed. Ecosystem management suggests the need for alternative conceptions that equalize the human–nature relationship, expand the concept of reason, broaden the scope of scientific inquiry, and create more equal social relations among humans.

Equalize the Human–Nature Relationship

A key criticism of Enlightenment thought is that the human–nature relationship has largely been defined by an attitude of domination and mastery, an attitude that has framed the allocation and management of resources for much of the last century. In the literature on the relationship between humans and nature, this view is generally described as anthropocentric, that is, a human-centered view in which reality is interpreted exclusively in terms of human values, experiences, and interests to the near exclusion of the nonhuman.[45] In contrast, ecosystem management, with its emphasis on maintaining and restoring ecological functions and protecting biodiversity, will require a more biocentric or life–earth centered perspective that redefines the relationship between humans and nature.

Under biocentric approaches, human goals are pursued in a manner that acknowledges the moral standing of the nonhuman world and seeks to ensure that it too may reveal itself in varied ways.[46] Such approaches include a belief that species, organisms, and ecosystems have intrinsic values of their own. Land is not simply inert, but in its natural state is already performing vital ecological services. Ultimately, the value of these services is both ethically and legally recognized.[47] Legal rights are given to "forests, oceans, rivers, and other so-called 'natural objects' in the environment—indeed, to the natural environment as a whole."[48] A new, symbiotic attitude toward nature no longer separates humans and nature by speaking of them as controller and controlled.

Biocentric conceptions move away from the traditional view that the natural world is simply a collection of natural resources that have no value except as a resource to meet human demands. History has taught us that the technical control of nature cannot be maintained because ecological problems result. Humans need not be either nature's master or its slave.[49] Under ecosystem management, an attitude of stewardship toward nature, not domination, is a more appropriate relationship between humans and the environment. It is prerequisite for resolving the paradoxes of sustainability, balancing the need to manage for both sustainability and development and for use and preservation.

Expand the Concept of Reason

Ecosystem management calls for an expanded conception of reason. The Enlightenment produced a narrow conception of reason, instrumental rationality, which gives little or no thought to the reasonableness of the ends sought. Since efficiency is most often the measuring rod, rationality is often determined by the aggregation of individual preferences. Moreover, the utilitarian rule of the greatest sum of benefits for the greatest number also promotes the assumption that as much value as possible should be extracted from scarce resources.[50] In contrast, ecosystem management requires direct examination of the ends sought. It requires society, as a whole, to determine the goals of resource management. The choices that need to be made cannot be made through instrumental reason because social decisions involve more than choosing among predetermined policy options. A shared effort within the larger community is needed to find common ground on what are reasonable ends.

Alternative models of rationality can be identified that seek to broaden the concept of reason. Rationality, for example, can include the concepts of freedom, equity, and autonomy. Primary weight can be given to judgments based on ethical choices between competing values; normative viewpoints can be incorporated into analysis.[51] Communicative rationality, for example, is based in dialogue and found through interactions between people.[52] Building on communicative rationality, one modern critical theorist calls for a new rationality called "ecological rationality" or "green reason." This type of rationality requires discovering ecological principles and incorporating these principles into natural resource decisions.[53] Developing an ecological rationality would be an interactive and adaptive process of interacting with the natural world through science, but in a social context. It requires a new, and more accurate, sense of the ways humans reason, interact, and learn about the natural world. It may require accepting the idea "that reason may not be as pure as most of us think or wish it were, that emotions and feelings may not be intruders in the bastion of reason at all: they may be enmeshed in its networks, for worse *and* for better."[54] An ecological rationality calls for the integration of the elements of discursive democracy, a public character, aesthetics, and other qualities, including human imagination and an ability to acknowledge the sublime.

Broaden the Scope of Scientific Inquiry

An attitude of stewardship toward nature and a richer conception of rationality suggest that changes in scientific inquiry are in order. As proposed, ecosystem management requires the integration of political and social factors with scientific information, that is, a more holistic and integrated science. Yet compartmentalization, specialization, and separation are characteristics of modern scientific life. It will be difficult to integrate political and social factors as required by ecosystem management with traditional modes of scientific inquiry.

Changes in scientific inquiry will mean new methods and research questions and new roles for scientists, some of whom can barely communicate across disciplines because of jargon or notions of academic supremacy. Academics themselves have played a large part in the general decline of scientific discourse and they have a responsibility to speak plainly. This entails democratizing the expert culture to include more avenues for direct public participation in the scientific enterprise, creating, in effect, a "civic science." Such a civic science addresses the paradox of expert versus open decision making by encouraging citizens to serve as lay scientists. Science is not just relegated to scientists working within universities and agency laboratories.[55]

Ecosystem management will also clearly require an effort to address the split in paths between the social and natural sciences and between theory and practice. As proposed under ecosystem management, management practices will be forged through a mix of theory and practice, on-the-ground experimentation, and multidisciplinary cooperation. Under this type of approach, inductive reasoning would be reemphasized. While deductive reasoning, the heritage of Enlightenment science, moves from stated premises or self-evident truths, inductive reasoning is grounded in observations and moves from the specific to the general. Not all relationships, especially social and political relationships, can be established by deductive reasoning. Ecosystem science would more explicitly recognize it is impossible to separate values from the context of analysis and that universal rational truths such as freedom or the sanctity of private property are themselves social constructions. It would explicitly acknowledge that science doesn't deliver truth that is nonarguable.

Ecosystem management requires the examination of social values and the questioning of normative assumptions. It requires answers to questions such as: Does nature have an intrinsic value of its own? Do animals and plants have rights? Can species be chosen for extinction? These questions cannot be answered without philosophy and ethics, two areas of study not generally included within mainstream scientific studies.

In a promising move, a leading scientist has called for a new social contract among scientists who are committed to helping society move toward a more sustainable future.[56] This contract would recognize the interdependence of issues that have been generally thought as independent of the environment, such as social justice, the economy, human health, and national security. It would forge new linkages among students of these issues and students of ecosystem structures and processes. More emphasis would be placed on linking scientific priorities to the social challenge of attaining sustainability and on facilitating faster and better communication of scientific knowledge to policy makers and the public. The contract would signify renewed scientific commitment to providing policy-relevant information as society makes the social and ethical decisions that shape sustainability. The scope of scientific inquiry is thus broadened considerably.

Create More Equal Relations among Humans

Underlying ecosystem management is an appeal for a restructuring of society's institutions. In modern society, social domination and hierarchy are instilled in our social institutions.[57] Social institutions in many respects reinforce patterns of domination in relationships among humans. Ironically, "those institutions that made rational discussion possible in the past and guaranteed the integrity of the public sphere (freedom of speech, assembly, and communication) today undermine it."[58] For example, the negative way the press frames coverage of government stimulates cynicism rather than public mindedness.[59] The public agencies charged with involving the public in resource management too often define the initial bounds of a conflict and the preferred set of options, greatly limiting the scope of public input.

However, ecosystem management, with its emphasis on collaborative decision making, social learning, and cooperative approaches to resource management, implies quite different social relationships. Rather than domination, the relationship suggested is one of interdependence and more equal relations. This interdependence is also suggested as a result of a new relationship with nature on the basis of stewardship. Under this view, humans are interdependent in the context of their relationship with the natural world. It is a much different picture of social relations than traditionally found in resource management, where powerful interests often collude in closed arenas, leaving little room for meaningful participation by the public.

Interdependence in social relations suggests a shift in emphasis from the individual to the community; a renewed conception of public life is called for. For example, diverse writers commenting on American society have noted the lack of a public place, or public sphere, where people can deliberate. In contrast to Aristotlean society, there is no publicly shared forum for discussing our politics philosophically. The absence of, but need for, a public sphere for communal discussion suggests the need to reestablish the democratic community and to create public places where individuals can congregate and discuss political life and choices. Professional groups, private groups, and citizens themselves, as well as public agencies, must work to create opportunities for this discourse to ensure governmental accountability and responsiveness and to balance tensions within the paradoxes of decision making. But to realize this ideal, new institutions that disperse power and authority more widely and equally among citizens and that encourage diverse individuals to develop critical thinking skills will be crucial.[60]

Developing Policy in Concert with Theory

Ecosystem management requires us to ask what kind of society we want and correspondingly what kind of relationship with nature we want. Because philosophy underlies our laws, institutions, and societal structures, including the institution of science, any new approach to natural resource policy must be developed in concert with political theory.

By focusing on Enlightenment thought, we have evaluated resource policy within the context of Western political thought and illustrated significant differences between ecosystem management and traditional resource management along four dimensions: the relationship between humans and nature, the concept of rationality, the role and structure of science, and the social relations among humans. The Enlightenment instilled in American society devotion to freedom, commitment to self-governance, trust in science, and belief in the power of reason. Yet, the dark side of the Enlightenment illuminated by the critical theorists—human mastery of nature, a narrow conception of reason, science as positivism, and domination of humans over humans—is also apparent in modern society and the traditional paradigm of resource management. Alternatively, the philosophy of ecosystem management suggests equalizing human–nature relationships, expanding the concept of reason, broadening the scope of scientific inquiry, and creating more equal relations among humans. It must be explicitly recognized that how we approach natural resource policies and how we define resource problems and their solutions are largely based on our own values, which in turn reflect basic theoretical principles. Each of us has deep-seated views on the questions posed earlier on the role of government and the role of citizens in resource decision making. These are not esoteric questions encountered only in ivory-tower discussions of political theory. They form the basis on which policies are formulated and structure how we address the paradoxes of political life. The growth and development of political society depend on their constant reassessment. We personally live answers to these questions every day.

NOTES

    1. Quarles, "The failure of federal land planning," pp. 16–17, emphasis in original.

    2. Much of this chapter draws on material adapted from Wallace et al. (used by per-

mission of the *Journal of Forestry*, published by the Society of American Foresters, 5400 Grosvenor Lane, Bethesda, Maryland 20814. Not for further reproduction.); and Wallace et al., "Moving toward ecosystem management" (used by permission).

3. Reich, *The Power of Public Ideas*, p. 1.

4. Cawley and Freemuth call these perspectives the "Mother Earth script" and the "Tree Farm script." Cawley and Freemuth, "Tree farms, mother earth, and other dilemmas."

5. Bird, "The social construction of nature"; Cawley and Freemuth, "Tree farms, mother earth, and other dilemmas"; and Leiss, *The Domination of Nature*.

6. See Cahn and O'Brien, *Thinking About the Environment*.

7. Gay, *The Enlightenment*.

8. Commager, *The Empire of Reason*.

9. Meyers, *The Mind of the Founder*, p. xxv. The other influences on the Founding Fathers that have been suggested include forms of Republicanism, both English and Classical, Medieval thought, the governance structures of the Iroquois Indians, and also economic and class factors present at the time. See Lutz, *A Preface to American Political Theory*.

10. Connolly, *Political Theory and Modernity*, p. 107.

11. Gay, *The Enlightenment*, p. 3.

12. Hulme and Jordanova, p 1.

13. O'Neill, "Enlightenment as autonomy," p. 186.

14. Aristotle, in a view that has influenced political theorists through time, saw humans as political animals who need the polis (the Greek word for a city-state) to achieve full *eudaimonia*. *Eudaimonia* is the Greek word for happiness, a word that connotes a rich happiness found by living a good life.

15. Cited in O'Neill, "Enlightenment as autonomy," p. 195. See also Connolly, *Political Theory and Modernity*, p. 100.

16. Hawthorn, *Enlightenment and Despair*, p. 13; and Jordanova, "The authoritarian response."

17. Such critical theorists include, for example, Horkheimer and Adorno writing in the 1940s and 1950s and Marcuse writing in the 1950s and 1960s. The most prominent modern critical theorist is Jurgen Habermas, who takes a much different perspective than the early critical theorists, deemphasizing the relationship between humans and nature. The critical theorists have been influenced in part by the early writings of Karl Marx, who is considered the founding father of critical theory. The critical theorists carried the same spirit of critique Marx used toward political economy, but instead focused on culture, science, and particularly the concept of reason. While many are familiar with his ideas concerning communism, few realize that Marx began his writing with a commitment to the critique of society. See Kellner, *Critical Theory, Marxism, and Modernity*. Rousseau's discussion of the inequalities imposed on humans by society in "Discourse on the origins of inequality," and his discussion of the limitations of science in "Discourse on science and arts," may also be considered early critiques of Enlightenment thought. See Rousseau, *The Basic Political Writings*.

18. Horkheimer and Adorno, *Dialectic of Enlightenment*. See also, Ophuls *Requiem for Modern Politics*.

19. Horkheimer and Adorno, *Dialectic of Enlightenment*, p. 248.

20. Horkheimer and Adorno, *Dialectic of Enlightenment*, p. 4. White, in an alternative theory, argues that the source of domination over nature is the Judeo-Christian religion. White argues, in essence, that "To a Christian a tree can be no more than a physical fact." White, "The historical roots of our ecological crisis," p. 1206. Moncrief, "The cultural basis of our environmental crisis"; Dubos, "A theology of earth"; and Steffen, "In defense of dominion," all take issue with White.

21. Marcuse, *One-Dimensional Man*, p. 240.

22. Tribe, "The limits of instrumental rationality," p. 618.

23. Heineman et al., *The World of the Policy Analyst*, pp. 38–39; and Horkheimer, *The Eclipse of Reason*, p. 3.

24. Horkheimer, *The Eclipse of Reason*, pp. 23, 108.

25. Dryzek, John, *Discursive Democracy*, pp. 5–6.

26. Horkheimer and Adorno, *Dialectic of Enlightenment*, pp. 82–83.

27. Horkheimer and Adorno, *Dialectic of Enlightenment*, p. 6.

28. Horkheimer and Adorno, *Dialectic of Enlightenment*, p. 164.

29. Schneider and Ingram, *Policy Design for Democracy*, pp. 150, 156.

30. Marcuse, *One-Dimensional Man*.

31. Leiss, *The Domination of Nature*, p. 134.

32. Quoted in Ambrose, *Undaunted Courage*, p. 34.

33. Rocco, "Between modernity and postmodernity," p. 74; Horkheimer and Adorno, *Dialectic of Enlightenment*, p. xiv; and Marcuse, *One-Dimensional Man*.

34. Dryzek, "Green reason," p. 198.

35. Ingram and Wallace, "An 'empire of liberty.'"

36. Stegner, *The American West as Living Space*, p. 46.

37. Stegner, *The American West as Living Space*, p. 27.

38. U.S. Department of the Interior Bureau of Reclamation, *The Colorado River*, p. 25.

39. Wilkinson, *Crossing the Next Meridian*, pp. 286–287.

40. Curry-Roper and McGuire, "The individualist imagination and natural resource policy"; Ophuls, "Reversal is the law of the Tao"; and Orr and Hill, "Leviathan, the open society, and the crisis of ecology."

41. Bellah et al., *The Good Society*, p. 115; and Heineman et al., *The World of the Policy Analyst*, chapter 2.

42. Ingram and Wallace, "An 'empire of liberty.'"

43. Reich, "The unfinished agenda."

44. See Mitroff, "The myth of objectivity or why science needs a new psychology of science."

45. Katz and Oechsli, "Moving beyond anthropocentrism," p. 50.

46. Eckersley, *Environmentalism and Political Theory*, p. 26.

47. Sax, "Property rights and the economy of nature."

48. Stone, *Should Trees Have Standing?*, p. 9.

49. Dubos, "A theology of earth"; and Dryzek, *Rational Ecology*, p. 46; Di Norcia, "From critical theory to critical ecology," pp. 89, 91; and Rodman, "Paradigm change in political science," p. 61. Concerning a new land ethic philosophy see Nash, *The Rights of Nature*.

50. Heineman et al., *The World of the Policy Analyst*, p. 87.

51. Leiss, *The Domination of Nature*; and Heineman et al., *The World of the Policy Analyst*, pp. 88–91.

52. Habermas, *The Philosophical Discourse on Modernity.*

53. Dryzek, "Green reason"; and Dryzek, *Rational Ecology.*

54. Damasio, *Descartes' Error*, p. xii, emphasis in original.

55. See Shannon and Antypas, "Civic science is democracy in action"; Shannon and Antypas, "Open institutions"; and Agger, "Theorizing the decline of discourse or the decline of theoretical discourse," p. 138.

56. Lubchenco, "Entering the century of the environment." The article is based on Lubchenco's presidential address at the 1997 annual meeting of the American Association for the Advancement of Science.

57. Bellah, *The Good Society*, p. 11.

58. Rosenau, *Post-Modernism and the Social Sciences*, p. 101.

59. Nye et al., *Why People Don't Trust Government.*

60. Rosenau, in *Post-Modernism and the Social Sciences*, p. 101, describes the public sphere as a place where citizens can debate and deliberate separate from the state in an effort to seek a "judicious, wise, thoughtful agreement about society's needs and the best policy for a nation." See also Dryzek, *Discursive Democracy*, p. 220; MacIntyre, *After Virtue*, p. 138; Stanley, "The rhetoric of the commons"; Shannon, "Community governance"; and Leiss, *The Domination of Nature*, p. 197.

Chapter 6

Collaborative Stewardship in Action: Building a Civic Society

The collaborative decision-making principle of ecosystem management evokes images of Aldo Leopold's land ethic in action: the citizenry, individually and collectively, stewarding the land and its resources. Citizens are called on to come together across disciplinary, management, and ownership boundaries to collectively determine management goals, develop management plans, implement those plans, and monitor and adjust as necessary. To do so, they must embrace a new form of governance, based in direct, or participatory, democracy theory. Participatory democracy is centered on the public forum, in which citizens discuss issues and set policy.[1] Chapter 5 addressed the philosophical changes involved in realizing such a democratic vision. In this chapter, we begin discussing the pragmatics of achieving civic involvement for collaborative ecosystem management.

The Citizen's Role in Government

Proponents of ecological stewardship are not the first to view civic involvement as necessary for effective action. Since Greek times, citizen participation has been recognized as a distinguishing characteristic of democratic governance. Thus the Greek philosopher Pericles wrote, "We do not say that a person who takes no interest in politics is one who minds his own business; we say that he has no business here at all."[2] Democracy is frequently referred to as "self-rule," because the supreme power of the state is vested in its citizens. It follows, then, that without citizen involvement in governance, there is no democracy.[3] The price of individual freedom is participation in governance;

this is part of the social contract between citizens and the state. Rousseau, champion of government by the people, argued that electing representatives to make decisions for oneself is tantamount to relinquishing one's freedom.[4]

Even within a representative democracy, citizen participation is held up as a measure of both social and political health. Over 100 years ago, in *Democracy in America*, Alexis de Tocqueville identified Americans' participation in civic organizations as critical to maintenance of American democracy. de Tocqueville also warned that American individualism could prove a threat to democracy by breaking down the civic organizations that connect individuals to central government, thereby allowing a sort of administrative despotism to evolve.[5]

Citizen participation in civic organizations is considered important to democracy in part because it is through participation in these voluntary institutions that people develop the trust and skills needed for participation in political groups. Citizens' capacity and willingness to engage in governance depend on a reserve of social capital, which, to reiterate, are those features of social life—networks, norms, and trust—that facilitate citizen association and enable participants to act together more effectively to pursue shared objectives. Social capital influences citizens' collective ability "to respond to external and internal stresses; to create and take advantage of opportunities; and to meet the needs of residents, diversely defined."[6] The collection of characteristics encompassed by the concept of social capital is enhanced by the presence of existing social networks, such as clubs, professional associations, religious organizations, and other groups—the "associations" de Tocqueville viewed as critical to American democracy. Through participation in these associations, citizens realize their collective power to change local conditions and influence society.[7]

Yet many observers note that Americans' civic activism, and citizen involvement in social institutions in general, have been in decline since World War II.[8] Policy analysts are divided over the reasons for this decline. According to some, the problem is social: the citizenry itself is to blame for neglecting individual and collective responsibilities while being overly concerned with individual rights. Others see it as a structural problem, placing the blame for citizen disinterest on an increasingly bureaucratic government characterized by inaccessibility and indifference.

Citizen Apathy

Americans prize highly their civil rights and liberties, such as the right to free speech, to privacy, to assembly, and to own property. As discussed in the previous chapter, these values stem in large measure from the influence of the Enlightenment writers on the framers of the Constitution. The amendments to the Constitution known as the Bill of Rights explicitly restrict the liberties of the national government in order to protect the liberties of individual citizens. Later amendments to the Constitution further restrict government liberties, for example by setting term limits and by expanding civil rights, such as the right to vote.[9] However, some observers claim that Americans have become overly concerned with protecting their individual rights and fail to recognize their civic responsibilities under a democratic system.[10]

Voting is perhaps the most basic mechanism by which citizens in a representative democracy express values and preferences and shape the direction of government policy. Notably, the participation rate for the 1992 presidential election was only 76 percent of all registered voters and a shocking 55 percent of all eligible voters. The percentage of Americans who made it to the polls in the 1996 presidential election was the lowest since 1924;[11] voting turnout was much higher in the latter half of the nineteenth century. It is considered a "good" year for voter turnout when approximately 65 percent of eligible voters actually vote. The last time this happened was in 1960. In state and local elections voter turnout is much lower, usually around 25 percent or less of the eligible electorate. As one analyst observes, "our generation values the right to vote over the duty to vote and the right to a trial by jury over the obligation to serve as juror."[12] Declining involvement in political parties, ethnic organizations, local business organizations, unions, and publicly minded churches and synagogues—the associations de Tocqueville saw as essential to American democracy—is held up as further evidence of eroding democracy in the United States.[13]

Inaccessible Government

Yet while some have argued that the decline in voter turnout is a reflection of citizens' social and political disconnectedness, others maintain that lower voter turnout is a logical choice made by citizens who do not believe their vote counts.[14] What appears to be citizen apathy actually may be citizens' rational evaluation of the costs and benefits of participating in a representative form of government.[15] Studies have shown most Americans consider government inaccessible and unresponsive to local needs and concerns and believe it is ruled by organized interest groups and power players. According to one study of American democratic practices, "Rather than being apathetic or unconcerned, citizens are angry and frustrated by politics as usual. They feel cut out of the process and unheard; they do not see how they can have any real impact on public affairs."[16] Furthermore, opportunities for participation in American governance have diminished as government has grown larger and more centralized.[17]

Some social and political theorists, particularly proponents of participatory democracy, suggest that to improve citizen participation, Americans need a less bureaucratic state that gives the public more direct input to governance. Rejecting the concept of citizens as consumers, driven only by self-interest, these scholars claim citizens are motivated to act for the good of the larger society, but lack appropriate vehicles for doing so. Given an appropriate public forum, it is argued, citizens will choose to participate in government and will support the policies they have helped create.[18]

Recent Trends in Citizen Involvement

The claim that citizens would participate in governance given appropriate opportunities is supported somewhat by other observations of citizen activism. For instance, while environmental issues are likely to be far down on the list of reasons citizens vote for a particular candidate, citizens do utilize initiatives and referendums, Progressive Era innovations that provide a way for citizens to vote directly on environmental and natural resource issues. These mechanisms provide citizens ways to express their values directly and to have those values enacted into law.

In many places, the American citizenry has taken governance on itself, developing new civic institutions, such as community health projects, neighborhood watch programs, and community dispute resolution projects. While citizens may be less interested in traditional social organizations and political parties, they apparently are still interested in forming associations around issues they find more relevant. Some social analysts have dubbed the tendency to form such groups the "community" movement.[19]

Citizens build community by identifying and organizing around common concerns. Thus communities are defined by the active involvement, or commitment, of their individual members as well as members' identification with a common place or issue. "A community is the means by which people live together. Communities enable people to protect themselves and to acquire the resources that provide for their needs."[20]

The community movement began primarily as community organizing in urban neighborhoods, where residents share common problems such as crime, inadequate schooling, pollution, and decaying infrastructure.[21] The federal government's "War on Poverty" programs of the 1960s, which sought to empower individual citizens and mandated "maximum feasible participation" in federal housing and urban renewal programs, were modeled on early urban community organizing efforts.[22]

Simply by gathering to discuss common concerns, communities have built political power and spurred community action.[23] In Baltimore, for example, a coalition of local churches, community-based organizations, and labor unions known as Baltimoreans United in Leadership Development (BUILD) surveyed neighborhoods on their political priorities, drafted its own agenda for the city, and then collected endorsements for its agenda from 70,000 citizens.[24] These endorsements significantly influenced local elections and city policies.

In the Bronx, grassroots community organizations developed in the 1980s to address problems of drugs, violence, and inadequate housing and social services. The Mid-Bronx Desperados is one of these organizations. The Desperados started out as a collection of block associations and other local groups "desperate" for a safer, cleaner neighborhood. Another organization, the Banana Kelly Community Improvement Association, was born from the bonding neighbors experienced when they joined hands to prevent the demolition of their tenement buildings. Together, these two groups have worked in a 100-block area to prevent further destruction of their homes and to rebuild those that had been lost to arson or city demolition crews. Slowly they gained credibility and the support of both the city and private funders. Between 1980 and 1995, the Desperados helped build or restore over 2,000 homes and organized social programs ranging from small loans programs to youth talent shows. Banana Kelly manages 45 buildings with over 1,000 units, filled with tenants carefully screened for their community values, and offers family and community enrichment courses to residents. Together, the two groups helped establish a children's health clinic and a separate doctor's office in the community.[25]

Starting in the 1960s and 1970s with toxics in the environment, communities also began organizing to effect change around environmental issues of local concern. In the 1980s, communities began addressing other environmental and natural resource management issues that federal laws enacted in the 1970s had neglected, such as nonpoint source pollution and protection and restoration of ecosystems.[26] By the 1990s, urban neighborhood organizations and local environmental groups abounded, frequently organized around environmental and land-use management issues.

More recently, a community-based conservation movement has arisen in rural communities, as citizens grapple with growing, and increasingly conflictual, pressures on the natural resource base.[27] Community-based conservation is characterized by a common sense of place and common concern for environmental or natural resource management issues. The landowners, commodity resource developers, and local environmentalists who come together in these communities share a belief that "experts do not know enough, can never know enough, and ultimately are not responsible for the outcomes that follow from their advice. It is the people with the problems who must determine what solution is right for them."[28] Community-based conservation efforts are said to enhance land use and natural resource management by drawing expertise and input from a wide range of individuals and groups who live in and intimately know the resource base and the local economy. Groups such as the Applegate Partnership and Trout Creek Mountain Working Group in Oregon and the Quincy Library Group in California's Sierra Nevadas have gained national acclaim for forging agreements on resource management among local industry, environmental, and agency representatives in areas with a long history of fierce confrontation.

In the Trout Creek case, the issue was 250,000 acres of high desert grasslands, home to the endangered native Lahontan cutthroat trout and used for grazing by local ranchers. The ranchers wanted their livelihoods protected, the environmentalists wanted the trout protected, and both were threatening to sue the Bureau of Land Management. Doc and Connie Hatfield, ranchers who believed that cattle and Lahontan could coexist, were able to help people see that they had some shared concerns. For instance, all participants agreed that the health of the watershed and its streams had degraded to the point that the future of both the trout and the ranching community and culture were in danger of extinction. Remarkably, soon after its formation, the Trout Creek Mountain Working Group "was able to build enough understanding of the immediate need for watershed improvement that the ranchers involved voluntarily removed their cattle for a three-year period of rest, at considerable personal cost."[29] Throughout this period of voluntary rest, the Trout Creek Mountain Group met regularly to work on a land management plan that would include grazing and protection of critical habitat. During these meetings, participants slowly began to understand each others' heartfelt hopes and fears, and also began to recognize a shared concern for the health of the Trout Creek Mountain ecosystem. The group painstakingly debated and refined the ecological improvements needed for healthy trout habitat conditions. After two years, they had drafted a mutually acceptable plan designed to benefit the watershed and the fish and to permit continued grazing. The test of their plan came in 1992 when, "in the seventh year of the worst drought since the 30s, cattle were returned to the mountain to graze pastures containing endangered Lahontan cutthroat trout." After two years of grazing, the group conducted a tour of the watershed, where they concluded "major positive changes on the land are a reality for everyone to see today."[30]

Community groups addressing local issues have come to be known as "communities of place," to differentiate them from national "communities of interest" such as Washington, D.C.-based environmental organizations and industry associations. The communities of place assert their right to participate fully in ecosystem management: "The social process of gathering stakeholders, communities of place, and land management agency expertise is very important to ecosystem planning. Ecosystems and social systems are equally unique and complex."[31] Some have even claimed communities of place should have a greater say in ecosystem management decisions than national groups, arguing, "problems of goals and problems of scale cannot be resolved in the abstract; they must emerge from a local process of dialogue and debate.... Thus an important function of environmental management is to work with local regions to develop, by discussion and careful experimentation, a set of goals that express the local culture even as they protect the contextual features important to its continuance."[32] Experiences with community-based conservation in other countries and early ecosystem management efforts in this country "illustrate the importance of increasing communities' authority and responsibility in [resource] management decisions and actions. This must be done so that humans can interact with [their] ecosystems without destroying them."[33]

Toward a Civic Society

Community-based conservation efforts appear to model the public involvement and stewardship requirements of ecosystem management and also hold hope for rebuilding society through what appears to be a resurgence in citizen involvement in governance. However, creating community groups and integrating their efforts with those of resource management bureaucracies raise problems of both insufficient community capacity and bureaucratic barriers to civic involvement in governance.

Because they believe the primary problem is citizens' lack of experience in civic involvement, some social scientists recommend fostering social capital through civic discourse and collective learning. By working collectively toward a common goal, people learn to overcome conflict and their fear of those different from themselves. They also learn that their self-interest includes seeking a common good. Equally important, collective action builds social networks that can expedite community action.

Involvement in community organizations does not always equate to citizens working well with government, however. Citizen groups frequently cite bureaucratic barriers such as agency inertia, administrative red tape, lack of interagency coordination, jurisdictional conflicts, and "reactionary policies" as impediments to their efforts.[34] Agency personnel at the local level who want to be involved in community processes frequently find they lack support from their administrative superiors in the agency. Community-based conservation efforts that are primarily organized and undertaken by local residents may be supported by a "shadow community" of agency employees, activists, and academics working steadily behind the scenes to support their activities.[35] These individuals offer input but avoid the limelight, in part to encourage the development of local leadership, but also because laws such as FACA, promotion policies, and employer allocation of their time discourage them from direct participation. As a result, experiments in small-scale, place-based governance are often undertaken outside the existing governance system:

> Faced with a paucity of formal options for engaging constructive-
> ly with governing institutions around issues of shared concern, cit-
> izens are relying on themselves for leadership and initiative. . . . It
> is a deeper, more intimate and inclusive kind of democracy—more
> direct than representative, more consensual than voting. . . .
> Citizens no longer defer to elected leaders or experts, trusting
> instead in their own capacity to work together and their deep com-
> mitment to each other and where they live.[36]

However, operating outside the existing governance system comes at a cost. Community-based conservation groups have had to re-create several basic governance functions to ensure equity and accountability, design procedures for decision making and record-keeping, and find financing. These tasks are daunting, and community-based conservation efforts frequently fail for reasons such as a lack of clear purpose, unrealistic goals or deadlines, disproportionate power, and lack of legal authority. An important challenge for ecosystem management will be finding ways to weave concepts of participatory democracy into organizational cultures and the laws and policies governing natural resource management. The following sections explore in more detail some of these proposed social and structural changes.

Civic Discourse

From a participatory democracy perspective, "full and free interchange between the people and their elected representatives, as well as between the people and appointed administrators, clearly is essential to responsible and well-informed public decision making and to responsive government."[37] Active dialogue allows the needs and concerns of each interested group or individual to be addressed during the planning process and permits the various participants to gain an understanding of each other's values, interests, and concerns, as well as the legal and policy constraints on agency decision making.[38] In addition to improving the information base on which decisions are made, improved dialogue is said to aid participants in the revision and refinement of their own values and interests. Such a process can assist in collective definition of goals, objectives, and decision-making criteria.[39]

In order to achieve civic discourse, however, communities must identify, and in many cases create, a safe, neutral public meeting space. Building on experiments in the 1980s, some community-based conservation groups have developed alternative forums for citizen discourse and decision making. The Quincy Library Group, for instance, identified the local library as a neutral place where environmentalists, foresters, and other community members could gather to discuss and debate economic and ecosystem needs. Such forums encourage broader participation because they are local, frequently located in a familiar community building, and are structured to encourage participation from all members.

Creating a forum for civic discourse involves more than identifying a meeting space. Effective civic discourse requires communication skills such as active listening, respecting others' opinions, accepting emotions as valid expressions, and presenting ideas clearly. Comparative studies of community-based conservation efforts have shown that citizens, scientists, resource managers, and representatives of diverse interests are often lacking these skills.[40] Agencies, for instance, are paralyzed not only by their bureaucracies but also by internal organizational cultures that demand strict adherence to "long-standing traditions and a 'we-know-best' attitude."[41] Many individuals and communities lack a willingness to accept controversy, accept others' views as valid, and depersonalize different stands on issues.[42] Given the contentious history of land management planning and private property regulation, a history of conflict among stakeholders is more than likely. Communities need tools, and frequently training, to help them overcome the mistrust rampant among agencies, scientific disciplines, as well as interest groups, and between the public and government.[43]

Collective Learning

Those implementing early ecosystem management efforts have further found that both the public and agency personnel lack basic knowledge of ecological and social systems, as well as the ability to see resource management activities in the broader context of ecosystem linkages and time frames. For example, residents of urban areas need a better understanding of the places that supply their electricity, water, and wood and paper products and the places that serve as repositories of their wastes. Citizens, scientists, and managers all need to develop the ability to learn from mistakes, take a long-term focus, and understand complex social and biophysical interactions, such as ecological links outside the immediate area.[44] Promoting compatible human uses of the ecosystem and developing a common understanding of ecosystem structures and functions are additional challenges for ecosystem management.

Some groups have had significant success developing a learning environment that allows people with different skill levels and areas of expertise to learn from one another and come to collective decisions.[45] Tools such as community visioning, mapping, and mediation are commonly used means of furthering discourse within communities. Community visioning is a process by which individuals share and explore their values and hopes for the future to achieve a common future goal and shared values.[46] Community mapping, in which community members together identify critical resource areas and define boundaries, has proven highly successful both in involving people in environmental planning and in dissipating conflict; attention is focused on the resources, rather than ideologies.[47] Mediation and other forms of conflict resolution have been applied at the community level to break down traditionally polarized stances and encourage constructive dialogue among adversaries. Each of these tools provides a means for citizens to become intimately involved in planning and decision making for their social and ecological environments within the limits of existing institutional frameworks. Collective learning methods such as these can address the paradox of expert and open decision making by respecting the unique knowledge and perspective that each citizen brings to the table and ensuring that all are privy to the same information.[48]

Some community efforts are attempting to address social and economic needs in concert with ecosystem restoration and maintenance. In urban neighborhoods from New York City to Los Angeles, community revitalization projects such as street tree planting and neighborhood gardens link ecological stewardship with stewardship of human communities. By bringing neighbors together in a positive setting to address a common concern for their environment, these projects have been used to develop community cohesiveness and have given residents a sense of pride in place.[49]

One proponent of sustainable societies says that as effective ecosystem stewards, citizens must become "students of their places.... They will need to know a great deal about new fields of knowledge such as restoration ecology, conservation biology, ecological engineering, and sustainable forestry and agriculture. They will need a more honest economics that allows them to account for all of the costs of economic–ecological transactions."[50] Achieving intensive, community-wide ecosystem science learning remains a major challenge for ecosystem management.

Making Bureaucracy Citizen Friendly

Changing the governance structure to enhance a community's political authority and vertical networks to regional, state, or national powers is equally
important to building a civic society.[51] Ecosystem management should
empower the citizenry:

> There are important things to do and decide. Rather than merely
> standing back and criticizing, one becomes part of a constructive
> process, and gains access to the resources that government, indus-
> try, and other nongovernmental organizations can contribute.
> Citizens work within a decision-making process that addresses
> their interests, and they have opportunities to play a part in imple-
> menting those decisions.[52]

Citizen involvement in governance thus becomes "not a one-shot affair but
a continuing network of interaction with others."[53]

As discussed in chapter 2, however, the existing bureaucratic structure of
government and its domination by the politics of interest present considerable
barriers and disincentives to increased citizen involvement in governance.[54]
Lack of access to state and federal government clearly is a major barrier to the
localized community-based decision making needed for ecosystem management. Statements at public hearings and written comments on draft plans, two
established methods of eliciting public comment, can exclude people uncomfortable about public speaking or formal letter-writing. The financial and time
requirements of planning are frequently cited as barriers to public participation as well. Whether or not government actions are considered to be "in the
public good," citizens want direct access to the decision-making process to
ensure that their interests are represented.[55]

In order for citizens to participate effectively in ecosystem management,
government processes must include forums where public deliberation can
occur. This will require a major restructuring of information and how it is
communicated. Agency planning and decision-making processes must be
capable of accommodating new forms of knowledge and multiple sources of
information, balancing both expert and lay input.[56] Effective management will
involve citizens and stakeholder groups at the earliest possible planning stages
and throughout the planning process, including problem definition, data gathering and analysis, and monitoring.[57] Agency procedures, and likely also regulations, will have to be adjusted to include citizens in determining management goals and procedures.

An example from the Sandhills of Nebraska illustrates the link between

early and ongoing public involvement and the development of politically feasible plans and projects. Wishing to preserve the unique dune ecosystem of
Nebraska's Sandhills, in the early 1980s the U.S. Fish and Wildlife Service
drafted a plan to purchase conservation easements on the unique wetlands
between the dunes. The plan was vehemently opposed by local landowners and
eventually abandoned. Ten years later, however, the agency hired a "Sandhills
Coordinator" to develop a program *with* the landowners. A task force of
agency representatives and representatives of locally active organizations and
landowners was formed to develop a mutually acceptable management plan.
"After much initial distrust between the landowners and agency representatives, participants discovered commonalities between landowner and wildlife
needs. Subsequently, the task force has developed into a team of people who
respect and trust one another, and who make decisions by consensus."
Operating by consensus, the task force developed a management plan "to
enhance the sandhill wetland–grassland ecosystem in a way that sustains prof-
itable private ranching, wildlife and vegetative diversity, and associated water
supplies." Importantly, the task force members remained active to help implement the management plan they collectively developed.[58]

All-party monitoring is one approach advocated by some community-
based conservation groups that addresses the paradoxes of expert and open
decision making and bureaucracy and accountability. By having representatives
from each stakeholder group, including national interests, collectively monitor
the implementation of a land management decision, all parties are assured that
their interests are being met.[59]

Local Empowerment

Some proponents of community-based conservation advocate a more significant devolution of decision-making authority and economic power to local
communities. From the perspective of participatory democracy theory, "It is
clear that a government which claims to rest on the belief that citizens are
capable of self-government must provide opportunities for citizens to exercise
that capability."[60] If citizens are expected to help implement and enforce
resource management decisions, it is argued, they should be given some
authority in making those decisions. Power must be transferred from the federal or state to the local level of government—and this means more than placing representatives of centralized government in local areas.[61]

Specifically, some proponents of community-based conservation argue
that local communities should have greater control over at least some financial decisions and revenue-raising activities, the authority to negotiate with
entities outside the community, and the power to make and enforce sanctions

and reward good stewardship.[62] For reasons of equity as well as sustainability, "an adequate portion of revenues obtained from extracting resources ... should be reinvested back into areas of origin for current and cumulative management needs."[63] Furthermore, industries should be "value added," refining harvested resources and manufacturing products locally, providing substantially higher revenues than exporting raw materials from the community.

At the same time, long-term government support may be required for the transition from external to local leadership, and some believe locals should be compensated, perhaps indefinitely, if ecosystem management decisions are to require a significant decline in resource extraction. Certainly, economic incentives can be powerful motivators for citizen involvement, particularly in cases where people are being asked to forego economic production for the sake of the environment.[64]

These arguments are strongly opposed by some, particularly national interest groups and federal agencies uncomfortable with the devolution of political power to local communities; they warn against a return to the days when locals dictated environmental and public land management standards. Many in the increasingly urban American society also consider rural communities likely to favor resource extraction at the expense of ecosystem health. Many also believe resource extraction industries have long been inappropriately subsidized and oppose the idea of subsidizing those same industries to no longer practice unsustainable activities.

An even more controversial issue concerns the influence of multinational corporations on local economies and governments. Many communities, particularly those rich in natural resources, experience exploitation by centralized government and outside corporations that export resources and revenues to the federal treasury or to investments in distant areas. As a result, "our globalized economy means that huge corporations can reach into rural areas throughout the world to claim the trees, the water, the fish, the land."[65] Such outside interests, seeking to maximize profits for their stakeholders or the "national interest," discourage local economic self-determination.[66] These conditions cause some to call for reassessment of the "global nature of economic forces and the way that local communities may be devastated by fluctuations on a futures market on the other side of the world."[67] Without addressing the corporate global economy, it is said, we will remain "caught in the paradox that we cannot save the world without saving particular places. But neither can we save our places without national and global policies that limit predatory capital and that allow people to build resilient economies, to conserve cultural and biological diversity, and to preserve ecological integrities."[68] Many proponents of ecosystem management shy away from such statements, however, considering community-based conservation, or ecosystem management at the local level, to be viable without radical changes in global economic institutions or the national governance structure. Attacking economic powers is seen as unpopular and impractical.

Evolving Civic Involvement

American civic involvement is continuously evolving. We can trace patterns of civic involvement that mirror the patterns of governance described in chapter 2. Early Americans were focused on independence, freedom, and self-reliance. The constitutional framers designed a system of government that represented a compromise between their commitment to popular sovereignty and their fear of placing too much direct power in the hands of the masses. In the late 1800s, the Progressive movement emerged in response to a public perception of inequitable and corrupt politics. The Progressive movement introduced the initiative, referendum, and recall, thus providing citizens with more avenues for involvement in governance. As bureaucracy built more complex governing structures, however, civic involvement was taken over by interest groups in what we have called the "politics of interest." Today, many people, including advocates of ecosystem management, are calling for more direct civic involvement in governance.

The image of collaboration in ecosystem management contrasts starkly with a common depiction of citizen involvement in governance, however. American citizens are often characterized as apathetic or hostile, rather than civic-minded. Some recent social trends, from low voting turnouts to "gated" communities to the private property rights movement, reinforce these images. Blaming everything from bureaucratic government to television for the current lack of citizen involvement in governance, many social scientists point out that since the 1950s the trend has been away from citizen involvement in local clubs, religious organizations, and other associations.

Yet we are currently experiencing another social trend, variously characterized as the new citizenship, civic renewal, or community movement, in which groups of citizens are organizing to address local issues such as crime, schooling, and environmental justice. In the realm of natural resource management, this movement is known as community-based conservation and involves local residents working together to resolve resource management conflicts and ensure themselves a healthy and productive environment. When local community concerns are at issue, there appears to be a resurgence in civic-mindedness.

Our models of citizen stewardship are as yet nascent and undeveloped. They do suggest some needed changes, however, both social and structural, to build a civic society. Socially, we need to develop the capacity for civic discourse and collective learning. Tools such as community visioning and mapping, collaborative learning, and mediation help develop these social skills and networks. Structurally, we need to break down the barriers to public involvement imposed by excessive bureaucracy, while remaining accountable to all stakeholders, present and potential. Open decision-making processes and all-party monitoring are tools that may address the paradoxes of expert and open decision making and bureaucracy and accountability. Increasing the governance authority of local communities and drastically reducing the power of large corporations could also foster renewed civic activism and possibly help balance decentralized and centralized governance, but risk undermining national policy and alienating important sectors of society.

Today, citizens are demanding not only the ability to set policy (as through initiatives and referendums), but also more direct participation throughout political decision-making processes, in the form of collaborative decision making through civic discourse. Collaborative, community-based ecosystem management presents one means of addressing both environmental concerns for ecological sustainability and democratic concerns for justice and economic equity without rejecting our representative form of government.[69] The extent to which we achieve it will depend on the extent to which we develop social capital and refine bureaucracy.

NOTES

1. Pateman, *Participation and Democratic Theory*; Bachrach and Botwinick, *Power and Empowerment*; Shannon, "Community governance"; and Tipple and Wellman, "Life in the fishbowl."

2. Pericles, *Funeral Oration*, quoted by Kemmis, *The Good City and the Good Life*, p. 183.

3. Aristotle argued that the converse was true, also; that is, social and political institutions—the polis—are essential to forming good citizens. Aristotle, *Politics*.

4. Cronin, *Direct Democracy*, pp. 38–39.

5. Bellah et al., *Habits of the Heart*, pp. vii, 38.

6. Kusel, "Well-being in forest-dependent communities," p. 369. Kusel lists physical and human capital as other determinants of community capacity.

7. Machlis, "The tension between local and national conservation groups in the democratic regime," p. 272. Involvement in civic organizations is considered critical to democracy because it is in such institutions that "citizens learn respect for others as well as self-respect; . . . where we develop the skills of self-government as well as the habit of governing ourselves." Etzioni, "The responsive communitarian platform," p. 11.

8. Putnam, "The strange disappearance of civic America"; Putnam, "Bowling alone"; and Boyte, "Citizenship as public work."

9. Amendments XIII, XIV, and XV, passed between 1865 and 1870, extended the

right of citizenship to persons of any race or color born or naturalized in the United States, including former slaves; in 1920 amendment XIX extended this right to women, and in 1971 Amendment XXVI extended it to those eighteen or older. Other twentieth-century amendments imposed term limits on the president and provided for direct election of senators.

10. This claim is most frequently made by proponents of Communitarianism, a movement that "emerged in the 1980s in response to the limits of liberal theory and practice. Its dominant themes are that individual rights need to be balanced with social responsibilities, and that . . . unless we begin to redress the balance toward the pole of community, . . . our society will continue to become normless, self-centered, and driven by special interests and power" seekers. Civic Practices Network, "Communitarianism." Communitarians have been criticized for advocating the imposition of social controls based on their own value system (e.g., mandatory AIDS testing) and blaming national civil rights advocacy for the breakdown of community in minority neighborhoods. See, for example, Walker, "The communitarian cop-out."

11. Baker, "An all-time high for ballot box no-shows," p. 11.

12. Oaks, "Rights and responsibilities," p. 40.

13. Putnam, "The strange disappearance of civic America."

14. See Teixeira, *The Disappearing American Voter*, on the former, and Downs, *An Economic Theory of Democracy*, on the latter.

15. Kathlene and Martin, "Enhancing citizen participation"; and Chrislip, "American renewal."

16. Chrislip, "American renewal," p. 25, citing Richard Harwood, *Citizens and Politics.* See also Advisory Commission on Intergovernmental Relations, *Citizen Participation in the American Federal System*; Greider, *Who Will Tell the People?*; and Pateman, *Participation and Democratic Theory.*

17. Ostrom, "A communitarian approach to local governance."

18. Sirianni and Friedland, "Social capital and civic innovation"; Stanley, "The rhetoric of the commons"; and Reich, *The Power of Public Ideas.*

19. Also referred to as the "civic renewal" or "new citizenship" movement.

20. Moore, "What is community?" p. 30. See also Kusel, "Well-being in forest-dependent communities."

21. Civic Practices Network, "The new citizenship movement"; and Siriani and Friedland, "Social capital and civic innovation."

22. Greider, *Who Will Tell the People?*, p. 224. Section 202 of the Economic Opportunity Act of 1964 defined "community action program" as one "which is developed, conducted, and administered with the maximum feasible participation of residents of the areas and members of the groups served."

23. Greider, *Who Will Tell the People?*

24. Greider, *Who Will Tell the People?*, p. 223. See also McDougall, *Black Baltimore.*

25. Breslin, "On these sidewalks of New York, the sun is shining again."

26. Sirianni and Friedland, "Social capital and civic innovation"; and John, *Civic Environmentalism*, p. 40.

27. Western and Wright, *Natural Connections*; Yaffee et al., *Ecosystem Management in the United States*; Sample et al., *Building Partnerships for Ecosystem Management on Mixed Ownership Landscapes*; and Natural Resources Law Center, *The Watershed Source Book.*

28. Moore, "What is community?" p. 29. See also Kusel, "Well-being in forest-dependent communities."

29. Hatfield and Hatfield, *History of the Trout Creek Mountain Group*, p. 10.

30. Hatfield and Hatfield, *History of the Trout Creek Mountain Group*, pp. 13, 15.

31. Lead Partnership Group, "Restoration on forested land," p. 23.

32. Norton, "A new paradigm for environmental management," pp. 36–37.

33. White et al., "Lessons to be learned from experience," p. 107.

34. Yaffee and Wondolleck, "Building bridges across agency boundaries"; and Yaffee et al., *Ecosystem Management in the United States*.

35. John, *Civic Environmentalism*, pp. 261–262. According to John the term "shadow community" was coined by Stephen Light of the Southern Florida Water Management District.

36. Chrislip, "American renewal," p. 26; and Greider, *Who Will Tell the People?*

37. Advisory Commission on Intergovernmental Relations, *Citizen Participation in the American Federal System*, p. 292.

38. Wondolleck, "The importance of process in resolving environmental disputes."

39. Wondolleck, "Resolving forest management planning disputes"; Wondolleck, "The importance of process in resolving environmental disputes"; Bachrach and Botwinick, *Power and Empowerment*; Reich, "Public administration and public deliberation"; and Shannon, "Public participation in the RPA process."

40. Yaffee and Wondolleck, "Building bridges across agency boundaries"; and Flora, *Vital Communities*.

41. Yaffee and Wondolleck, "Building bridges across agency boundaries," p. 56.

42. Flora, *Vital Communities*.

43. Yaffee et al., *Ecosystem Management in the United States*; Yaffee and Wondolleck, "Building bridges across agency boundaries"; and Wright, "Recommendations."

44. Yaffee et al., *Ecosystem Management in the United States*.

45. For instance, the collaborative learning approach encourages joint fact-finding and discourages using information in a competitive manner; encourages exploration of underlying values; provides opportunities for relationship building; and focuses parties on interests rather than positions. Walker and Daniels, "Collaborative learning." See also Moore et al., *Creating Dialogue between Decision-Makers and Communities*.

46. Gardner et al., *The Community Visioning and Strategic Planning Handbook*.

47. Moore et al., *Creating Dialogue between Decision-Makers and Communities*.

48. For example, the collaborative learning method of public involvement is based on the premise that "learning and thinking systematically are critical to planning, making decisions about, and managing complex systems." See Daniels et al., "Using collaborative learning in fire recovery planning," p. 7; and Walker and Daniels, "Collaborative learning."

49. See, for example, Burch and Grove, "People, trees, and participation on the urban frontier"; Aloff, "Where to cool both the soul and the heels"; Lowenthal, "Rolling on the river"; and Tamez, "The urban forest ecosystem and cultural values on the urban frontier."

50. Orr, "A world that takes its environment seriously," p. 133.

51. Flora, *Vital Communities*, p. 10.

52. Institute for Research on Environment and Economy, *Community Empowerment in Ecosystem Management*, irregular pagination.

53. Bachrach and Botwinick, *Power and Empowerment*, p. 29.

54. See, for example, Greider, *Who Will Tell the People?*; and Chrislip, "The failure of tra-ditional politics."

55. Advisory Committee on Intergovernmental Relations, *Citizen Participation in the American Federal System*; Blahna and Yonts-Shepard, "Public involvement in resource plan-ning"; Facaros, "Public involvement in national forest planning"; Feller, "Grazing man-agement on public lands"; Wondolleck, *Public Lands Conflict and Resolution*; Wondolleck, "The importance of process in resolving environmental disputes"; Fortmann and Lewis, "Public involvement in natural resource management"; Amy, *The Politics of Environmental Mediation*; Carpenter and Kennedy, *Managing Public Disputes*; Arnstein, "A ladder of citizen participation"; Achterman and Fairfax, "The public participation requirements of the Federal Land Policy and Management Act"; and Advisory Commission on Intergovernmental Relations, *Citizen Participation in the American Federal System*.

56. Shannon and Antypas, "Open institutions"; Orr, *Ecological Literacy*; Blahna and Yonts-Shepard, "Public involvement in resource planning"; Kweit and Kweit, "The poli-tics of policy analysis"; Stanley, "The mystery of the commons"; Stanley, "The rhetoric of the commons"; Stankey, "Ecosystem management"; and Cortner and Shannon, "Embedding public participation in its political context."

57. Wright, "Recommendations," p. 526; also see Little, "The link between local par-ticipation and improved conservation"; and Blahna and Yonts-Shepard, "Public involve-ment in resource planning."

58. Frentz et al., *Ecosystem Management in the U.S.*, p. A-87.

59. Lead Partnership Group, "Social and economic monitoring in rural communi-ties."

60. Kweit and Kweit, "Citizen participation," p. 197.

61. Little, "The link between local participation and improved conservation," p. 363. According to Little, "indicators of genuine decentralization include the extent to which financial decisions and revenue-raising activities are given over to local communities; com-munity authority to negotiate with external bodies … and agencies; and community power to sanction offenders."

62. Little, "The link between local participation and improved conservation"; and Seymour, "Are successful community-based conservation projects designed or discov-ered?"

63. Lead Partnership Group, "Opportunities for community and national interests around reinvestment," p. 30.

64. Little, "The link between local participation and improved conservation"; Seymour, "Are successful community-based projects designed or discovered?"; and White et al., "Lessons to be learned."

65. Korten, "Amid signs of fear and hope, rural people brace for the next millenni-um," p. 4.

66. Korten, *When Corporations Rule the World*; and Walker, "The communitarian cop-out."

67. Smith, "Community-arianism," irregular pagination.

68. Orr, "A world that takes its environment seriously," p. 138.

69. Korten, "Amid signs of fear and hope, rural people brace for the next millenni-um," p. 7.

Chapter 7

Effective Governmental Policies and Structures

While statesmen of another era could write, "when I pay taxes, I buy civilization,"[1] Americans today are in a tax cutting mode, skeptical of bureaucratic efficiency, and distrustful of government and its officials. Yet, they are also increasingly demanding more governmental services than decades ago. We are thus confronted with yet another paradox of political life: the paradox of both distrusting and burdening government. In 1930, Felix Frankfurter, later to become U.S. Supreme Court Justice, commented about this paradox:

> [It] reveals some unresolved inner conflict about the interaction of government and society. I suspect that it implies an uncritical continuance of past assumptions about government and society. We have not adjusted our thinking about government to the overwhelming facts of modern life, and so carry over old mental habits, traditional school-book platitudes and campaign slogans as to the role, the purposes, and the methods of government.[2]

While the paradox may not be new, it has, arguably, intensified during the last two decades of the twentieth century. If we are to get fair value for the civilization we buy with future tax dollars, the design and operation of our governmental institutions will need to be examined critically and adjusted to the facts of modern life that are unfolding as we move into a new century.

Ecosystem management challenges Americans to confront the paradoxes of decision making and scale that are exacerbated by our governance structures. It challenges us to think about how to revise institutions to work toward resolving paradoxes within the context of ecosystem management. It also challenges us to rethink human–nature relationships and relationships among humans and how those relationships are structured through social and governmental institutions. Ecosystem management depends as much on building effective governmental structures as it does upon building social capital. Chapter 6 focused on individual responsibilities as citizens and community members, the building of social capital, and innovative opportunities for citizens to engage in community-based ecosystem management. This chapter discusses governmental policies and structures to enhance governmental performance and the pursuit of democratic values and ecological sustainability. At a minimum, four general areas deserve attention: reexamining laws; rethinking property rights and responsibilities; changing administrative organizations; and aligning market operations with the goal of sustainability.

Reexamining Laws

Although existing environmental and natural resource laws support fragments of ecosystem management concepts, there is no explicit mandate for ecosystem management.[3] Consequently, it may well be time to reexamine the suitability of the current legal framework in relation to ecosystem management.

An Ecosystem Management Law Review Commission?

While ecosystem management has been adopted as policy by federal agencies and projects are being undertaken under the existing framework of laws, if ecosystem management is to be more than an incremental adjustment to the traditional paradigm, a comprehensive reexamination of law will be necessary. According to a former chief of the Forest Service:

> The applicable laws should be evaluated *in total*, and restructured to remove conflicts while radically simplifying management processes. More 'quick fixes' of amendments to various acts seem likely to cause increased instability over the long term. Changes, piece meal, in applicable laws could cause even more problems due to the upset in the balance of the myriad case law.[4]

It may be an appropriate time to convene an ecosystem management law review commission that would be similar to the Public Land Law Review Commission of the 1960s.[5] Congress established this commission in 1964 to make a comprehensive review of all laws, rules, and regulations pertaining to lands under federal control (Indian reservations were excluded). The commission's 1970 report, *One Third of the Nation's Land*, served as a focal point throughout that decade for discussion about the future management of the public domain lands.[6] The process established by a new ecosystem management law review commission could be structured to provide innovative forums for citizen deliberation. This commission could review existing legislation through the lens of ecosystem management; identify conflicting legal requirements; look for novel ways to address the paradoxes of decision making, scale, and sustainability; and make recommendations to the Congress and president for new and corrective legislation.

The commission could consider two categories of laws that have significant implications for implementation of ecosystem management: (1) those specific and particular to natural resources; and (2) those directly applicable to a host of other policy areas as well as to natural resources.

Laws Specific to Natural Resources

In the first category—laws specific and particular to natural resources—consider the following criticisms. The General Mining Act of 1872 promotes commodity production and is clearly an anachronism from a time when government sought to encourage development by offering land and resources at bargain basement prices and when there was little concern for environmental consequences. Similarly, the Multiple-Use–Sustained-Yield Act of 1960, which embraces the multiple-use–sustained-yield paradigm, may have outlived its usefulness. The rational-comprehensive planning approaches outlined in laws such as the National Forest Management Act and the Federal Land Policy and Management Act and their implementing regulations may be too rigid, inflexible, expensive, and inimical to adaptive management. Laws such as the Clean Water Act and the Clean Air Act may be so complex that it is doubtful if the administrative capacity to fully implement them can ever be fully developed. Finally, the Endangered Species Act's species-by-species approach may be counterproductive to efforts to look at species distribution and mix over larger ecosystems.[7] These criticisms merit further public debate in the specific context of ecosystem management.

In addition to reviewing existing legislation, proposed new legislation to further the principles of ecosystem management should also be evaluated. Among the proposals: site-specific legislation governing the management of specific ecosystems; a new federal ecosystem management law; and a constitutional amendment establishing a fundamental obligation for all levels of government to protect the environment.[8]

Laws at the state and local level also merit examination. At the state level, for example, many state lands are held in trust to benefit education and are constitutionally required to be managed for maximum financial return. While the trust doctrine under which these lands are managed arguably does not preclude managing for ecosystem or amenity benefits, implementation of the state trust responsibility has tended to favor commodity uses.[9]

Laws Applying to Natural Resources and Other Policy Areas

In the second category are laws that directly apply to a host of other policy areas as well as to resource management. The Federal Advisory Committee Act (FACA) discussed in chapter 4 falls into this category, and is routinely cited as a law needing further amendment to remove barriers to participation. Two other examples of laws in this category are federal antitrust laws and international trade policies.

Antitrust laws, which can be traced to the Sherman Act of 1890, are specially designed to prevent trade restraint and price fixing in all sectors of the economy, and cover, for example, oil companies, lumber manufacturers, and even university boards of regents.[10] While ecosystem management emphasizes cooperation, collaboration, and partnerships, "the only environment that matters for antitrust purposes is the *competitive* environment."[11] Thus, private owners may be in violation of antitrust laws if they jointly develop ecosystem management plans that reduce or defer outputs from their lands. While it is uncertain how much of a problem antitrust will prove to be in practice, clarifying legislation may still be in order.[12] Global markets and international trade policies not only affect the financial climate in which resource management takes place, but also the way companies and agencies manage and produce resource outputs. International trade agreements, such as the North American Free Trade Agreement (NAFTA), are increasingly imposing environmental obligations on American business and government.

NAFTA, for example, approved by Mexico, Canada, and the United States in 1993 as a regional free trade agreement, includes extensive environmental provisions that protect domestic environmental laws and commit countries to undertake trade and investment in a manner consistent with environmental protection. As a condition of President Clinton's support for NAFTA, supplemental "side" agreements on labor and the environment were drafted and signed as part of the NAFTA package. The presence of such environmental concerns in a trade agreement is unprecedented.[13] One side agreement, the North American Agreement on Environmental Cooperation, established the Commission for Environmental Cooperation as the body charged with monitoring the environmental provisions of NAFTA. A separate agreement between Mexico and the United States created the Border Environmental Cooperation Commission and the North American Development Bank. The Border Commission is charged with cleaning up water ways and sewage waste within 100 kilometers of the U.S.–Mexican border. The bank finances projects certified by the Commission. These new institutions have been both lauded as innovative opportunities to address the trade–environment linkage and criticized for being ineffective. There are concerns, for example, that they lack the fiscal resources, political will power, and jurisdiction necessary to identify and solve environmental problems.[14]

A popular slogan is to "act locally but think globally." However, the magnitude of global problems means it is necessary to act globally as well as to think globally.[15] While some envision a "world that takes its environment seriously,"[16] critics worry that a "new world order" raises the specter of world government and loss of national sovereignty. Nonetheless, the global economy and the agreements that set the conditions for world trade can do much to either facilitate or impede ecosystem management and the quest for ecological sustainability.

The Prospects for Reform

A number of interesting alternatives for revising and expanding the legal basis for ecosystem management have thus been suggested and deserve further study and public deliberation. Proposals to revise or add laws, however, are bound to be fraught with intensive controversy and fought by constituencies who fear change from the status quo or who distrust the policy orientations of those doing the rewriting. Environmentalists, for example, fear the gutting of procedural protections they have used in lawsuits to make commodity-oriented agencies more environmentally sensitive. Multiple-use has become the mantra for the prodevelopment Wise Use movement; suggesting elimination or revision of the Multiple-Use–Sustained-Yield Act is likely to be viewed as verification that ecosystem management portends the elimination of all extractive resource production. Likewise, passage of a general ecosystem management law is likely to be opposed by a coalition of disparate interests, including: those who fear that the law would only be symbolic; those who fear that its provisions would be substantive, trumping existing legislation protective of their interests; those who fear the trampling of private property rights; and those who believe decentralized approaches rather than more federal legislation is the appropriate path to achieving sustainability. Nonetheless, if structured to encourage informed public deliberation, such debate could serve a

useful social function, using the tension of the paradox of conflict and collaboration in constructive fashion to work toward understanding the goals
people have in common and as an incentive to develop innovative solutions.[17]

Other Laws Affecting Resource Management

The attention of those interested in natural resources is typically directed
toward laws in the first, and to a lesser degree, second category. Yet, there are
laws in a third category—laws that do not directly apply to resource management but that nonetheless structure the overall social and political environment—that also cannot be ignored. These laws reflect social values, impact
patterns of resource use, and affect citizen trust and confidence in governmental institutions. Examples include: immigration laws and policies that
define the cultural make-up of the population whose values and resource use
patterns must be considered in resource management; worker leave and retire-
ment laws that impact leisure time and hence recreational demands; and campaign finance laws that determine who has access and influence in decision
making. Although laws such as these likely would be outside the purview of
an ecosystem management law review commission, they nonetheless affect the
political demands the public places on resource management as well as public
attitudes toward government and governance structures in general.

Campaign finance laws, for example, are in serious need of reform at all
levels of government. As political campaigns become more expensive, candidates have been forced to raise significant amounts of money from special
interests. In effect, candidates are put up for sale to special interests, who in
turn receive inordinate access and power. In the aftermath of the 1996 presidential election, egregious examples were revealed, including sleep-overs in the
White House Lincoln bedroom rewarded to major contributors and foreign
campaign contributions targeted to influence U.S. foreign policy.

Public financing of campaigns, free air time, spending limits, and controls on political action committees (PACs) are all proposed solutions.[18]
Campaign finance reform is introduced in every session of Congress, but no
significant legislation has ever been passed. Because incumbents are typically
favored with campaign cash by interests who hedge their bets on proven winners, campaign finance reform is most ardently pushed by challengers cam-
paigning for office, not incumbents. Maintaining the status quo is the result,
not only in terms of revising campaign financing, but also in terms of per-
petuating the politics of interest. However difficult, campaign finance reform
may be one of the most significant steps that can be taken to restore political
health and public confidence in the political system.

Rethinking Property Rights and Responsibilities

While efforts to manage at a landscape scale will fail unless both public and private lands are part of the management picture, management plans cannot be divorced from ownership realities and the different objectives of private and public landowners or they will become mired in constitutional and political conflict.[19] U.S. society places a high cultural and legal value on private property rights, which is one of the most tenaciously protected American liberties. The nation's founders believed republican government was dependent on a broad distribution of property. Because "power follows property," property ownership was necessary to ensure that wealth did not become concentrated in a few, thus undermining the economic and political bases of representative government.[20]

The property rights movement of the last several years is indicative of the extremely deep feelings that people have about private property. During the 1990s, a number of groups organized to advance property rights. Along with groups allied with the Wise Use movement, these interests have actively pursued legislative and judicial strategies to ensure that private property owners are compensated when the government imposes environmental regulations. Issues surrounding such "regulatory takings" have become extremely controversial in the last decade. Between 1991 and 1996, at least 52 property rights measures were adopted in 26 states in all regions of the country.[21]

Under the ancient concept of eminent domain, government has the right to take private property for public use. However, under the Fifth Amendment of the U.S. Constitution, no property can be taken without just compensation. Constitutional law has also determined that under the general police powers of the state—the powers to regulate for public health, safety, morals, and general welfare—government can impose reasonable regulations on the use of property without compensation. Zoning, for example, has been repeatedly upheld by the courts as a valid use of police power. The question then becomes: when is the burden of governmental regulations of such a magnitude that in effect government has "taken" property and the landowner is deserving of compensation? Recent decisions by the U.S. Supreme Court have tended to favor private property rights claims.[22]

The right to use and own property is an institutional process characterized by continuity and change. Property is a social construction that is undergoing continual modification through court rulings, new philosophical and ethical currents, and changing societal values about labor and capital. As the debate over private property and takings signifies, too often public debate, policy, and research focus on the dichotomy of private versus public property and miss the complexity and richness of the hybrid forms of land ownership that already exist.[23] In reality, property tenure systems in today's society are dynamic and diverse. These changes in the institutions of property warrant deeper analysis as they relate to ecosystem management. In the future, public–private cooperation and new types of property, such as shared land ownership, may well result in further changes in the way society views private and public property.

In addition to the prospect that more or less stringent regulation may be placed on fee-simple ownership rights, managing across boundaries may also imply, as chapter 4 discussed, opening public lands to more private uses. This implies rethinking the concept of public property. Changing property conceptions, as the previous chapter discussed, might well entail giving local communities greater access to, and control over, decisions affecting adjacent public lands.

Property is also a classic example of the responsibilities that attend rights. Under law one may have the right to use one's land as one pleases, but not to the point that it becomes a nuisance to others. It is generally accepted, for instance, that pollution spewing uncontrolled from an effluent pipe or smokestack may be regulated for the greater good. More recently, the legal responsibilities of landowners have been found to include a responsibility to resident endangered species and their habitat.

Societal understanding of property rights and the appropriate extent of government regulation should be expected to evolve, just as the definition of good stewardship changes as more is learned about ecosystems.[24] For example, societal perception of wetlands has shifted considerably in recent years. Not long ago wetlands were considered unproductive wastelands best drained and reclaimed for productive use. Today, wetlands are highly valued as wildlife habitat and water purifiers, among other things, and under current law landowners no longer have the right to drain swamps at will.[25] As population has grown and the technological capacity to do significant ecological damage has increased, there are simply a lot more instances where doing what one wants with property hurts someone else.[26]

Although arguments are frequently heard about "too much regulation," Aldo Leopold reminds us that those who rail against government regulations are often those who are failing in their own obligations to practice stewardship:

> Individual landowners and users, especially lumbermen and stockmen, are inclined to wail long and loudly about the extension of government ownership and regulation of land, but (with notable

exceptions) they show little disposition to develop the only visible alternative: the voluntary practice of conservation on their own lands.[27]

The modern reality is that landowner responsibilities are simply greater than they once were, and regulation is often the price paid for failure to attend to the responsibilities attached to property rights. Recognizing the increasing responsibilities of landowners and changing citizens' philosophical orientation to nature to acknowledge responsibilities for stewarding public and private resources can do much to ensure that property rights serve both ecological sustainability and democracy, and reduce the need for government regulation.

Changing Administrative Organizations

The importance of organizational change, especially change in how resource agencies relate to one another and to the public, is crucial to the adoption of an ecosystem approach and to resolving the paradoxes of decision making and scale. Resource agencies are being asked to reinvent themselves to increase efficiency, accountability, and public trust. Governmental institutions will have to become more flexible and open in decision making and embrace new models of leadership and coordination.[28] Agency culture will need to be modified, coordination mechanisms strengthened, and new institutional arrangements contemplated.

Agency Cultures
Agency cultures are a substantial barrier to ecosystem management. Professional norms affect the identification of management goals and the formulation and adoption of the means for achieving those goals. A strong professional ethos can serve an agency well, giving it purpose and making it cohesive. But such insularity can also be damaging when professional beliefs and myths persist in the face of either new scientific evidence or markedly changing social values.[29] Agencies become wedded to routine and deeply resistant to any alteration that doesn't agree with their own professional view of what should be done. Issues become framed as "them versus us," and professional divisions between the professional expert and the public are sharpened.

Incentives and rewards systems in resource management agencies traditionally have been heavily weighted toward commodity production; efforts toward improving ecological conditions have not been rewarded. Management incentives also exist to control information.[30] When faced with conflict, conformity rather than dissent and innovation is rewarded. Agency cultures have yet to foster a spirit of cooperation and a willingness to give up resources and hence power to other agencies and entities. Agencies have been reluctant to shift from linear step-by-step approaches to public participation to those that are flexible, open, and encourage a rich public discourse. Innovation and new forms of leadership have been impeded by hierarchical decision-making structures, the risk aversion found in upper levels of decision making, and standards for organizational promotion. However, efforts to diversify the workforce by discipline, gender, ethnicity, and philosophy have brought new attitudes and perceptions that are providing support for new approaches.[31] Moreover, employee loyalty is increasingly not to the organization but to issues such as protection of resources or to the employee's own sense of personal ethics. While such individuals are simultaneously praised as brilliant entrepreneurs and lambasted as deviant insubordinates, they are indicative of attempts by lower- and mid-level employees to shape organizational change.[32]

Overcoming organizational biases and rigidity, however, is not a trivial task. Proponents of participatory democracy note that opening resource management decision making will require a shift from the current agency/government focus on efficiency. "The criteria for evaluating policy in a democratic process are the accessibility of the process and/or the responsiveness of the policy to those who are affected by it, rather than efficiency or rationality of the decision."[33] Rather than simple, linear, cause and effect models, organizational cultures will need to move toward more complex and integrated systems thinking.[34]

Coordination Mechanisms

As long as multiple agencies and levels of government remain protective of their own turf and define their own visions and management objectives apart from each other, it will be difficult to effectively manage at larger spatial scales. Interagency and intergovernmental coordination is needed to meet the greater data and research requirements of ecosystem management, reduce repetition, ensure data comparability, and share results. Resource managers will need to acknowledge mutual responsibility for ecosystem components and coordinate processes that transcend conventional boundaries.[35] Since water, plants, animals, pollutants, and people are in large part oblivious to administrative boundaries and cross them at will, ecosystem management combined with society's growing penchant for decentralized institutions will intensify the paradoxes of scale. Strengthening existing institutional mechanisms for interagency and intergovernmental coordination is another way to build the political capacity to manage the problems of fragmentation and address the paradoxes of scale.

While there is no single statute that provides authority for federal agencies to coordinate with other federal entities or with state and local governments and Indian tribes, many pieces of legislation mandate coordinative activities. The National Environmental Policy Act (NEPA) is, of course, very specific about the need for coordination, requiring that the federal government cooperate with state and local governments and other concerned public and private organizations in carrying out the purposes of the act.[36] Coordination requirements are also contained within legislation specific to the mission of an agency. For example, the Resources Planning Act (RPA) and National Forest Management Act (NFMA) require the USDA Forest Service to coordinate its land and resource management plans with the planning processes of state and local governments and other federal agencies. The Federal Land Policy and Management Act (FLPMA) has a similar requirement, but additionally requires the Bureau of Land Management to ensure its plans are consistent with state and local plans.

Federal legislation may also provide state or local agencies comanagement responsibilities (e.g., the shared federal–state responsibility for fish and game management), require federal entities to comply with state and local requirements (e.g., air and water quality standards), or provide incentives for cooperation. Section 6 of the Endangered Species Act (ESA), for example, encourages states to enter into cooperative agreements with the federal government and requires the Secretary of the Interior to enter into such agreements if the state's proposed program is in accordance with ESA criteria. At the state level, zoning, land-use planning, environmental quality, and game and fish legislation all frequently require interagency and intergovernmental cooperation.

There are a variety of informal and formal coordination techniques available as well.[37] Aside from informal linkages and networks sustained by telephone calls or ad hoc issue-related meetings, the most informal methods of intergovernmental coordination involve development of local, grassroots agreements among local and regional land managers. Informal opportunities for discourse are proving to be an important means for including grassroots members of the policy community.[38] Another form of coordination, particularly at the state or regional scale, is the memorandum of agreement, in which organizations agree to coordinate management policies and practices. These formal memoranda are more lasting and effective than local agreements, but they require extensive preparation and negotiation. Moreover, such "good faith efforts" are easily broken.[39]

Bureaucratic efforts to protect agency domains have long been recognized as one of the main impediments to coordination. Turf battles persist among agencies and different levels of government; specialists in one agency don't trust similar specialists in another. Cultural barriers divide managers and scientists.[40] Even within agencies there may be competition among specialists or different parts of the agency; better external coordination can occur only when there is better internal coordination.[41]

Requirements for coordination are not the same thing as opportunities for coordination. Coordination is both a process and a structure of relationships that distributes power, access, and resources. Too often in the past, coordination has been treated as a formal procedure to meet requirements that can be satisfied by notice and consultation. Coordination can be strengthened by making it frequent, personal, and ongoing.[42]

New Institutions

Concerns that resource management is fragmented among too many agencies with conflicting policy and management goals, and that the current agencies are too entrenched to reinvent themselves, have led to many proposals to reorganize, consolidate, and eliminate natural resource agencies. These proposals often point in significantly divergent directions. One set of analysts, for example, advocates consolidating three Department of the Interior agencies—the Bureau of Land Management, the Bureau of Reclamation, and the U.S. Fish and Wildlife Service—into a new Western Ecosystems Management Agency;[43] another analyst recommends consolidating the Forest Service and the Bureau of Land Management;[44] and yet another calls for breaking up the Department of the Interior, including giving most of the National Park Service to state and local governments or nonprofit groups.[45]

Another proposal is to transfer federal lands to the states. Such proposals, however, have usually been scuttled by a combination of concerns, including: state management would be governed by state constitutional provisions to maximize economic return; the federal framework of environmental laws would no longer apply; the states would eventually dispose of the lands to private interests; and the states have neither the financial nor political willingness to commit to management and environmental protection.[46] Past efforts at comprehensive reorganization of natural resource agencies at the federal level have also been repeatedly rebuffed.[47]

While reorganization and state transfers may prove undesirable or infeasible, there are still a number of other innovative institutional forms that can be contemplated. Ecosystem study boards,[48] quasi-official citizen councils,[49] new river basin commissions,[50] and new forms of cooperative regional land management to integrate management of small units of public and private land[51] have all been suggested. A number of analysts favor spatially targeted approaches over blanket regulation or centralized planning of large blocks of land. Taking a regional approach, critical areas of importance would be identified and singled out for special management through a variety of either regulatory or market mechanisms—a "spatial solution to a spatial problem."[52] Some argue small-scale institutions would be more responsive to community concerns.[53] The concept of localized decision making, however, again raises the paradox of centralization and decentralization and the perennial question of how national interests can be reconciled with local interests.

However, experiments with new institutional arrangements in places like the Applegate watershed in Southern Oregon and the Columbia River Gorge in Washington and Oregon, are beginning to yield information on how this paradox might be approached. The Applegate Partnership, for example, illustrates how the creation of a voluntary organization can set a standard for community-based conservation The Partnership, which emerged during the highly charged timber wars in the Pacific Northwest, has been a key player in working toward resolution of that debate. Another institutional alternative is the creation of legislation and agencies that combine local, state, and federal authority and responsibility. The Columbia River National Scenic Area Act, for example, attempts to balance national and local interests and area protection with economic development. The act created a 295,000-acre area— which is not a national park, national forest, or wilderness area—to be managed by a partnership among the USDA Forest Service, a bi-state regional planning agency (the Columbia River Gorge Commission), the states of Washington and Oregon, and the area's six counties. The act also calls for interagency and tribal coordination and cooperation. A comprehensive development plan and several economic development projects have been completed since passage of the act. Not all residents are happy with the new institutional arrangement, however. A small billboard at the turnoff to two of the area's new economic development projects, Skamania Lodge and the Columbia Gorge Interpretive Center, declares:

> At the expense of the citizens who live here the Columbia River Scenic Act was created through collusion, conflict of interest, deceit and downright crookedness by our U.S. Senators, Congressmen, state Attorney Generals, Governors, Gorge Commission and other Skunks with the help and cajoling force of the lobbying groups known as the 'friends quislings' of the Columbia Gorge and the 1,000 friends quislings of Oregon.

Aligning Market Operations with the Goal of Sustainability

As the paradoxes of sustainability illustrate, the operation of economic systems have often been in opposition to the goal of ecological sustainability.
Resolving these paradoxes means exploring how ecosystem management will
evolve in economic terms, including an analysis of the role that markets can
play in facilitating ecosystem management on both public and private lands.
The goal is to recognize that economics is also a vital part of the solution and
to align market operations with the goal of sustainability, allowing markets to
work in a positive manner.[54] Markets are themselves political institutions, and
the availability of goods and services and the prices at which those goods and
services are bought and sold are heavily influenced by government policy.
Consequently, changes in government policy can create an institutional climate
in which market forces are used to reinforce ecosystem management goals and
reward the private sector for producing ecosystem benefits and pursuing long-
term ecological sustainability. Government can establish market-based incentives through tax and spending policy and other economic incentives, it can
privatize certain governmental functions through the creation of marketable
rights and permits, and it can revise budgetary and accounting policies and
practices.

Market-Based Incentives

Instead of command and control regulation (i.e., legislatures issue laws or
agencies issue regulations and then put into place an elaborate system for
enforcing compliance), market-based approaches use economic *incentives* to
achieve the desired effect. The importance of economic incentives should not
be underestimated. Economic incentives are critical to motivating local
landowners and other community members, particularly in cases where local
citizens are being asked to forego economic production for the benefit of the
environment.[55]

Tax and Spending Policy

One way government policy can provide economic incentives is by changing
tax and spending policies that are not compatible with the goal of ecological
sustainability.[56] For example, estate tax laws that often force landowners to
break environmentally sensitive lands into smaller, less environmentally valu-
able parcels can be revised.[57] Spending policies can also eliminate a whole
range of subsidies, including those that encourage the construction of costly
and environmentally destructive water projects, the expansion of automobile
use, and revenue-losing timber, mining, and grazing practices.

Another way to use taxing policy is to create strong positive incentives for firms and individuals to ameliorate the costs of preservation and reflect the societal costs of polluting and other environmentally damaging activities. For instance, taxes can be used to reward private owners that forego environmentally damaging development to preserve open space resources. In the Seattle metropolitan area, for example, a public benefits rating system gives landowners points for providing open space resources that protect aquifers, salmon habitat, shorelines, trail linkages, historical sites, and the like. Property tax reductions are given, depending on the number of accumulated points.[58] An alternate method is to place taxes on each unit of pollution discharged into the environment. Such taxes, it is argued, would make pollution a cost of production; as long as the tax is more than the cost of control, a firm would have a strong incentive to improve its pollution control efforts.[59]

Nontax Economic Incentives

A number of nontax market incentives have also been suggested to replace traditional command and control approaches. The use of transferable development rights, for example, is advocated as a way to preserve ecologically sensitive lands. In turn, for not developing a particular piece of property, a landowner is given development rights in an off-site area where development may be suitable at higher densities than local zoning currently allows. The Pine Barrens Commission of New York, for example, has used transferable development rights as part of a program to preserve Long Island's rare pitch pines and scrub oak forest.[60]

Another nontax market tool is the tradeable pollution discharge permit. In this case, the government issues pollution permits that allow so many units of pollution to be discharged during a given time period. Dischargers are able to buy and sell permits among themselves. Tradeable emission permits differ from the pollution tax discussed above in that the cost of polluting is determined by supply and demand in the market rather than by government.[61]

Government policies that affect the setting of prices for regulated commodities, such as water and power, can also be revised so that those goods are delivered closer to their true economic and environmental costs. Since usage is sensitive to price (the price elasticity of demand), increasing price can lower demand and encourage conservation. As with tradeable pollution units, government policies can be changed to permit the creation of markets where none currently exist, as in water markets that enable the voluntary transfer and exchange of water rights.[62]

Finally, green certification and environmental labeling can create market incentives. As a price for trading in international markets, for example, participants are increasingly expected to meet certain "green production" standards. Private landowners who have sought and received certification under standards developed by the International Forest Stewardship Council, for example, hope to have new markets opened to them or obtain price premiums for their products.

Privatization

In the 1980s, government policy sought to turn back the tide of government expansion by deregulating certain policy areas, such as airlines and telecommunications, and by proposing that many government functions be privatized (i.e., turned over to the private sector). Proposals for privatization have been suggested for many areas of government, from social security to public lands.

Highly controversial proposals to privatize public lands range from creating marketable rights to water or forage resources to complete divestiture of such lands to private control. Arguments for privatization are based on the premise that markets are a more efficient means than government to manage resource systems, protect public goods, and achieve ecological stewardship.[63] The failures of federal land and water policy are seen as a failure to use markets.

Opponents of privatization are not persuaded that private ownership will result in ecologically sustainable management. The current regulatory framework was created in response to public demands for intervention precisely because the private sector caused and refused to correct many environmental abuses. The corporate economy is seen as interested only in short-term economic gain and remote and insensitive to economically, socially, or ecologically vital communities.[64] Many fear that the public lands they are accustomed to using, are attached to emotionally, and consider they own in common with all Americans would soon sprout "keep out" signs. Despite such criticisms, there are instances of privatization, especially in countries like New Zealand, that can provide instructive lessons.

Beginning in 1984, New Zealand restructured its economy, deregulating and privatizing many government assets. As part of this restructuring, New Zealand dissolved its national forest service. All state-owned indigenous forests were placed in a new department of conservation along with former reserves, national parks, and those portions of Crown lands suitable for reserves. These forests are off limits to timber production and are managed under a conservation management strategy to protect soil, water, and ecological values, while permitting some recreation and controlled tourism.[65] A publicly-owned forestry corporation was created to manage the remaining forest lands, which consisted of approximately 1.3 million acres of plantation forests, comprised largely of exotic stands of radiata pine. By 1987, the government had decided to move toward full privatization, and most of the forests managed by the corporation were sold to private interests. Regional and district councils were established in 1989 to be responsible for local resource policies, planning, and management oversight, and in 1991 fundamental reordering of resource legislation resulted in the comprehensive Resource Management Act, which now effectively governs nearly all resource use in New Zealand. The principal purpose of the act is to "promote the sustainable management of natural and physical resources."

In effect, New Zealand wiped out the multiple-use concept and replaced it with a dominant-use system that separated resource production from resource protection.[66] While it may be too early to be certain of the outcomes of the New Zealand changes, the New Zealand experience nonetheless has interesting implications for U.S. policymakers. Yet, it is also important that Americans recognize the differences between the U.S. and the New Zealand situations. In New Zealand, the total acreage is quite small; the exotic pine plantations have always been well defined and distinct from the indigenous forests and their functions as production well accepted; and the parliamentary form of government, where the executive and legislative branches are controlled by the same party, is perhaps more conducive to making rapid and dramatic change.[67]

Budgeting and Accounting

As the paradox of doing more with less illustrates, the costs of managing the environment based on ecological prescriptions will require significant investments in labor and capital for monitoring and managing ecosystem conditions, integrating management activities, developing and nurturing partnerships, fostering public deliberation, and coordinating across jurisdictions. Yet, smaller budgets and workforce reduction are likely to be the norm at least for the near future. Given this budgetary climate, changes in governmental budgeting policy will need to occur to align budgetary incentives with the principles of ecosystem management.

Budgetary processes that remain fragmented and tied to functional activities will need to be revamped.[68] Ecosystem management is a multigenerational process that requires secure, consistent funding. Annual budgeting and appropriations are unreliable and can serve as a disincentive for cooperation. To rectify such problems, one study group recommended that the land management agencies, Congress, and state legislatures all study the benefits of multiyear budgeting.[69] Innovative budget augmentation strategies will also be required, including partnerships with industry or charitable foundations and means for securing volunteer labor for monitoring and remediation work.

Such changes will not come easily. Budget processes do not usually capture the same kind of public attention as the more visible planning and decision-making processes.[70] Interest groups that benefit from subsidies or depend on funds to advance favorite projects are the most attentive to budget processes. These interests have a strong grip on appropriation processes and are resistant to changes in the processes of budgeting that would minimize their influence.

Economic theory influences how we use conventions, such as the discount rate (which assumes that the value of a dollar or a resource is less in the future than in the present), and how we construct and use indicators of economic health, such as the gross national product and the consumer price index. Some economists are now developing models for valuing ecological assets. One study, for example, estimates that the worldwide dollar value of nature's services is $33 trillion annually, compared to the $18 trillion generated by human produced goods and services.[71] Others assert, however, that it is immoral to put dollar values on nature's services, because nature, like life itself, cannot be priced. Some question whether such devices are methodologically sufficient.[72] Nonetheless, changes will be needed in government policy and regulations that have institutionalized often outmoded economic theory and accounting practices, and to correct for the inevitable market failures that occur on the landscape level.[73]

Linking the Economic Marketplace and Political Marketplace

A persistent debate exists among those who favor market solutions and those who favor command and control regulation. The debate has too often been painted as either/or. The most ardent supporters of markets often portray government as bad and environmental regulation as ecofascism; the Progressive Era is said to have initiated a century-long romance with "sylvan socialism" that "featured centralized planning by Platonic despots."[74] Ardent feelings on the other side also abound, with markets painted as always capitulating to corporate and private greed.[75] Market-based tools such as the tradeable emissions permit are criticized as rewarding polluters to pollute.

However, the market is *now* a highly controlled social institution, a fact that must be more explicitly recognized in discussions of market and nonmarket approaches. Furthermore, the economically and politically high costs of command and control regulation must be balanced against the benefits that can be realized by other means. Political and economic policies cannot be considered in isolation from one another. Rather than the either/or debate, what is needed are better linkages between the economic marketplace and the political marketplace. Experimentation will be needed to determine where and when it might be more appropriate to use one approach and where and when it is more appropriate to use another or a mix of approaches.

Moving Resource Management into the Next Century

There is already a rich stew of ideas and ongoing experiments that suggests how to improve governmental performance in a world where the principles of ecosystem management guide natural resource management. These ideas and experiments center around reexamining laws, rethinking basic concepts of property, changing administrative organizations, and aligning market operations with the goal of sustainability.

Many of these ideas, such as, for example, improving public participation processes and interagency coordination mechanisms, have been around for quite some time; others, such as the idea for a new Western Ecosystems Management Agency and a constitutional amendment on the environment, are more recent. Some, such as revisions to the General Mining Act of 1872 or the planning procedures of the National Forest Management Act, are specific to laws and policies governing natural resources; others, like campaign finance reform, are generic to the overall political climate, but will nonetheless also affect efforts to implement ecosystem management. Some appear to be more politically feasible than others. Repeated proposals to transfer public lands to private ownerships, for example, have never fared well, while experiments in the use of tax and spending policy, tax incentives, green accounting, and dollar valuation of nature's services are already occurring. Some are rather bold, such as making adjustments in our long-held thinking about private property rights and responsibilities. But bold and revolutionary changes will be needed to fully implement ecosystem management and resolve the paradoxes of ecosystem management. This will require looking hard at existing and alternative strategies, such as convening an ecosystem management law review commission. Not all of these ideas are necessary for ecosystem management to succeed, and not all will prove workable.

A paradigm shift does not require sweeping rejection of all existing policies. What it does require is their careful reevaluation in light of changing management goals and philosophies. Integrating the goal of ecological sustainability into economic approaches, for example, can do much to resolve the paradoxes of sustainability by avoiding the inadequacies of traditional economic conventions. New institutional arrangements, more effective interagency and intergovernmental coordination mechanisms, and changes in organizational culture can also move toward resolution of the paradoxes of scale and decision making. Combined with changes in the philosophical postulates that underlie natural resource policy and the building of social capital, these policy changes can be more than incremental adjustments to the status quo.

NOTES

1. Justice Oliver Wendell Holmes as cited in Gaus, *Reflections on Public Administration*, p. 19.

2. Felix Frankfurter, *The Public and Its Government*, p. 170.

3. Robert Keiter has written extensively on the adequacy of existing natural resource and environmental laws to meet the requirements of ecosystem management. See, for example: Keiter, "NEPA and the emerging concept of ecosystem management on the public lands"; Keiter, "Toward legitimizing ecosystem management on the public domain"; Keiter, "Taking account of the ecosystem on the public domain"; Keiter et al., "Legal perspectives on ecosystem management"; Keiter, "Ecological policy and the courts"; and Keiter, "Beyond the boundary line." On law also see Flick and King, "Ecosystem management as American law"; and Meidinger, "Organizational and legal challenges for ecosystem management."

4. Thomas, "The instability of stability," p. 8, emphasis in original.

5. See, for example, Cawley and Freemuth, "A critique of the multiple use framework in public lands decisionmaking," p. 40; and Thomas, "The instability of stability."

6. Cawley and Freemuth, "A critique of the multiple use framework in public lands decisionmaking," p. 40. The Federal Land Policy and Management Act of 1976 is cited as embodying most of the recommendations of the Public Land Law Review Commission. The commission's most controversial and rejected recommendation, however, dealt with dominant use. In some instances, the commission argued, certain areas should not be managed for multiple use but for maximum benefit of a dominant use. Other uses would be managed to "avoid interference with fulfillment of such dominant use." See Public Land Law Review Commission, *One Third of the Nation's Land*, p. 3.

7. Klyza, *Who Controls Public Lands?*; Wilkinson, *Crossing the Next Meridian*; Behan, "The irony of the multiple-use/sustained-yield concept"; Behan, "Multiresource forest management"; Gordon, "From vision to policy"; Keiter et al., "Legal perspectives on ecosystem management"; Rosenbaum, *Environmental Politics and Policy*; Rohlf, "Six biological reasons why the Endangered Species Act doesn't work—and what to do about it"; and Franklin, "Preserving biodiversity."

8. Keiter et al., "Legal perspectives on ecosystem management." Prominent environmental scholar and the intellectual force behind the environmental impact statement requirement of NEPA, Lynton Caldwell, has proposed a constitutional amendment on the environment.

9. For discussion generally of state trust lands and the argument that management for ecological benefit is not precluded, see Souder and Fairfax, *State Trust Lands*; and Fairfax et al., "The school trust lands." Also discussing the issues involved in balancing the interests of the trust's beneficiaries versus other public interests are: Bassett, "Utah's school trust lands"; Beaver, "Management of Wyoming's state trust lands from 1890–1990";

McCormack, "Land use planning and management of state school lands"; and O'Laughlin, *Idaho's Endowment Lands.*

10. For cases involving such entities see: *United States v. Socony-Vacuum Oil Co, Inc.*, 310 U.S. 150 (1940); *American Column Co. v. United States*, 257 U.S. 377 (1921); *NCAA v. Board of Regents of University of Oklahoma*, 468 U.S. 85 (1984). On antitrust more generally, see Parzych, *Public Policy and the Regulatory Environment*; Gundlach and Mohr, "Collaborative relationships"; and Stelzer and Kitt, *Selected Antitrust Cases.*

11. Smith, "Antitrust and ecosystem management," emphasis in original.

12. See Meidinger, "Organizational and legal challenges for ecosystem management," pp. 375–376.

13. Magraw, "NAFTA's repercussions." See also Vogel, "International trade and environmental regulation."

14. Shannon, "Report blasts NAFTA environmental legacy along U.S.–Mexico border"; Wheat, "Troubled NAFTA waters"; and Charnovitz, "Environment and trade."

15. Eckersley, *Environmentalism and Political Theory*, p. 174.

16. Orr, "A world that takes its environment seriously."

17. In the area of forest policy, for example, the Seventh American Forest Congress used regional roundtables and a national meeting to develop a vision and principles for management of the nation's forests, a process that could also serve as a template for discussion of legislation for ecosystem management. See Bentley and Langbein, *Final Report— Seventh American Forest Congress*; and Bentley, "Scarcity, political economy, and the forest congress process."

18. Rivlin, "Values, institutions, and sustainable forestry"; and McCain, "How to clean up the mess." Lijphart, "Unequal participation," p. 2 footnote 1 notes that making financial contributions to campaigns is characterized by an income bias that is greater than for any other mode of political participation. However, he also notes that this can be equalized by complete and exclusive public financing of political parties and campaigns, however difficult this is to achieve in countries like the United States that do not have strong and disciplined political parties.

19. Flick et al., "Public purpose and private property." Many Americans citing the Fifth Amendment do not accept any restrictions on the use of private land. See Hargrove, "Anglo-American land use attitudes"; and Cribbet, "Concepts in transition."

20. Howe, "Republican thought and the political violence of the 1790s," p. 150.

21. Emerson, "A comparative study of state property rights legislation," p. 3. According to Emerson, "poor states with greater dependence on natural resources, where Republicans and 'neo-legislators' dominate the statehouse and where limited institutional resources have been invested in environmental and natural resource policies are most likely to adopt property rights measures, particularly strong measures." As a result, this study concludes, "we are not facing a sweeping reversal of our regulatory property regime in this country. Instead, we may be witnessing a growing differentiation between those states committed to environmental regulation and those intent on limiting regulatory encroachments."

22. See, for example, *First English Evangelical Lutheran Church v. Los Angeles County*, 482 U.S.

304(1987); *Lucas v. South Carolina Coastal Council,* 505 U.S. 1003 (1992); and *Nollan v. California Coastal Commission,* 483 U.S. 825 (1987).

23. Geisler and Kittel, "Who owns the ecosystem?"

24. Cribbet, "Concepts in transition"; and Sax, "Property rights and the economy of nature."

25. "For example, as a society we at first applauded, and then treated as part of the general order of things, the destruction of the first 50 percent of the wetlands in the continental United States.... [But] we have begun to understand as a society that those who are destroying the wetlands that yet remain in this country are hurting the rest of us.... [It is reasonable, therefore, that the law] now must hold that swamp owners don't have the right to use their property in that way...draining swamps means something different now from what it once meant to society." Weeks, *Beyond the Ark,* p. 135.

26. Weeks, *Beyond the Ark,* pp. 134–135.

27. Leopold, *A Sand County Almanac and Sketches Here and There,* p. 213.

28. Boyle et al., *Policies and Mythologies of the U.S. Forest Service;* and Lee and Stankey, "Evaluating institutional arrangements for regulating large watersheds and river basins."

29. Schiff, *Fire and Water;* and Kennedy and Dombeck, "The evolution of public agency beliefs and behavior toward ecosystem-based stewardship." See Clarke and McCool, *Staking Out the Terrain,* on the role of professionalism as a source of agency power. For discussion of organizational culture and change in resource agencies, see also Kennedy and Thomas, "Exit, voice, and loyalty of wildlife biologists in public natural resource/environmental agencies"; Kennedy, "Legislative confrontation of groupthink in U.S. natural resource agencies"; Kennedy and Roper, "Status of and need for career development research in natural resource agencies"; Hodges and Durant, "The professional state revisited"; Twight et al., "Constituency bias in a federal career system?"; and Brown and Harris, "Professional foresters and the land ethic, revisited."

30. Boyle et al., *Policies and Mythologies of the U.S. Forest Service.*

31. Boyle et al., *Policies and Mythologies of the U.S. Forest Service.*

32. O'Leary, "The bureaucratic politics paradox."

33. Kweit and Kweit, "The politics of policy analysis," p. 22.

34. Kennedy and Dombeck, "The evolution of public agency beliefs and behavior toward ecosystem-based stewardship"; and Senge, *The Fifth Discipline.*

35. Keiter, "Beyond the boundary line"; and Keiter, "Taking account of the ecosystem on the public domain."

36. Federal officials preparing environmental impact statements must consult and obtain comments from other federal agencies having jurisdiction or other special expertise regarding any identified environmental impact. Environmental impact statements are to be made available to appropriate state, local, and federal agencies authorized to develop and enforce environmental standards, as well as to the public. For discussion of NEPA and ecosystem management see Keiter, "NEPA and the emerging concept of ecosystem management on the public lands."

37. See, for example, Alexander, "Interorganizational coordination"; Cowart and Fairfax, "Public lands federalism"; and Fulk et al., *Effectiveness of Planning Coordination.*

38. Hoover and Shannon, "Building greenway policies within a participatory democracy framework."

39. Grumbine, "Cooperation or conflict?" p. 29.

40. Forest Ecosystem Management Assessment Team (FEMAT), *Forest Ecosystem Management*, pp. VII–105.

41. Sample et al., *Building Partnerships for Ecosystem Management on Mixed Ownership Landscapes*, p. 63.

42. Cowart and Fairfax, "Public lands federalism"; and Fulk et al., *Effectiveness of Planning Coordination*, pp. 8–9, 26.

43. Clarke and McCool, *Staking Out the Terrain*, pp. 228–229.

44. Wood, "Ecosystem management," p. 11.

45. Nelson, *Public Lands and Private Rights*, pp. 319–328.

46. Clarke and McCool, *Staking Out the Terrain*, p. 227, argue that turning the federal lands over to the states "would set back natural resources management in the United States by one hundred years. It was not a good idea in 1929, it wasn't a good idea in 1981, and it is an even worse idea in 1995, since we are just now developing the capability to manage entire watersheds and ecosystems." The last large-scale and nationally significant movement to divest public states to the states occurred in 1979 when the state of Nevada mounted an effort to lay claim to the public lands within its borders, and was subsequently joined by several other western states. The so-called Sagebrush Rebellion was in effect diffused by the election of President Reagan, but transfer proposals regularly resurface. See Cawley, *Federal Land, Western Anger*; Fairfax, "Riding into a different sunset"; and Cortner and Ingram, "The case of the Sagebrush Rebellion."

47. See Convery et al., *Reorganization*, for discussion of President Jimmy Carter's proposal to create a new department of natural resources, as well as for perspectives on earlier reorganization attempts.

48. Dworsky, "Ecosystem management." In the case of the Great Lakes, an ecosystem study board would assess the need for new institutions as well as take other steps to remove obstacles to integrated ecosystem management.

49. Caldwell, "The state as a work of art," p. 661. Such councils, argues Caldwell, would consider "issues of basic concern to the future of the nation," advance social learning, and help restore social capital.

50. Morrison et al., *The Sustainable Use of Water in the Lower Colorado River Basin*, for example, call for the establishment of an International Colorado River Basin Commission to develop a "comprehensive, integrated environmentally sustainable, long-term management plan for the Colorado River," pp. 66–67.

51. Reidel and Richardson, "A public/private cooperative paradigm for federal land management." Shannon and Anderson, "Institutional strategies for landscape management," compare and contrast two models—ad hoc organizations and the more structured council form—that could be used for ecosystem management in the Quileute/Hoh watershed.

52. Gottfried et al., "Institutional solutions to market failure on the landscape scale"; and Wear et al., "Ecosystem management with multiple owners." These studies draw on an interdisciplinary examination of the Southern Appalachian watershed.

53. Shannon, "Community governance"; and Lee, "Ecologically effective social organization as a requirement for sustaining watershed ecosystems."

54. See, President's Council on Sustainable Development, *Sustainable America*, p. 44.

55. Little, "The link between local participation and improved conservation"; and Seymour, "Are successful community-based conservation projects designed or discovered?"

56. President's Council on Sustainable Development, *Sustainable America*, p. 47.

57. Keystone Center, *The Keystone National Policy Dialogue on Ecosystem Management*, p. 40.

58. Keystone Center, *The Keystone National Policy Dialogue on Ecosystem Management*, p. D2–D3.

59. Freeman, "Economics, incentives, and environmental regulation," p. 198.

60. President's Council on Sustainable Development, *Sustainable America*, p. 45.

61. Each polluter would need to trade off the cost of purchasing a ticket in order to pollute, the cost of making changes to production processes to reduce the amount of pollution for which a permit would be required, and the revenue foregone if the permit was sold. See Freeman, "Economics, incentives, and environmental regulation," pp. 198–199.

62. "Like water banking schemes, if developed with environmental considerations in mind, water transfers and exchanges represent potential net benefits for aquatic ecosystems and could lead to more sustainable patterns of water use." Morrison et al., *The Sustainable Use of Water in the Lower Colorado River Basin*, p. 63.

63. Advocates of privatization view government bureaucracies as self-aggrandizing, seeking to maximize their own budgets, and reacting to perverse incentives that result in resource damage rather than resource protection. See Anderson, "Prices, property rights, and profits"; Anderson and Leal, *Free Market Environmentalism*; Stroup and Baden, *Natural Resources*; O'Toole, *Reforming the Forest Service*; Baden, "After a century, Forest Service requires reform"; Nelson, *Public Lands and Private Rights*; and Hess, "Political rights and policy wrongs." For a critical summary of privatization arguments, see Lehmann, *Privatizing Public Lands*. Throughout the nation's history there have been periodic movements mounted to transfer federal lands to private ownership. Many of these efforts have been led by ranchers dissatisfied with government control of grazing on public domain lands. When the Reagan Administration took office in 1981, there was hope in some quarters that the federally controlled public lands would be privatized either by direct transfer to private owners or by transfer to the states for later transfer to private owners.

64. Korten, *When Corporations Rule the World*.

65. See Field, "Evolution of resource planning and management in New Zealand with particular reference to new administration, procedures, public participation in environmental planning, and forestry," for an overview of the structure for resource management in New Zealand.

66. Field, "Evolution of resource planning and management in New Zealand with particular reference to new administration, procedures, public participation in environmental planning, and forestry," p. 25.

67. Richardson and Stankey, "Privatizing forest land in New Zealand." For an analysis of the effects of privatizing the national forests in the United States, see Hyde and Chamberlain, "Who would gain from privatizing the national forests?" Hyde and Chamberlain conclude that "We anticipate that large-scale land transfers would have neither the generalized favorable effect on economic development that some market proponents anticipate, nor cause the uncompensated destruction that some environmentalists predict," p. 25.

68. Sample, "Budget reform and integrated resource management."

69. Keystone Center, *The Keystone National Policy Dialogue on Ecosystem Management*, p. 39. Experience with Section 6 of the Endangered Species Act, for example, which encourages state–federal cooperative agreements, shows that unreliable funding can strain cooperative relationships. See Ernst, "Federalism and the act," p. 99.

70. Yaffee, *The Wisdom of the Spotted Owl*, p. 242, notes that while environmental and citizen groups were heavily involved in forest planning activities at the local level, the real choices impacting the harvesting of old-growth forests and spotted owl habitat were being made by appropriations committees in Washington as they set timber harvest levels.

71. Costanza et al., "The value of the world's ecosystem services and natural capital"; and Daily, *Nature's Services.*

72. Christensen and Simpson, "A world of change." For discussion of the arguments for and against discounting the interests of future generations, see Peterson, "Time preference, the environment and the interests of future generations."

73. Gottfried et al., "Institutional solutions to market failure on the landscape scale."

74. Baden, "After a century, Forest Service requires reform."

75. Korten, *When Corporations Rule the World.*

Chapter 8

The Future of
Ecosystem Management

Lady Bird Johnson, former First Lady and environmental leader, said, "The environment is where we all meet; where we all have a mutual interest; it is one thing that all of us share. Whatever its condition, it is, after all, a reflection of ourselves—our tastes, our aspirations, our successes, and our failures."[1] Politics is the process by which our values are collectively and authoritatively stamped on the environment, and patterns of land settlement and resource use reflect political history. For example, remnants of the "wild and free" era of westward settlement and resource exploitation are revealed in much of today's mining and western water law. However, it is the twentieth-century politics that developed from the Progressive Era reforms that have made the largest imprint on the environment.

Progressive Era reforms arose from concerns about unbridled accumulation of wealth in a few hands, the rise of monopolies, concentration of political power in wealthy magnates and industrialists, and rampant exploitation of the nation's resources. Progressive Era leaders responded with a set of sweeping political reforms, and of course, the birth of the conservation movement. People were redefining how they wanted their governance institutions to operate and how they wanted the nation's natural resources to be used. The Progressive Era was a time of transformation and experimentation, and the conservation policies of that era reflected the new social consensus of the time.[2] Noteworthy accomplishments ensued, including the birth of resource professions, scientific analysis, laws to protect wilderness and to control pollution, and more efficient development of natural resource products for human betterment.

However, in the face of changes in social values, technologies, and demographics—the raw material of politics—the framework for natural resource management that has evolved from that earlier transformation does not currently fare well under critical assessment. It is not sufficient for achieving either ecological sustainability or democratic sustainability. A politics of expertise, a politics of maximum sustained yield, and a politics of interest have created inaccessible bureaucracies staffed by aloof civil servants, resource depletion, and interest group polarization. As a consequence, scientists, managers, and citizens are increasingly advocating a radical shift from the model that has dominated resource management for most of the twentieth century to an ecosystem management model.

Ecosystem management differs in many ways from traditional resource management policies and practices. Most notably, it makes ecological sustainability—long-term maintenance of ecosystem productivity and resilience—a primary goal of resource management. Ecosystem management also recognizes a critical interdependence between social and ecological vitality, including humans and human societies in resource management to an unprecedented extent. Ecosystem management breaks new ground in resource management by making the social and political basis of natural resource management goals explicit and by encouraging their development through an inclusive and collaborative decision-making process. Ecosystem management is based on an ecosystem science that integrates many disciplinary approaches and addresses ecological issues at very large temporal and spatial scales. Given the recognized complexity and dynamic nature of ecological and social systems, ecosystem management is adaptive management, constantly being reassessed and revised as new information becomes available. As this book has shown, adopting ecosystem management will require dramatic changes in the existing American governance system. The extent to which these changes are adopted in the twenty-first century will determine whether ecosystem management truly represents a paradigm shift in natural resource management.

Understanding and addressing the paradoxes of ecosystem management will be key to crafting new, innovative policies to facilitate its implementation. Resolving these apparent contradictions first requires recognizing them as paradoxes that can be reconciled. By readjusting our focus, we may be able to see, for instance, that conflict and collaboration can be complementary, not mutually exclusive, and that expert decision making and social discourse can both be found in a science-informed, open decision-making process. Society will also have to address other paradoxes of decision making: flexibility and consistency, inclusiveness and accountability, and bureaucracy and responsiveness. The paradoxes of scale will not easily be resolved, particularly the paradox of maintaining consistent national standards and protecting national interests while empowering locals to steward natural resources; nor will the ultimate paradox of ecosystem management, the paradox of sustainable development. Resolving paradoxes requires looking at the world in a new way and questioning some of our most basic assumptions.

To move toward ecological sustainability, we will have to recognize humans as part of, not apart from, nature. As "mere citizens" of our ecosystems, humans will have to develop new respect for the importance of other species and the health of ecological systems and develop an attitude of stewardship toward nature. Ecosystem management requires us to reject an utilitarian view of nature and management practices judged mainly by the criterion of economic efficiency, and instead adopt an experimental, adaptive approach to resource management based on an exploration of ecological principles. A primarily reductionist science must be replaced by a more holistic, integrative science that recognizes the role of social values in science and embraces inductive research. Relationships among humans and social institutions will have to become open and integrative, encouraging public dialogue and political debates. Because of the recognized interdependence of social sustainability and ecological sustainability, science, interpersonal relations, and public policy, all must be developed with a consciousness of the political philosophies that underlie them.

A new kind of democracy, based on open deliberation and easy access to government, and a newly involved citizenry will be key to making ecosystem management decisions. One such model is community-based conservation. It is characterized by civic associations organized to determine societal as well as ecological needs and goals, resolve natural resource management disputes, and undertake environmental restoration and management projects that also address social needs. In order to be fully functional, these civic associations will have to be integrated into the governance structure, particularly the regulation and management of natural resources and land use. Citizens will have to be motivated and empowered by being given opportunities to participate in making critical environmental and social choices that address their interests. New forums for collective learning and information sharing will have to be developed. Agency decision-making processes will have to be revised to accommodate new forms of knowledge and multiple sources of information, balancing both expert and lay input. Citizens will have to be given direct access to governmental, industry, and interest group resources. Citizen empowerment may well require fundamental restructuring of our economic system to break the power monopolies of centralized governments and large corporations.

Some of our most time-honored governance institutions will also have to be reworked. Federal, state, and local laws will have to be reexamined, and in many cases revised, in order to ensure they support the principles of ecosystem management. For instance, rigid, inflexible, and prescriptive natural resource management laws will likely impede the adaptive and holistic science required for ecosystem management. Current administrative practices may not permit open and inclusive decision-making forums. Private property rights, one of the oldest and most tenaciously protected American governance institutions, may have to be reshaped to ensure uniform consideration of ecological concerns. At the very least, the stewardship responsibilities of private property ownership will have to be made more explicit. The concept of public property may also change, as society struggles to meet social as well as ecological imperatives. Agency cultures will need to be modified to reward ecological restoration and open decision making and to reduce the sense of "ownership" some agencies have over the land or resources they manage. Planning and decision-making processes will become more complex and chaotic as they attempt to integrate a wider array of information, including changing social and ecological information. Better mechanisms for interagency and public–private coordination will have to be developed and enforced to redistribute power, access, and resources. New governmental agencies or other organizations may have to be created to achieve the level of coordination and broad-scale planning required for ecosystem management. Finally, we will have to struggle with social decisions and government structures to address human population growth and economic systems that threaten the goal of ecological sustainability.

Future Scenarios

Many are appalled at the extent of the proposed changes and reject ecosystem management altogether. Considerable opposition to ecosystem management comes from those who espouse multiple use, but, in essence, defend dominant use (e.g., timber production as the first and foremost use of forests or water supply as the first and foremost use of rivers). These opponents see themselves in direct opposition to the values, goals, and issues of the environmental movement. Many in this camp believe that decision making about resources ought to be entrusted to professional experts, not opened to more public input. However, we believe politics has changed to the extent that this reactionary view will not prevail. The principles of ecosystem management reflect emergent social values that accept the tenets of environmentalism, increased scientific understanding of ecological systems, and professional experience with new technologies and leadership models. Environmental values are now core societal values, and the public expects biodiversity and other ecosystem functions to be protected. The public will continue to distrust experts and will demand to participate equally in crafting policies responsive to their concerns. Attention will continue to be placed on correcting the ecological mistakes of past practices. Sustainability, biodiversity, social welfare, and equality will remain dominant social values. There is no turning back.

American society, however, may choose to define ecosystem management as an incremental addition to the concept of multiple-use–sustained-yield, adopting what we have called a "sustain-all-uses" approach to ecosystem management. In this case, the production of goods and services will remain paramount, although it will be done with a greater appreciation of the constraints imposed by ecological processes. When push comes to shove, human uses, whether a new elementary school, world-class research facility, mine, wilderness recreation, or gambling casino, will still dominate over protecting ecosystem integrity. The geographic and temporal scales of consideration will continue to expand, and resource management will become more collaborative. Under this scenario, while more people may embrace civic engagement and live lightly on the land, these practices will not become major forces in our society or in global politics. The political will may not be sufficient to create a context in which nature's needs are on par with human needs, and short-term, immediate socioeconomic gains are routinely foregone in order to achieve long-term ecological gains. In this case, policy changes will be made to accommodate the heightened focus on ecosystems and human communities, but the political and resource management changes that occur will not be revolutionary. Critics call this the "have-your-cake-and-eat-it-too" approach to ecosystem management, since it implies that all uses can be maintained within a framework in which ecological sustainability is given substantially greater consideration but is not the primary goal. Thus the prognosis in this instance is for continued incremental change—a little more appreciation of ecosystems, a little more civic engagement, and some tinkering with laws and policies. These changes are important, but they will not create a society that lives in balance with nature or protects ecosystems from irreparable damage.

If ecological sustainability is to assume a dominant position in natural resource management, American society must embrace sweeping and profound changes, not only in natural resource management practices, but in our policies, institutions, notions of citizenship, and politics. Such changes are necessary not only for ecological sustainability, but the health of democracy itself. Attention must be directed toward building the social capital that is requisite for effective involvement in a civic society, as well as improving the art of statecraft so that our governmental institutions more effectively link ecosystems, citizens, and government. Commodity production and other short-term economic gains may well have to be sacrificed to protect biodiversity or prevent degradation of the productive capability of land or waters. Intergenerational equity will be an essential factor in the decision-making process. The tensions between human and nature's needs will be made explicit, and when those tensions cannot be appropriately balanced, society will more often decide in nature's favor. It is this view of ecosystem management that truly represents a paradigm change in natural resource management.

The Challenge Ahead

There is tangible evidence that we are moving toward the principles and philosophy of ecosystem management. There is a considerable volume of published literature on ecosystem management. Ecosystem management research and demonstration projects have been undertaken. Extensive professional and public discussion have sought to further the adoption of ecosystem management principles. After many years of decline in civic involvement, there are also encouraging signs that Americans may again be beginning to "come out of their houses" and participate in community groups focused on issues such as crime and the environment.[3] New types of organizations and groups are forming, reflecting a desire on the part of many citizens to be civically engaged and to participate directly in governance issues. Likewise, administrative organizations are experimenting with new organizational designs, leadership models, and communication forums. Agencies have endorsed the concept of ecosystem management, and new laws have been proposed that would explicitly address ecological sustainability. Yet, because of significant criticisms and many unresolved paradoxes, ecosystem management is still in a preparadigm stage: moving forward, but still not totally accepted either by professionals or by the public.

In the midst of the American depression of the 1930s, Franklin D. Roosevelt observed, "The country needs, and, unless I mistake its temper, the country demands bold, persistent experimentation. It is common sense to take a method and try it. If it fails, admit it frankly and try another. But above all, try something."[4] The temper of the times may again be conducive for bold, persistent experimentation in resource management as well as in politics. There is potential to build on the American ideals of self-governance and to try innovations that will improve both management of natural resources and the health of American democracy, revamping how power and authority are distributed, how social institutions shape the character of the citizenry, and how collective responsibilities are balanced with individual rights or interests. Such experimentation will not require us to discard out of hand all of the political institutions that have developed through years of trial and error. While aspects of current democracy, science, rationality, and economics are all part of the problem and require significant revision, they are also part of the solution.

A paradigm shift to ecosystem management that would truly embrace the goal of ecological sustainability is not impossible, but will not occur without explicit societal recognition and acceptance of the political changes that will necessarily accompany it. The political challenges of ecosystem management cannot be ignored, for political choice by both individuals and institutions will determine how ecosystem management evolves in the future. Because our environment is a reflection of ourselves, the results will be manifest not only on the political landscape but on the physical landscape as well.

NOTES

1. Johnson and Lees, *Wildflowers Across America*, p. 264
2. Freemuth, "The emergence of ecosystem management," pp. 412–413.
3. Kettering Foundation, *Meaningful Chaos*; and Greider, *Who Will Tell the People?*
4. As cited in Hofstadter, *The American Political Tradition*, p. 315.

References

Achterman, Gail L., and Sally K. Fairfax. 1979. The public participation requirements of the Federal Land Policy and Management Act. *Arizona Law Review* 21 (2):501–539.

Adams, P. W., and W. A. Atkinson. 1992. *Watershed Resources: Balancing Environmental, Social, Political, and Economic Factors in Large Basins.* Corvallis, OR: Oregon State University Forest Engineering Department.

Advisory Commission on Intergovernmental Relations. 1979. *Citizen Participation in the American Federal System.* Washington, D.C.: Government Printing Office.

Agee, James K., and Darryll R. Johnson. 1988a. A direction for ecosystem management. In *Ecosystem Management for Parks and Wilderness*, edited by James K. Agee and Darryll R. Johnson, 226–232. Seattle, WA: University of Washington Press.

Agee, James K., and Darryll R. Johnson, eds. 1988b. *Ecosystem Management for Parks and Wilderness.* Seattle, WA: University of Washington Press.

Agger, Ben. 1991. Theorizing the decline of discourse or the decline of theoretical discourse. In *Critical Theory Now*, edited by Philip Wexler, 118–144. London, England: The Falmer Press.

Alexander, Ernest R. 1993. Interorganizational coordination: theory and practice. *Journal of Planning Literature* 7 (4):328–343.

Allin, Craig W. 1982. *The Politics of Wilderness Preservation.* Westport, CT: Greenwood Press.

Aloff, Mindy. 1997. Where to cool both the soul and the heels. *New York Times.* August 22, B1, B26.

Alston, R. M. 1991. Are sustained yield and sustainable forests equivalent? Paper read at the 1991 National Convention of the Society of American Foresters, August 4–7, at San Francisco, CA.

Ambrose, Stephen E. 1996. *Undaunted Courage: Meriwether Lewis, Thomas Jefferson, and the Opening of the American West.* New York, NY: Simon and Schuster.

American Forest and Paper Association. 1993. *Ecosystem Management: A New Approach to Federal Forest Management and Planning.* Washington, D.C.: Forest Resources Board American Forest Products Association.

American Forest and Paper Association. 1994. Sustainable Forestry Principles and Implementation Guidelines, as Approved by AF&PA Board of Directors, October 14, 1994. Washington D.C.: American Forest and Paper Association.

Amy, Douglas. 1987. *The Politics of Environmental Mediation.* Washington, D.C.: Columbia University Press.

Anderson, Terry L. 1992. Prices, property rights, and profits: market approaches to federal land management. In *Multiple Use and Sustained Yield: Changing Philosophies for Federal Land Management (the Proceedings and Summary of a Workshop Convenved on March 5 and 6, 1992)*, edited by Library of Congress Congressional Research Service, 173–189. Washington, D.C.: Government Printing Office.

Anderson, Terry L., and D. R. Leal. 1991. *Free Market Environmentalism.* San Francisco, CA: Pacific Research Institute for Public Policy and Westview Press.

Aristotle. 1962. *Politics,* translated and edited by Ernest Barker. New York, NY: Oxford University Press.

Arnstein, Sherry. 1969. A ladder of citizen participation. *Journal of the American Institute of Planners* 35 (4):216–224.

Atkinson, William A. 1992. Silvicultural correctness: the politicalization of forest science. *Western Wildlands* 17 (4):8–12.

Bachrach, Peter, and Aryeh Botwinick. 1992. *Power and Empowerment: A Radical Theory of Participatory Democracy.* Philadelphia, PA: Temple University Press.

Baden, John. 1997. After a century, Forest Service requires reform. *Arizona Daily Star.* February 21.

Bailey, Eric A. 1989. Good forest management for the future: sustained yield and sustainable development aren't the same thing. *Environment News* 12 (2):11–14.

Baker, Peter. 1996. An all-time high for ballot box no-shows. *Washington Post National Weekly.* November 11, 11–17.

Banning, Lance. 1986. Madison, James. In *Encyclopedia of the American Constitution*, edited by Leonard W. Levy, Kenneth L. Karst, and Dennis J. Mahoney, 1189–1194. New York: Macmillan.

Banzhaf, W. H. 1995. The videoconference: moving the discussion forward. *Journal of Forestry* 93 (5):3.

Barton, William J. 1992. Telling our story (commentary). *Journal of Forestry* 90 (1):3.

Bass, Rick. 1997. On wilderness and Wallace Stegner. *The Amicus Journal* 19 (1):23–27.

Bassett, Kedric A. 1989. Utah's school trust lands: dilemma in land use management and the possible effect of Utah's trust land management act. *Journal of Energy Law and Policy* 9:195–212.

Beaver, Clinton D. 1991. Management of Wyoming's state trust lands from 1890–1990: a running battle between good politics and the law. *Land and Water Law Review* 26 (1):69–92.

Behan, R.W. 1966. The myth of the omnipotent forester. *Journal of Forestry* 64 (6):398–407.

———. 1988. A plea for constituency-based management. *American Forests* 94 (7–8):46–48.

———. 1990. Multiresource forest management: a paradigmatic challenge to professional forestry. *Journal of Forestry* 88 (4):12–18.

———. 1992. The irony of the multiple-use–sustained-yield concept: nothing is so powerful as an idea whose time has passed. In *Multiple Use and Sustained Yield: Changing Philosophies for Federal Land Management (the Proceedings and Summary of a Workshop Convened on March 5 and 6, 1992)*, edited by Library of Congress Congressional Research Service, 95-106. Washington, D.C.: Government Printing Office.

———. 1997. The obsolete paradigm of professional forestry. *Renewable Resources Journal* 15 (1):14–19.

Bellah, Robert N., Richard Madsen, William M. Sullivan, Ann Swidler, and Steven M. Tipton. 1985. *Habits of the Heart: Individualism and Commitment in American Life.* Berkeley, CA: University of California Press.

———. 1991. *The Good Society.* New York, NY: Alfred A. Knopf.

Bentley, William R. Forthcoming. Scarcity, political economy, and the Forest Congress process. *Forum for Applied Research and Public Policy.*

Bentley, William R., and William D. Langbein. 1996. *Final Report—Seventh American Forest Congress.* New Haven, CT: Yale University Office of the Seventh American Forest Congress.

Berry, Joyce K., and John C. Gordon. 1993. *Environmental Leadership: Developing Effective Skills and Styles.* Washington, D.C.: Island Press.

Bhat, Vasanthakumar N. 1996. *The Green Corporation: The Next Competitive Advantage.* Westport, CT: Quorum Books.

Bird, Elizabeth Ann R. 1987. The social construction of nature: theoretical approaches to the history of environmental problems. *Environmental Review* 11 (Winter):255–264.

Blahna, Dale J., and Susan Yonts-Shepard. 1989. Public involvement in resource planning: toward bridging the gap between policy and implementation. *Society and Natural Resources* 2 (3):209–227.

Block, Peter. 1993. *Stewardship: Choosing Service Over Self Interest.* San Francisco, CA: Berrett-Koehler Publishers.

Bormann, F. Herbert, and Gene Likens. 1979. *Pattern and Processes in a Forested Ecosystem.* New York, NY: Springer-Verlag.

Bosso, Christopher J. 1997. Seizing back the day: the challenge to environmental activism in the 1990s. In *Environmental Policy in the 1990s: Reform or Reaction?*, edited by Norman J. Vig and Michael E. Kraft, 53–74. Washington, D.C.: Congressional Quarterly Press.

Boyle, Brian J., Margaret A. Shannon, Robert A. Rose, Kathleen Halvorsen, and H. Stuart Elway. 1994. *Policies and Mythologies of the U.S. Forest Service: A Conversation with Employees.* Seattle, WA: University of Washington College of Forest Resources Institute for Resources in Society.

Boyte, Harry C. 1995. Citizenship as public work. Paper read at the PEGS Conference (World Wide Web: http//www.cpn.org/), February 11–12, 1995.

Bradley, Dennis P., and Bernard J. Lewis. 1992. Ecological economics: integrating natural and social dimensions. *Journal of Forestry* 90 (2):30–33.

Breckenridge, Lee P. 1995. Reweaving the landscape: the institutional challenges of ecosystem management for lands in private ownership. *Vermont Law Review* 19:363–422.

Breslin, Patrick. 1995. On these sidewalks of New York, the sun is shining again. *Smithsonian* 26 (1):100–110.

Brewer, Gary D. 1983. Some costs and consequences of large-scale social systems modeling. *Behavioral Science* 28 (2):166–185.

Brooks, David J., and Gordon E. Grant. 1992. New approaches to forest management: background, science issues, and research agenda (parts one and two). *Journal of Forestry* 90 (1 and 2):25–28 and 21–24.

Brown, Greg, and Chuck Harris. 1998. Professional foresters and the land ethic, revisited. *Journal of Forestry* 96 (1):4–12.

Brown, Lester R., Christopher Flavin, and Hilary French. 1997. *State of the World 1997: A
Worldwatch Institute Report on Progress Toward a Sustainable Society.* New York, NY: W.W.
Norton.

Brown, Lester R., ed. 1991. *State of the World 1991: A Worldwatch Institute Report on Progress
Toward a Sustainable Society.* New York, NY: W.W. Norton.

Brown, R. Steven, and Karen Marshall. 1996. Ecosystem management in state governments. *Ecological Applications* 6 (3):721–723.

Burch, W. R. Jr., and J. M. Grove. 1993. People, trees, and participation on the urban
frontier. *Unasylva* 173 (44):19–27.

Cahn, Matthew Alan, and Rory O'Brien. 1996. *Thinking About the Environment: Readings on
Politics, Property, and the Physical World.* Armonk, NY: M.E. Sharpe.

Caldwell, Lynton K. 1970. The ecosystem as a criterion for public land policy. *Natural
Resources Journal* 10 (2):203–221.

———. 1988a. Implementing an ecosystems approach. In *Perspectives on Ecosystem
Management for the Great Lakes: A Reader,* edited by Lynton Keith Caldwell, 1–29. Albany,
NY: State University of New York Press.

———. 1988b. *Perspectives on Ecosystem Management for the Great Lakes: A Reader.* Albany, NY:
State University of New York Press.

———. 1996. The state as a work of art: statecraft for the 21st century. *PS: Political Science
and Politics* 29 (4):657–664.

Caldwell, Lynton K., Charles F. Wilkinson, and Margaret A. Shannon. 1994. Making
ecosystem policy: three decades of change. *Journal of Forestry* 92 (4):7–10.

Carpenter, Susan L., and W. J. D. Kennedy. 1988. *Managing Public Disputes: A Practical Guide
to Handling Conflict and Reaching Agreements.* San Francisco, CA: Jossey-Bass.

Carson, Rachel. 1962. *Silent Spring.* Boston, MA: Houghton Mifflin Company.

Catlin, George. 1990. An artist proposes a national park. In *American Environmentalism:
Readings in Conservation History,* edited by Roderick Frazier Nash, 31–35. New York, NY:
McGraw-Hill.

Cawley, R. McGreggor. 1993. *Federal Land, Western Anger: The Sagebrush Rebellion and
Environmental Politics.* Lawrence, KS: University Press of Kansas.

Cawley, R. McGreggor, and John Freemuth. 1993. Tree farms, mother earth, and other
dilemmas: the politics of ecosystem management in Greater Yellowstone. *Society and
Natural Resources* 6:41–53.

———. 1997. A critique of the multiple use framework in public lands decisionmaking.
In *Western Public Lands and Environmental Politics,* edited by Charles Davis, 32–44. Boulder,
CO: Westview.

Charnovitz, Steve. 1994. Environment and trade: talking across cultures. *Environment* 36
(2):14.

Chrislip, David D. 1993. The failure of traditional politics. *National Civic Review* 82
(3):234–245.

———. 1994. American renewal: reconnecting citizens with public life. *National Civic
Review* 83 (1):25–31.

Christensen, Norman L., Ann M. Bartuska, James H. Brown, Stephen Carpenter, Carla

D'Antonio, Robert Francis, Jerry F. Franklin, James A. MacMahon, Reed F. Noss, David J. Parsons, Charles H. Peterson, Monica G. Turner, and Robert G. Woodmansee. 1996. The report of the Ecological Society of America Committee on the Scientific Basis for Ecosystem Management. *Ecological Applications* 6 (3):665–691.

Christensen, Norman L. Jr., and R. David Simpson. 1996–97. A world of change. *Renewable Resources Journal* 14 (4):18–20.

Civic Practices Network. 1997a. Communitarianism. (World Wide Web http://www. cpn.org/sections/tools/models/communitarianism.html.)

———. 1997b. The new citizenship movement: an overview. (World Wide Web http://www.cpn.org/sections/new_citizenship/new_citizenship_intro.html.)

Clark, Mary E. 1991. Rethinking ecological and economic education: a gestalt shift. In *Ecological Economics: The Science and Management of Sustainability*, edited by Robert Costanza, 400–415. New York, NY: Columbia University Press.

Clark, Tim W., Elizabeth D. Amato, Donald G. Wittemore, and Ann H. Harvey. 1991. Policy and programs for ecosystem management in the greater Yellowstone ecosystem: an analysis. *Conservation Biology* 5 (3):412–422.

Clark, Tim W., and S. C. Minta. 1994. *Greater Yellowstone's Future.* Moose, WY: Homestead Publishing.

Clarke, Jeanne Nienaber, and Daniel C. McCool. 1996. *Staking Out the Terrain: Power and Performance Among Natural Resource Agencies.* 2nd ed. Albany, NY: State University of New York Press.

Clary, David A. 1986. *Timber and the Forest Service.* Lawrence, KS: University Press of Kansas.

Coggins, George Cameron. 1998. Of Californicators, quislings and crazies. *Chronicle of Community* 2 (2):27–33.

Collins, Ronald K. L., and David M. Skover. 1996. *The Death of Discourse.* Boulder, CO: Westview Press.

Commager, Henry Steele. 1977. *The Empire of Reason: How Europe Imagined and America Realized the Enlightenment.* Garden City, NJ: Doubleday.

Commission on Research and Resource Management Policy in the National Park System. 1989. *National Parks: From Vignettes to a Global View.* Washington, D.C.: National Park Service.

Connolly, William E. 1988. *Political Theory and Modernity.* New York, NY: Basil Blackwell.

Convery, Frank J., Jack P. Royer, and Gerald R. Stairs. 1979. *Reorganization: Issues, Implications and Opportunities for U.S. Natural Resources Policy.* Durham, NC: Duke University Center for Resource and Environmental Policy Research.

Cooperrider, Allen Y. 1996. Science as a model for ecosystem management—panacea or problem? *Ecological Applications* 6 (3):736–737.

Cornett, Zane J. 1995. Birch seeds, leadership, and a relationship with the land. *Journal of Forestry* 93 (9):6–11.

Cortner, Hanna J., and Helen M. Ingram. 1982. The case of the Sagebrush Rebellion. In *Energy and the Western United States: Politics and Development*, edited by James L. Regens, Robert W. Rycroft and Gregory A. Daneke, 113–130. New York, NY: Praeger.

Cortner, Hanna J., and Margaret A. Moote. 1992. Sustainability and ecosystem management: forces shaping political agendas and public policy. In *American Forestry—An*

Evolving Tradition. Proceedings of the 1992 Society of American Foresters National Convention, 310–316. Bethesda, MD: Society of American Foresters.

————. 1994. Trends and issues in land and water resources management: setting the agenda for change. *Environmental Management* 18 (2):167–173.

Cortner, Hanna J., and Dennis L. Schweitzer. 1983. Institutional limits and legal implications of quantitative models in forest planning. *Environmental Law* 13 (2):493–516.

Cortner, Hanna J., and Margaret A. Shannon. 1993. Embedding public participation in its political context. *Journal of Forestry* 91 (7):14–16.

Cortner, Hanna J., Margaret A. Shannon, Mary G. Wallace, Sabrina Burke, and Margaret A. Moote. 1996. *Institutional Barriers and Incentives for Ecosystem Management: A Problem Analysis.* Portland, OR: USDA Forest Service Pacific Northwest Research Station.

Costanza, Robert. 1991. *Ecological Economics: The Science and Management of Sustainability,* edited by Robert Costanza. New York, NY: Columbia University Press.

Costanza, Robert, Herman E. Daly, and Joy A. Bartholomew. 1991. Goals, agenda, and policy recommendations for ecological economics. In *Ecological Economics: The Science and Management of Sustainability,* edited by Robert Costanza, 1–20. New York, NY: Columbia University Press.

Costanza, Robert, Ralph d'Arge, Rudolf de Groot, Stephen Farber, Monica Grasso, Bruce Hannon, Karin Limburg, Shahid Naeem, Robert V. O'Neill, Jose Paruelo, Robert G. Raskin, Paul Sutton, and Marjan van den Belt. 1997. The value of the world's ecosystem services and natural capital. *Nature* 387 (May 15):253–260.

Coufal, J. E. 1989. The land ethic question. *Journal of Forestry* 87 (6):23–24.

Council on Environmental Quality. 1991. *Twenty-First Annual Report of the Council on Environmental Quality.* Washington, D.C.: Council on Environmental Quality Executive Office of the President.

Cowart, Richard H., and Sally K. Fairfax. 1988. Public lands federalism: judicial theory and administrative reality. *Ecology Law Quarterly* 15:375–476.

Craig, R., Z. Cornett, J. Difley, J. E. Force, E. W. Frazer, and N. E. Linnartz. 1992. Land ethic canon proposal: a report from the task force. *Journal of Forestry* 90 (8):40–41.

Cribbet, John Edward. 1986. Concepts in transition: the search for a new definition of property. *University of Illinois Law Review* 1 (1):1–42.

Cronin, Thomas E. 1989. *Direct Democracy: The Politics of Initiative, Referendum, and Recall.* Cambridge, MA: Harvard University Press.

Cronon, William. 1983. *Changes in the Land: Indians, Colonists, and the Ecology of New England.* New York, NY: Hill and Wang.

————. 1991. *Nature's Metropolis: Chicago and the Great West.* New York, NY: W.W. Norton.

Curry-Roper, Janel M., and Steven McGuire. 1993. The individualistic imagination and natural resource policy. *Society and Natural Resources* 6:259–272.

Czech, Brian. 1995. Ecosystem management is no paradigm shift: let's try conservation. *Journal of Forestry* 93 (12):17–23.

Daily, Gretchen C. 1997. *Nature's Services: Societal Dependence on Natural Ecosystems.* Washington, D.C.: Island Press.

Daly, Herman E. 1993. Sustainable growth: an impossibility theorem. In *Valuing the Earth: Economics, Ecology, Ethics,* edited by Herman E. Daly and K. N. Townsend, 267–274. Cambridge, MA: MIT Press.

Damasio, Antonio R. 1994. *Descartes' Error: Emotion, Reason, and the Human Brain.* New York, NY: G.P. Putnam.

D'Amato, Anthony. 1990. Do we owe a duty to future generations to preserve the global environment? *American Journal of International Law* 84 (1):190–198.

Dana, Samuel Trask, and Sally K. Fairfax. 1980. *Forest and Range Policy: Its Development in the United States.* 2nd ed. New York, NY: McGraw-Hill.

Daniels, Steven E., and Gregg B. Walker. 1996. Collaborative learning: improving public deliberation in ecosystem-based management. *Environmental Impact Assessment Review* 16 (2):71–102.

Daniels, Steven E., Gregg B. Walker, Matthew S. Carroll, and Keith A. Blatner. 1996. Using collaborative learning in fire recovery planning. *Journal of Forestry* 94 (8):4–9.

de Tocqueville, Alexis. 1900. *Democracy in America*, translated by Henry Reeve, revised ed. Vol. II. New York, NY: Colonial Press.

Deason, Jonathan P. 1996–97. Changing world attitudes on environmental values and sustainability: implications for educational institutions. *Renewable Resources Journal* 14 (4):6–11.

Dewey, John. 1927. *The Public and Its Problems.* Denver: Alan Swallow.

Dietz, Thomas, and Linda Kalof. 1992. Environmentalism among nation-states. *Social Indicators Research* 26 (4):353–366.

Diggins, John Patrick. 1986. Progressive constitutional thought. In *Encyclopedia of the American Constitution*, edited by Leonard W. Levy, Kenneth L. Karst, and Dennis J. Mahoney, 1481–1482. New York, NY: Macmillan.

Di Norcia, Vincent. 1974. From critical theory to critical ecology. *Telos* 22:85–95.

Dionne, E. J. Jr. 1991. *Why Americans Hate Politics.* New York, NY: Simon and Schuster.

Dove, Lisa B. 1992. *Multiple Use, Sustained Yield, and Other Philosophies of Federal Land Management: A Selected Bibliography.* Washington, D.C.: U.S. Congress, Library of Congress, Congressional Research Service.

Downs, Anthony. 1957. *An Economic Theory of Democracy.* New York, NY: Harper and Row.

Dryzek, John. 1987. *Rational Ecology.* Oxford: Basil Blackwell.

———. 1990a. *Discursive Democracy: Politics, Policy, and Political Science.* Cambridge, England: Cambridge University Press.

———. 1990b. Green reason: communicative ethics for the biosphere. *Environmental Ethics* 12 (3):195–210.

Dubos, Rene. 1973. A theology of earth. In *Western Man and Environmental Ethics*, edited by Ian Barbour, 43–54. Reading, MA: Addison-Wesley.

Dudley, Nigel, Chris Elliott, and Sue Stolton. 1997. A framework for environmental labeling. *Environment* 39 (6):16-20, 42–45.

Duerr, William A., and Jean B. Duerr. 1975. The role of faith in forest resource management. In *Social Sciences in Forestry: A Book of Readings*, edited by Fay Rumsey and William A. Duerr, 30–40. Philadelphia, PA: W. B. Saunders Co.

Dunlap, Riley E. 1987. Polls, pollution, and politics revisited: public opinion on the environment in the Reagan era. *Environment* 29 (6):6–11, 32–37.

Dunlap, Riley E., and Angela G. Mertig, eds. 1992. *American Environmentalism: The U.S. Environmental Movement, 1970–1990.* Philadelphia, PA: Taylor and Francis.

Dunlap, Riley E., and Kent D. Van Liere. 1978. The 'new environmental paradigm': a proposed measuring instrument and preliminary results. *Journal of Environmental Education* 9 (4):10–19.

Dworsky, Leonard B. 1993. Ecosystem management: Great Lakes perspective. *Natural Resources Journal* 33 (2):347–362.

Easton, David. 1965. *A Framework for Political Analysis.* Englewood Cliffs, NJ: Prentice-Hall.

Eckersley, Robyn. 1992. *Environmentalism and Political Theory: Toward an Ecocentric Approach.* Albany, NY: State University of New York Press.

Ehrenfeld, David. 1992. Ecosystem health and ecological theories. In *Ecosystem Health: New Goals for Environmental Management,* edited by Robert Costanza, Bryan G. Norton, and Benjamin D. Haskell, 135–143. Washington, D.C.: Island Press.

Ehrlich, Paul R. 1968. *The Population Bomb.* New York, NY: Ballantine Books.

Ehrlich, Paul R., Anne H. Ehrlich, and Gretchen C. Daily. 1995. *The Stork and the Plow: The Equity Answer to the Human Dilemma.* New York, NY: Putnam's.

Emerson, Kirk. 1997. A comparative study of state property rights legislation: accounting for variation in policy responses. Paper read at the Western Political Science Association, March 13–15, at Tucson, AZ.

Ernst, John P. 1991. Federalism and the act. In *Balancing on the Brink of Extinction: The Endangered Species Act and Lessons for the Future,* edited by Kathryn A. Kohm, 98–113. Washington, D.C.: Island Press.

Etzioni, Amitai. 1995. The responsive communitarian platform: rights and responsibilities. In *Rights and the Common Good: The Communitarian Perspective,* edited by Amitai Etzioni, 11–23. New York, NY: St. Martin's Press.

Everhart, William C. 1983. *The National Park Service.* Boulder, CO: Westview Press.

Facaros, Nickolas. 1989. Public involvement in national forest planning: what the Council on Environmental Quality requires, the Forest Service neglects. *Journal of Environmental Law and Litigation* 4 (1):1–34.

Fairfax, Sally K. 1980. Riding into a different sunset: the sagebrush rebellion. *Journal of Forestry* 79 (8):516–520, 582.

———. 1993. Remarks made at the symposium, Creating a New Forestry for the 21st Century. Portland, OR.

Fairfax, Sally K., Jon A. Souder, and Gretta Goldenman. 1992. The school trust lands: a fresh look at conventional wisdom. *Environmental Law* 22:796–910.

Fedkiw, John. 1997. The Forest Service's pathway toward ecosystem management. *Journal of Forestry* 95 (4):30–34.

Feller, Joseph M. 1991. Grazing management on the public lands: opening the process to public participation. *Land & Water Law Review* 26 (2):571–596.

Ferejohn, J. 1974. *Pork Barrel Politics: Rivers and Harbors Legislation, 1947–1968.* Palo Alto, CA: Stanford University Press.

Field, David. 1995. Evolution of resource planning and management in New Zealand with particular reference to new administration, procedures, public participation in environmental planning, and forestry. In *Proceedings of the International Symposium on Public Participation and Environmental Conservation,* edited by Toshiyuki Tsuchiya and Hiroaki Kakizawa, 23–40. Tokyo, Japan: Japan Society of Forest Planning Press.

Fitzsimmons, Allan K. 1994. Federal ecosystem management: a "train wreck" in the making. *Policy Analysis* 217:33.

————. 1996. Sound policy or smoke and mirrors: does ecosystem management make sense? *Water Resources Bulletin* 32 (2):217–227.

Flick, Warren A., Allen Barnes, and Robert A. Tufts. 1995. Public purpose and private property: the evolution of regulatory taking. *Journal of Forestry* 93 (6):21–24.

Flick, Warren A., and William E. King. 1995. Ecosystem management as American law. *Renewable Resources Journal* 13 (3):6–11.

Flora, Cornelia Butler. n.d. *Vital Communities: Combining Environmental and Social Capital.* Ames, Iowa: Iowa State University North Central Regional Center for Rural Development.

Floyd, Don W., and William E. Frost. 1987. Measuring management objectives with condition classes: time for a change. *Rangelands* 9 (4):161–162.

Folke, Carol. 1995. Ecologists and economists can find common ground. *BioScience* 45 (4):283–284.

Force, Jo Ellen, and Kevin L. Williams. 1989. A profile of national forest planning participants: determining participant characteristics can help the Forest Service work with the public. *Journal of Forestry* 87 (1):33–38.

Forest Ecosystem Management Assessment Team (FEMAT). 1993. *Forest Ecosystem Management: An Ecological, Economic, and Social Assessment.* Washington, D.C.: Government Printing Office.

Fortmann, Louise, and Connie Lewis. 1987. Public involvement in natural resource management, unpublished manuscript. Berkeley, CA: University of California.

Foss, Philip D. 1960. *Politics and Grass: The Administration of Grazing on the Public Domain.* Seattle, WA: University of Washington Press.

Fox, Stephen. 1981. *The American Conservation Movement: John Muir and His Legacy.* Madison, WI: University of Wisconsin Press.

Francis, George. 1993. Ecosystem management. *Natural Resources Journal* 33 (2):315–345.

Francis, G. R., and H. A. Regier. 1995. Barriers and bridges to the Great Lakes Basin ecosystem. In *Barriers and Bridges to the Renewal of Ecosystems and Institutions*, edited by L. H. Gunderson, C. S. Holling, and S. S. Light, 239–291. New York, NY: Columbia University Press.

Frankfurter, Felix. 1930. *The Public and Its Government.* New Haven, CT: Yale University Press.

Franklin, Jerry F. 1990. Biological legacies: a critical management concept from Mount St. Helens. *Transactions of the North American Wildlife and Natural Resources Conference* 55: 216–219.

————. 1993a. The fundamentals of ecosystem management with applications in the Pacific Northwest. In *Defining Sustainable Forestry*, edited by Gregory H. Aplet, Nels Johnson, Jeffrey T. Olson, and V. Alaric Sample, 127–144. Washington D.C.: Island Press.

————. 1993b. Preserving biodiversity: species, ecosystems or landscapes? *Ecological Applications* 3 (2):202–205.

————. Forthcoming. Ecosystem management: an overview. In *Ecosystem Management Applications for Sustainable Forest and Wildlife Resources*, edited by A. Haney and M. S. Boyce, 21–53. New Haven, CT: Yale University Press.

Freeman, A. Myrick III. 1997. Economics, incentives, and environmental regulation. In

Environmental Policy in the 1990s: Reform or Reaction?, edited by Norman J. Vig and Michael E. Kraft, 187–207. Washington, D.C.: Congressional Quarterly Press.

Freemuth, John. 1996. The emergence of ecosystem management: reinterpreting the gospel? *Society and Natural Resources* 9 (4):411–417.

Frentz, Irene, Paul Hardy, Susanne Maleki, Ali Phillips, and Barbara Thorpe. 1995. *Ecosystem Management in the U.S.: An Inventory and Assessment of Current Experience.* Ann Arbor, MI: University of Michigan School of Natural Resources and the Environment.

Fri, Robert W. 1991. Sustainable development: can we put these principles into practice? *Journal of Forestry* 89 (7):24–26.

Frome, Michael. 1992. *Regreening the National Parks.* Tucson, AZ: University of Arizona Press.

Fulk, Thomas A., William G. Bradshaw, James M. Colby, Melody S. Mobley, M. Kent Nelson, Marcus G. Phelps, Joseph E. Stutler, and Tom Wardle. 1990. *Effectiveness of Planning Coordination.* Vol. 6, *Critique of Land Management Planning.* Washington, D.C.: USDA Forest Service Policy Analysis Staff.

Gale, Richard P., and Sheila M. Cordray. 1991. What should forests sustain? eight answers. *Journal of Forestry* 89 (5):31–36.

Gardner, John W., Chris Gates, Tyler Norris, Bill Potapchuk, Derek Okubo, and John Parr. 1997. *The Community Visioning and Strategic Planning Handbook.* Denver, CO: The National Civic League.

Gaus, John Merriman. 1947. *Reflections on Public Administration.* University, AL: University of Alabama Press.

Gay, Peter. 1969. *The Enlightenment: An Interpretation.* Vol. II, *The Science of Freedom.* New York, NY: Alfred A. Knopf.

Geisler, Charles C. 1992. Cultural factors in public land policy. Paper read at the 4th North American Symposium on Society and Resource Management, May 17–20, 1992, at Madison, WI.

————. 1993. Rethinking SIA: why ex-ante research isn't enough. *Society and Natural Resources* 6:327-338.

Geisler, Charles C., and Susan Kittel. 1994. Who owns the ecosystem? Property dimensions of ecosystem management. Paper read at the Institutional Problem Analysis Workshop, October 20–22, 1994, at Stevenson, WA.

General Accounting Office. 1994. *Ecosystem Management: Additional Actions to Adequately Test a Promising Approach, GAO RCED-94-111.* Washington, D.C.: Government Printing Office.

Gerth, H. H., and C. Wright Mills, eds. 1946. *From Max Weber: Essays in Sociology.* New York, NY: Oxford University Press.

Glenn, Don. 1995. Ecosystem management: voices of reason and common sense. *Rangelands* 17 (1):20–22.

Goergen, Michael T., Donald W. Floyd, and Peter G. Ashton. 1997. An old model for building consensus and a new role for foresters. *Journal of Forestry* 95 (1):8–12.

Golley, Frank Benjamin. 1993. *A History of the Ecosystem Concept in Ecology: More Than the Sum of the Parts.* New Haven, CT: Yale University Press.

Gordon, John C. 1993. Ecosystem management: an idiosyncratic overview. In *Defining Sustainable Forestry*, edited by Gregory H. Aplet, Nels Johnson, Jeffrey T. Olsen, and V. Alaric Sample, 240–244. Washington, D.C.: Island Press.

———. 1994. From vision to policy: a role for foresters. *Journal of Forestry* 92 (7):16–19.

Gottfried, Robert, David Wear, and Robert Lee. 1996. Institutional solutions to market failure on the landscape scale. *Ecological Economics* 18:133–140.

Gottlieb, Robert. 1988. *A Life of its Own: The Politics and Power of Water.* San Diego, CA: Harcourt Brace Jovanovich.

———. 1993. *Forcing the Spring: The Transformation of the American Environmental Movement.* Washington, D.C.: Island Press.

Greider, William. 1992. *Who Will Tell the People? The Betrayal of American Democracy.* New York, NY: Simon and Schuster.

Grumbine, R. Edward. 1990. Viable populations, reserve size, and federal lands management: a critique. *Conservation Biology* 4 (2):127–134.

———. 1991. Cooperation or conflict? Interagency relationships and the future of biodiversity for U.S. parks and forests. *Environmental Management* 15 (1):27–37.

———. 1994. What is ecosystem management? *Conservation Biology* 8 (1):27–38.

Gunderson, Lance H., C. S. Holling, and Stephen S. Light, eds. 1995. *Barriers and Bridges to the Renewal of Ecosystems and Institutions.* New York, NY: Columbia University Press.

Gundlach, Gregory T., and Jakki J. Mohr. 1992. Collaborative relationships: legal limits and antitrust considerations. *Journal of Public Policy and Marketing* 2 (2):101–114.

Habermas, Jurgen. 1992. *The Philosophical Discourse of Modernity.* Cambridge, MA: MIT Press.

Hagen, J. B. 1992. *An Entangled Bank: The Origins of Ecosystem Ecology.* New Brunswick, NJ: Rutgers University Press.

Hagenstein, Perry R. 1992. Some history of multiple use/sustained yield concepts. In *Multiple Use and Sustained Yield: Changing Philosophies for Federal Land Management (the Proceedings and Summary of a Workshop Convened on March 5 and 6, 1992)*, edited by Library of Congress Congressional Research Service, 31–43. Washington, D.C.: Government Printing Office.

Halvorson, William L., and Gary E. Davis, eds. 1996. *Science and Ecosystem Management in the National Parks.* Tucson, AZ: University of Arizona Press.

Hargrove, Eugene C. 1980. Anglo-American land use attitudes. *Environmental Ethics* 2 (Summer):121–148.

Harper, Stephen C., Laura L. Falk, and Edward W. Rankin. 1990. *The Northern Forest Lands Study of New England and New York.* Rutland, VT: USDA Forest Service.

Hart, S. L. 1994. How green production might sustain the world. *Illahee* 1:4–14.

Harwood, Richard. 1991. *Citizens and Politics: A View from Mainstreet America.* Dayton, OH: Kettering Foundation.

Hatfield, Doc, and Connie Hatfield. 1993. *History of the Trout Creek Mountain Working Group* (unpublished booklet).

Hawking, Stephen. 1988. *A Brief History of Time: From the Big Bang to Black Holes.* New York, NY: Bantam Books.

Hawthorn, Geoffrey. 1976. *Enlightenment and Despair: A History of Sociology.* Cambridge, England: Cambridge University Press.

Haynes, Richard W., Russell T. Graham, and Thomas M. Quigley, eds. 1996. *A Framework for Ecosystem Management in the Interior Columbia Basin and Portions of the Klamath and Great Basins.* Portland, OR: USDA Forest Service Pacific Northwest Research Station.

Hays, Samuel P. 1959. *Conservation and the Gospel of Efficiency: The Progressive Conservation Movement, 1890–1920.* New York, NY: Atheneum.

———. 1987. *Beauty, Health, and Permanence: Environmental Politics in the United States, 1955–1985.* Cambridge, England: Cambridge University Press.

Heifetz, R. A., and R. M. Sinder. 1990. Political leadership: managing the public's problem solving. In *The Power of Public Ideas*, edited by Robert Reich, 179–203. Cambridge, MA: Harvard University Press.

Heineman, Robert A., William T. Bluhm, Steven A. Peterson, and Edward N. Kearny. 1997. *The World of the Policy Analyst: Rationality, Values, and Politics.* 2nd ed. Chatham, NJ: Chatham House Publishers.

Held, David. 1987. *Models of Democracy.* Cambridge, England: Polity Press.

Hendee, John C., and Randall C. Pitstick. 1992. The growth of environmental and conservation-related organizations: 1980–1991. *Renewable Resources Journal* 10 (2):6–19.

Henning, Daniel H. 1970. Natural resources administration and the public interest. *Public Administration Review* 30 (2):134–140.

Henson, Larry, and H. M. Montrey. 1992. *Ecology Based Multiple-Use Management Strategy.* Albuquerque, NM: USDA Forest Service Southwestern Region and Rocky Mountain Forest and Range Experiment Station.

Hess, Karl J. 1992. *Visions Upon the Land: Man and Nature on the Western Range.* Washington, D.C.: Island Press.

———. 1997. Political rights and policy wrongs: the ecology of conflict on America's western public lands. *Human Ecology Review* 4 (1):9–16.

Hesse, Herman. 1972. *Magister Ludi (The Glass Bead Game).* New York, NY: Bantam Books.

Hirt, Paul. 1994. *A Conspiracy of Optimism: Management of the National Forests Since World War II.* Lincoln, NE: University of Nebraska Press.

Hodges, Donald G., and Robert F. Durant. 1989. The professional state revisited: twixt Scylla and Charybdis? *Public Administration Review* 49 (September/October):474–484.

Hofstadter, Richard. 1948. *The American Political Tradition.* New York, NY: Vintage.

Holling, C. S., ed. 1978. *Adaptive Environmental Assessment and Management.* New York, NY: John Wiley and Sons.

Holmes, Beatrice Hort. 1972. *A History of Federal Water Resources Programs and Policies, 1800–1960.* Washington, D.C.: USDA Economic Research Service.

———. 1979. *A History of Federal Water Resources Programs and Policies, 1961–1970.* Washington, D.C.: USDA Economic Research Service.

Hoover, Anne P., and Margaret A. Shannon. 1995. Building greenway policies within a participatory democracy framework. *Landscape and Urban Planning* 33:433–459.

Horkheimer, Max. 1947. *The Eclipse of Reason.* New York, NY: Oxford University Press.

Horkheimer, Max, and Theodor W. Adorno. 1995. *Dialectic of Enlightenment*, translated by John Cumming. New York, NY: The Continuum Publishing Company.

Howe, John R. Jr. 1967. Republican thought and the political violence of the 1790s. *American Quarterly* 19 (Summer):147–165.

Hulme, Peter, and Ludmilla Jordanova, eds. 1990. *The Enlightenment and its Shadows.* New York, NY: Routledge.

Hunt, Lee O. 1996. Forest management abandoned (letter to the editor). *Journal of Forestry* 94 (10):13.

Hyde, William F., and James L. Chamberlain. Who would gain from privatizing the national forests? *Journal of Forestry* 93 (8):22–25.

Inglehart, Ronald. 1977. *The Silent Revolution: Changing Values and Political Styles Among Western Publics.* Princeton, NJ: Princeton University Press.

Ingram, Helen, and Mary G. Wallace. 1997. An 'empire of liberty:' Thomas Jefferson and governing natural resources in the West. In *Thomas Jefferson and the Changing West: From Conquest to Conservation*, edited by James P. Ronda, 93–108. Albuquerque, NM: University of New Mexico Press for the Missouri Historical Society Press.

Institute for Research on Environment and Economy (IREE). 1996. *Community Empowerment in Ecosystem Management.* Ottawa, Ontario: University of Ottawa Institute for Research on Environment and Economy.

Interagency Ecosystem Management Task Force. 1995. *The Ecosystem Approach: Healthy Ecosystems and Sustainable Economies: Vol. I - Overview.* Springfield, VA: National Technical Information Service.

Irland, Lloyd D. 1993. Developing ethical reflection. *Journal of Forestry* 91 (4):11.

Iverson, Dave. 1993. An ecosystems approach to management—moving from old to new standards (unpublished manuscript). Ogden, UT: USDA Forest Service Intermountain Station.

Jaffe, Adam M. 1980. Benefit-cost analysis and multi-objective evaluations of federal water projects. *Harvard Environmental Law Review* 4:58–85, 70.

John, DeWitt. 1994. *Civic Environmentalism: Alternatives to Regulation in States and Communities.* Washington, D.C.: Congressional Quarterly.

Johnson, Darryll R., and James K. Agee. 1988. Introduction to ecosystem management. In *Ecosystem Management for Parks and Wilderness*, edited by James K. Agee and Darryll R. Johnson, 3–14. Seattle, WA: University of Washington Press.

Johnson, K. Norman, Richard Holthausen, Margaret A. Shannon, and Jim Sedell. 1995. Developing a forest plan for federal forests of the Pacific Northwest: FEMAT and its aftermath, paper read at the workshop Crossroads of Science, Management, and Policy: A Review of Bioregional Assessments. Portland, OR.

Johnson, K. Norman, Frederick Swanson, Margaret Herring, and Sarah Greene, eds. Forthcoming. *Bioregional Assessments: At the Crossroads of Science, Management, and Policy.* Washington, D.C.: Island Press.

Johnson, Lady Bird, and Carlton B. Lees. 1988. *Wildflowers Across America.* New York, NY: Abbeville Press.

Jones, Jeff R., Roxanne Martin, and E. T. Bartlett. 1995. Ecosystem management: the U.S. Forest Service's response to social conflict. *Society and Natural Resources* 8:161–168.

Jordanova, Ludmilla. 1990. The authoritarian response. In *The Enlightenment and its Shadows*, edited by Peter Hulme and Ludmilla Jordanova, 200–216. New York, NY: Routledge.

Kathlene, Lyn, and John A. Martin. 1991. Enhancing citizen participation: panel designs, perspectives and policy formation. *Journal of Policy Analysis and Management* 10 (1):46–63.

Katz, Eric, and Lauren Oechsli. 1993. Moving beyond anthropocentrism: environmental ethics, development and the Amazon. *Environmental Ethics* 15 (1):49–59.

Kaufman, H. 1994. The paradox of excellence. Paper read at the U.S. Forest Service Chief's Workshop, Preparing for the Future by Examining the Past, June 6, 1994, at Milford, PA.

Keiter, Robert. 1989. Taking account of the ecosystem on the public domain: law and ecology in the greater Yellowstone region. *University of Colorado Law Review* 60:923–1007.

———. 1990. NEPA and the emerging concept of ecosystem management on the public lands. *Land and Water Law Review* 25 (1):41–60.

———. 1994. Beyond the boundary line: constructing a law of ecosystem management. *University of Colorado Law Review* 65 (2):293–333.

———. 1996. Toward legitimizing ecosystem management on the public domain. *Ecological Applications* 6 (3):727–730.

———. 1997. Ecological policy and the courts: of rights, processes, and the judicial role. *Human Ecology Review* 4 (1):2–8.

Keiter, Robert B., Louise Milkman, and Ted Boling. 1995. Legal perspectives on ecosystem management: legitimizing a new federal land management policy. Paper read at the Ecological Stewardship workshop, at Tucson, AZ.

Keller, Morton. 1985. *Parties, Congress, and Public Policy.* Washington, D.C.: American Historical Association.

Kellner, Douglas. 1989. *Critical Theory, Marxism, and Modernity.* Cambridge, England: Polity Press.

Kemmis, Daniel. 1995. *The Good City and the Good Life.* New York, NY: Houghton Mifflin Company.

Kempton, Willett, James S. Boster, and Jennifer A. Hartley. 1995. *Environmental Values in American Culture.* Cambridge, MA: MIT Press.

Kennedy, James J. 1988. Legislative confrontation of groupthink in U.S. natural resource agencies. *Environmental Conservation* 15 (2):123–128.

Kennedy, James J., and Michael P. Dombeck. 1995. The evolution of public agency beliefs and behavior toward ecosystem-based stewardship. Paper read at the Ecological Stewardship Workshop, at Tucson, AZ.

Kennedy, James J., and Brett B. Roper. 1989. Status of and need for career development research in natural resource agencies: a Forest Service example. *Transactions of the North American Wildlife and Natural Resource Conference* 54:432–438.

Kennedy, James J., and Jack Ward Thomas. 1992. Exit, voice, and loyalty of wildlife biologists in public natural resource/environmental agencies. In *American Fish and Wildlife Policy—The Human Dimension*, edited by W. R. Mangun, 221–238. Carbondale, IL: Southern Illinois Press.

———. 1995. Managing natural resources as social value. In *A New Century for Natural Resources Management*, edited by Richard L. Knight and Sarah F. Bates, 311–321. Washington, D.C.: Island Press.

Kessler, Winifred B., and Hal Salwasser. 1995. Natural resource agencies: transforming from within. In *A New Century for Natural Resources Management*, edited by Richard L. Knight and Sarah F. Bates, 171–187. Washington, D.C.: Island Press.

Kessler, Winifred B., Hal Salwasser, Charles W. Cartwright Jr., and James A. Caplan. 1992. New perspectives for sustainable natural resources management. *Ecological Applications* 2 (3):221–225.

Kettering Foundation. 1993. *Meaningful Chaos: How People Form Relationships with Public Concerns.* Dayton, OH: Kettering Foundation.

Keystone Center. 1996. *The Keystone National Policy Dialogue on Ecosystem Management.* Keystone, CO: The Keystone Center.

Kimmins, J. P. 1990. Modeling the sustainability of forest production and yield for a changing and uncertain future. *The Forestry Chronicle* 66:271–280.

Klyza, Christopher McGrory. 1996. *Who Controls Public Lands? Mining, Forestry, and Grazing Policies, 1870–1990.* Chapel Hill, NC: University of North Carolina Press.

Knight, Richard L., and Sarah Bates, eds. 1995. *A New Century for Natural Resources Management.* Washington, D.C.: Island Press.

Knight, Richard L., and T. Luke George. 1995. New approaches, new tools: conservation biology. In *A New Century for Natural Resources Management*, edited by Richard L. Knight and Sarah F. Bates, 279–295. Washington, D.C.: Island Press.

Knott, Jack H., and Gary J. Miller. 1987. *Reforming Bureaucracy: The Politics of Institutional Choice.* Englewood Cliffs, NJ: Prentice-Hall.

Korten, David C. 1995. *When Corporations Rule the World.* San Francisco, CA: Berrett-Koehler Publishers.

Korten, Frances. 1996. Amid signs of fear and hope, rural people brace for the next millennium. *Practitioner (Newsletter of the National Network of Forest Practitioners)* 6 (December): 4, 7.

Kouzes, James M., and Barry Z. Posner. 1987. *The Leadership Challenge: How to Get Extraordinary Things Done in Organizations.* San Francisco, CA: Jossey-Bass.

Kuhn, T. S. 1970. *The Structure of Scientific Revolutions.* 2nd ed. Chicago, IL: University of Chicago Press.

Kusel, Jonathan. 1996. Well-being in forest-dependent communities, part I: a new approach. In *Sierra Nevada Ecosystem Project; Final Report to Congress, Volume II, Assessments and Scientific Basis for Management Options*, 361–374. Davis, CA: University of California, Centers for Water and Wildland Resources.

Kweit, Mary Grisez, and Robert W. Kweit. 1987. The politics of policy analysis: the role of citizen participation in analytic decision-making. In *Citizen Participation in Public Decision-Making*, edited by Jack Desario and Stuart Langton, 19–37. New York, NY: Greenwood Press.

Lackey, Robert T. 1997a. Ecological risk assessment: use, abuse, and alternatives. *Environmental Management* 21 (6):808–812.

———. 1997b. Ecosystem management: paradigms and prattle, people and prizes. In *Proceedings of the Conference: Forty Years of Controversy and Achievement in North American Fisheries.* Dearborn, MI: American Institute of Fishery Research Biologists.

———. 1998. Radically contested assertions in ecosystem management. Paper read at the conference Shared Waters/Shared Stewardship: Environmental Management in the Georgia Basin–Puget Sound, May 27–28, at Bellingham, WA.

———. Forthcoming. Seven pillars of ecosystem management. *Landscape and Urban Planning.*

Ladd, Everett Carll, and Karlyn Bowman. 1996. Public opinion on the environment. *Resources (A Newsletter of Resource for the Future)* 124 (Summer):5–7.

Lasswell, Harold D. 1961. *Politics: Who Gets What, When, and How.* New York, NY: Meridian.

Lawrence, Nathaniel, and Dennis Murphy. 1992. New perspectives or old priorities? *Conservation Biology* 6 (3):465–468.

Lead Partnership Group. 1996a. Opportunities for community and national interests around reinvestment. In *Proceedings of the Lead Partnership Group Northern California/Southern Oregon Regional Roundtable on Communities of Place, Partnerships, and Forest Health*, edited by J. Kusel, G. J. Gray, and M. J. Enzer, 27–32. Washington, D.C.: American Forests/Forest Community Research.

———. 1996b. Restoration on forested land: an opportunity for partnerships. In *Proceedings of the Lead Partnership Group Northern California/Southern Oregon Regional Roundtable on Communities of Place, Partnerships, and Forest Health*, edited by J. Kusel, G. J. Gray, and M. J. Enzer, 21–26. Washington, D.C.: American Forests/Forest Community Research.

———. 1996c. Social and economic monitoring in rural communities. In *Proceedings of the Lead Partnership Group Northern California/Southern Oregon Regional Roundtable on Communities of Place, Partnerships, and Forest Health*, edited by J. Kusel, G. J. Gray, and M. J. Enzer, 33–38. Washington, D.C.: American Forests/Forest Community Research.

Lee, Kai N. 1993. *Compass and Gyroscope: Integrating Science and Politics for the Environment.* Washington, D.C.: Island Press.

Lee, Robert G. 1992. Ecologically effective social organization as a requirement for sustaining watershed ecosystems. In *Watershed Management: Balancing Sustainability and Environmental Change*, edited by R. J. Naiman, 73–90. New York, NY: Springer-Verlag.

———. 1994. *Broken Trust, Broken Land.* Wilsonville, OR: Bookpartners.

Lee, R. G., and G. H. Stankey. 1992. Evaluating institutional arrangements for regulating large watersheds and river basins. In *Watershed Resources: Balancing Environmental, Social, Political and Economic Factors in Large Basins*, edited by P. W. Adams and W. A. Atkinson, 30–37. Corvallis, OR: Oregon State University Forest Engineering Department.

Lehmann, Scott. 1995. *Privatizing Public Lands.* New York, NY: Oxford University Press.

Leiss, William. 1974. *The Domination of Nature.* Boston, MA: Beacon Press.

Lemann, Nicholas. 1996. Kicking in groups. *Atlantic Monthly* 277 (4):22–26.

Leopold, Aldo. 1949. *A Sand County Almanac and Sketches Here and There.* Special Commemorative Edition. New York, NY: Oxford University Press.

Leshy, John D. 1992. Is the multiple use/sustained yield management philosophy still applicable today? In *Multiple Use and Sustained Yield: Changing Philosophies for Federal Land Management (the Proceedings and Summary of a Workshop Convened on March 5 and 6, 1992)*, edited by Library of Congress Congressional Research Service, 107–119. Washington, D.C.: Government Printing Office.

Liebman, Ernst. 1972. *The Water Resources Council.* Arlington, VA: U.S. National Water Commission.

Lijphart, Arend. 1997. Unequal participation: democracy's unresolved dilemma. *Presidential Address, American Political Science Association, 1996. American Political Science Review* 91 (1):1–14.

Likens, Gene E. 1992. *The Ecosystem Approach: Its Use and Abuse.* Luhe, Germany: Ecology Institute.

Lincoln, Yvonna S. 1985. Introduction. In *Organizational Theory and Inquiry: The Paradigm Revolution*, edited by Yvonna S. Lincoln, 29–42. Beverly Hills, CA: Sage Publications.

Lipset, Seymour Martin. 1995. Malaise and resiliency in America. *Journal of Democracy* 6 (3):4–18.

Lipset, Seymour Martin, and William Schneider. 1987. *The Confidence Gap.* Baltimore, MD: Johns Hopkins University Press.

Little, Peter D. 1994. The link between local participation and improved conservation: a review of issues and experiences. In *Natural Connections: Perspectives in Community-Based Conservation*, edited by David Western and R. Michael Wright, 347–372. Washington, D.C.: Island Press.

Loehr, Rodney C., ed. 1952. *Forests for the Future: The Story of Sustained Yield as Told in the Diaries and Papers of David T. Mason, 1907–1950*. St. Paul, MN: Minnesota Historical Society.

Long, F. J., and M. B. Arnold. 1995. *The Power of Environmental Partnerships*. New York, NY: The Dryden Press.

Lowenthal, Jeff. 1997. Rolling on the river: Chicago teens battle blight and neglect to help transform the banks of a notorious river into a neighborhood park. *Hope* (July/August):71–73.

Lowi, Theodore J. 1979. *The End of Liberalism: The Second Republic of the United States*. 2nd ed. New York, NY: W.W. Norton.

Lubchenco, Jane. 1998. Entering the century of the environment: a new social contract for science. *Science* 279 (January 23):491–497.

Lubchenco, Jane, Annette M. Olson, Linda B. Brubaker, Stephen R. Carpenter, Marjorie M. Holland, Stephen P. Hubbell, Simon A. Levin, James A. MacMahon, Pamela A. Matson, Jerry M. Melillo, Harold A. Mooney, Charles H. Peterson, H. Ronald Pulliam, Leslie A. Real, Philip J. Regal, and Paul G. Risser. 1991. The sustainable biosphere initiative: an ecological research agenda. *Ecology* 72 (2):371–412.

Lutz, Donald S. 1992. *A Preface to American Political Theory*. Lawrence, KS: University of Kansas Press.

Maass, Arthur. 1951. *Muddy Waters: The Army Engineers and the Nation's Rivers*. Cambridge, MA: Harvard University Press.

MacCleery, Douglas W., and Dennis C. Le Master. 1995. Producing and consuming natural resources within an ecosystem management framework: what is the proper context? Paper read at the Ecological Stewardship Workshop, at Tucson, AZ.

Machlis, Gary E. 1990. The tension between local and national conservation groups in the democratic regime. *Society and Natural Resources* 3:267–279.

MacIntyre, Alasdair. 1984. *After Virtue*. South Bend, IN: Notre Dame Press.

Magraw, Daniel. 1994. NAFTA's repercussions: is green trade possible? *Environment* 36 (2):14–20, 39–45.

Mahoney, Dennis J. 1986. Wilson, Woodrow. In *Encyclopedia of the American Constitution*, edited by Leonard W. Levy, Kenneth L. Karst, and Dennis J. Mahoney, 2070–2071. New York, NY: Macmillan.

Malthus, Thomas Robert. 1976. *An Essay on the Principle of Population*, edited by Philip Appleman, *Norton Critical Editions*. New York, NY: W.W. Norton & Company.

Manring, N. J. 1993. Reconciling science and politics in Forest Service decision making: new tools for public administrators. *American Review of Public Administration* 23 (4):343–359.

Marcuse, Herbert. 1964. *One-Dimensional Man*. Boston, MA: Beacon Press.

Marsh, George Perkins. 1965. *Man and Nature: Or, Physical Geography as Modified by Human Action*. Cambridge, MA: The Belknap Press.

Marsh, Lindell L. 1996. Conservation planning under the ESA: a new paradigm. In *Biodiversity and the Law*, edited by William J. Snape III, 59–66. Washington, D.C.: Island Press.

Maser, Chris. 1992. Do we owe anything to the future? In *Multiple Use and Sustained Yield: Changing Philosophies for Federal Land Management (the Proceedings and Summary of a Workshop Convened on March 5 and 6, 1992)*, edited by Library of Congress Congressional Research Service, 195–213. Washington, D.C.: Government Printing Office.

————. 1996. *Resolving Environmental Conflict: Towards Sustainable Community Development.* Delray Beach, FL: St. Lucie Press.

Maser, C., R. G. Anderson, K. Cromack, J. T. Williams, and R. E. Martin. 1979. Dead and down woody material. In *Wildlife Habitats in Managed Forests: the Blue Mountains of Oregon and Washington*, edited by J. W. Thomas, 78–95. Washington, D.C.: USDA Forest Service.

Maxey, William R. 1996. Foresters: another endangered species? *Journal of Forestry* 94 (8):44.

McCain, John. 1996. How to clean up the mess. *Newsweek* October 28, 1996.

McCloskey, Michael. 1995. The skeptic: collaboration has its limits. *High Country News* 28 (9):7.

McCormack, Wayne. 1982. Land use planning and management of state school lands. *Utah Law Review* 1982 (3):525–547.

McDougall, Harold A. 1991. *Black Baltimore: A New Theory of Community.* Philadelphia, PA: Temple University Press.

McIntosh, Robert P. 1985. *The Background of Ecology: Concept and Theory.* New York, NY: Cambridge University Press.

McLain, Rebecca. 1993. Toward more effective ecological learning: procedural guidelines for the USMAB Landscape Sustainability Project (draft manuscript). Seattle, WA: University of Washington College of Forest Resources.

McLain, Rebecca, and Robert G. Lee. 1994. Adaptive management: promises and pitfalls. Paper read at the 57th Annual Meeting of the Rural Sociological Society, August 11–14, at Portland, OR.

Meadows, Donella H., Dennis L. Meadows, Jorgen Randers, and William W. Behrens III. 1972. *The Limits to Growth.* New York, NY: Universe Books.

Meffe, Gary K., and C. Ronald Carroll. 1994. *Principles of Conservation Biology.* Sunderland, MA: Sinauer Associates.

Meffe, Gary K., and Stephen Viederman. 1995. Combining science and policy in conservation biology. *Renewable Resources Journal* 13 (3):15–18.

Meidinger, Errol E. 1997. Organizational and legal challenges for ecosystem management. In *Creating a Forestry for the 21st Century: The Science of Ecosystem Management*, edited by Kathryn A. Kohm and Jerry F. Franklin, 361–379. Washington, D.C.: Island Press.

Meine, Curt. 1988. *Aldo Leopold: His Life and Work.* Madison, WI: University of Wisconsin Press.

Meyers, Marvin. 1973. *The Mind of the Founder: Sources of the Political Thought of James Madison.* Indianapolis, IN: Bobbs-Merrill.

Milbrath, Lester W. 1984. *Environmentalists: Vanguard for a New Society.* Albany, NY: State University of New York Press.

Miller, Tim R. 1985. Recent trends in federal water resources management: are the "iron triangles" in retreat? *Policy Studies Review* 5 (2):395–411.

Mitroff, Ian I. 1972. The myth of objectivity or why science needs a new psychology of science. *Journal of Management Science* 18 (10):B613–B618.

Moncrief, Lewis. 1973. The cultural basis of our environmental crisis. In *Western Man and Environmental Ethics*, edited by Ian Barbour, 43–54. Reading, MA: Addison-Wesley Publishing Company.

Moore, Carl M. 1996. What is community? *Chronicle of Community* 1 (1):28–32.

Moore, Lucy, Richard Pacheco, Aaron Rael, and Rosemary Romero. 1996. *Creating Dialogue between Decision-Makers and Communities: Community Resource Mapping in Northern New Mexico*. Santa Fe, NM: Western Network.

Moote, Margaret A., and Mitchel P. McClaran. 1997. Implications of participatory democracy for public land planning. *Journal of Range Management* 50 (5):473–481.

Moote, Margaret A., Mitchel P. McClaran, and Donna K. Chickering. 1997. Theory in practice: applying participatory democracy theory to public land planning. *Environmental Management* 21 (6):877–889.

More, Thomas R. 1996. Forestry's fuzzy concepts: an examination of ecosystem management. *Journal of Forestry* 94 (8):19–23.

Morrison, Jason I., Sandra L. Postel, and Peter H. Gleick. 1996. *The Sustainable Use of Water in the Lower Colorado River Basin*. Oakland, CA: Pacific Institute for Studies in Development, Environment, and Security.

Morrissey, Wayne A., Jeffrey A. Zinn, and M. Lynne Corn. 1994. *Ecosystem Management: Federal Agency Activities*. Washington, D.C.: Library of Congress Congressional Research Service.

Nash, Roderick Frazier. 1973. *Wilderness and the American Mind*. Revised ed. New Haven, CT: Yale University Press.

———. 1989. *The Rights of Nature: A History of Environmental Ethics*. Madison, WI: The University of Wisconsin Press.

———. 1990. *American Environmentalism: Readings in Conservation History*. 3rd ed. New York, NY: McGraw-Hill.

National Performance Review. 1993. *Reinventing Environmental Management: Accompanying Report of the National Performance Review*. Washington, D.C.: Office of the Vice President.

National Research Council. 1990. *Forestry Research: A Mandate for Change*. Washington, D.C.: National Academy Press.

Natural Resources Law Center. 1996. *The Watershed Source Book: Watershed-Based Solutions to Natural Resources Problems*. Boulder, CO: University of Colorado Natural Resources Law Center.

Nelson, Robert, H. 1995. *Public Lands and Private Rights: The Failure of Scientific Management*. Lanham, MD: Rowman & Littlefield.

Newmark, W. D. 1985. Legal and biotic boundaries of Western North American national parks: a problem of congruence. *Biological Conservation* 33:197–205.

Norgaard, Richard B., and Richard B. Howarth. 1991. Sustainability and discounting the future. In *Ecological Economics: The Science and Management of Sustainability*, edited by Robert Costanza, 88–101. New York, NY: Columbia University Press.

Norris, Pippa. 1996. Does television erode social capital? a reply to Putnam. *PS: Political Science and Politics* 29 (3):474–480.

Norton, Bryan G. 1992. A new paradigm for environmental management. In *Ecosystem Health: New Goals for Environmental Management*, edited by Robert Costanza, Bryan G. Norton, and Benjamin D. Haskell, 23–41. Washington, D.C.: Island Press.

Noss, R. F. 1983. A regional approach to maintain diversity. *BioScience* 33:700–706.

Noss, R. F., and L. D. Harris. 1986. Nodes, networks and mums: preserving diversity at all scales. *Environmental Management* 10:299–309.

Nuszkiewicz, Michelle. 1992. Twenty years of the Federal Advisory Committee Act: it's time for some changes. *Southern California Law Review* 65:957–997.

Nye, Joseph S. Jr., Philip D. Zelikow, and David C. King. 1997. *Why People Don't Trust Government*. Cambridge, MA: Harvard University Press.

Oaks, Dallin H. 1995. Rights and responsibilities. In *Rights and the Common Good: The Communitarian Perspective*, edited by Amitai Etzioni, 37–44. New York, NY: St. Martin's Press.

Odum, E. P. 1971. *Fundamentals of Ecology*. Philadelphia, PA: W. B. Saunders.

O'Keefe, Timothy. 1990. Holistic (new) forestry: significant difference or just another gimmick? No paradigmatic shift in sight. *Journal of Forestry* 88 (4):23–24.

O'Laughlin, Jay. 1990. *Idaho's Endowment Lands: A Matter of Sacred Trust*. Moscow, ID: Idaho Forest, Wildlife, and Range Policy Analysis Group.

O'Leary, Rosemary. 1994. The bureaucratic politics paradox: the case of wetlands legislation in Nevada. *Journal of Public Administration Research and Theory* 4 (4):443–467.

Omernik, James M., and Robert G. Bailey. 1997. Distinguishing between watersheds and ecoregions. *Journal of the American Water Resources Association* 33 (5):935–949.

O'Neill, Onora. 1990. Enlightenment as autonomy: Kant's vindication of reason. In *The Enlightenment and its Shadows*, edited by Peter Hulme and Ludmilla Jordanova, 184–200. New York, NY: Routledge.

Ophuls, William. 1974. Reversal is the law of the Tao: the imminent resurrection of political philosophy. In *Environmental Politics*, edited by Stuart Nagel, 34–48. New York, NY: Praeger Publishers.

———. 1997. *Requiem for Modern Politics: The Tragedy of the Enlightenment and the Challenge of the New Millennium*. Boulder, CO: Westview Press.

Orians, Gordon H. 1990. Ecological concepts of sustainability. *Environment* 32 (9):10–15, 34–39.

Orr, David W. 1992. *Ecological Literacy: Education and the Transition to a Postmodern World*. Albany, NY: State University of New York Press.

———. 1995. A world that takes its environment seriously. In *A New Century for Natural Resources Management*, edited by Richard L. Knight and Sarah F. Bates, 123–141. Washington, D.C.: Island Press.

Orr, David W., and Stuart Hill. 1978. Leviathan, the open society and the crisis of ecology. *Western Political Quarterly* 31:34–48.

Ostrom, Elinor. 1993. A communitarian approach to local governance. *National Civic Review* (Summer):226–233.

O'Toole, Randal. 1988. *Reforming the Forest Service*. Washington, D.C.: Island Press.

Padover, Saul K., ed. 1939. *Thomas Jefferson on Democracy*. New York, NY: Mentor Books.

Paehlke, Robert C. 1989. *Environmentalism and the Future of Progressive Politics*. New Haven, CT: Yale University Press.

Page, Talbot. 1991. Sustainability and the problem of valuation. In *Ecological Economics: The Science and Management of Sustainability*, edited by Robert Costanza, 58–74. New York, NY: Columbia University Press.

Parker, Michael, James G. Thompson, Robert R. Reynolds Jr., and Michael D. Smith. 1995. Use and misuse of complex models: examples from water demand management. *Water Resources Bulletin* 31 (2):257–263.

Parry, B. Thomas, Henry J. Vaux, and Nicholas Dennis. 1983. Changing conceptions of sustained-yield policy on the national forests. *Journal of Forestry* 81 (3):150–154.

Parzych, Kenneth M. 1993. *Public Policy and the Regulatory Environment.* Lanham, MD: University Press of America.

Pastor, John. 1995. Ecosystem management, ecological risk, and public policy. *BioScience* 45 (4):286.

Pateman, Carole. 1970. *Participation and Democratic Theory.* Cambridge, England: Cambridge University Press.

Patton, M. Q. 1975. *Alternative Evaluation Research Paradigm.* Grand Forks, ND: University of North Dakota Press.

Payne, Daniel G. 1996. *Voices in the Wilderness: American Nature Writing and Environmental Politics.* Hanover, NH: University Press of New England.

Pennsylvania Bureau of Forestry. n.d. *Penn's Woods: Sustaining Our Forests.* Harrisburg, PA: Department of Environmental Resources, Bureau of Forestry.

Perlin, John. 1991. *A Forest Journey: The Role of Wood in the Development of Civilization.* Cambridge, MA: Harvard University Press.

Perry, David A., and Michael P. Amaranthus. 1997. Disturbance, recovery, and stability. In *Creating a Forestry for the 21st Century: The Science of Ecosystem Management,* edited by Kathryn A. Kohm and Jerry F. Franklin, 31–56. Washington, D.C.: Island Press.

Peterson, E. Wesley F. 1993. Time preference, the environment and the interests of future generations. *Journal of Agricultural and Environmental Ethics* 6 (2):107–126.

Peterson, Merrill D. 1986. Jefferson, Thomas. In *Encyclopedia of the American Constitution,* edited by Leonard W. Levy, Kenneth L. Karst, and Dennis J. Mahoney, 1014–1018. New York, NY: Macmillan.

Pinchot, Gifford. 1910. *The Fight for Conservation.* Garden City, NY: Harcourt Brace.

———. 1947. *Breaking New Ground.* Washington, D.C.: Island Press.

Pinchot, Gifford, and Elizabeth Pinchot. *The End of Bureaucracy and the Rise of the Intelligent Organization.* New York, NY: Doubleday, Page.

President's Council on Sustainable Development. 1996. *Sustainable America: A New Consensus for Prosperity, Opportunity, and a Healthy Environment for the Future.* Washington, D.C.: Government Printing Office.

Press, Daniel. 1994. *Democratic Dilemmas in the Age of Ecology: Trees and Toxics in the American West.* Durham, NC: Duke University Press.

Press, Daniel, and Daniel A. Mazmanian. 1997. The greening of industry: achievement and potential. In *Environmental Policy in the 1990s: Reform or Reaction?* edited by Norman J. Vig and Michael E. Kraft, 255–277. Washington, D.C.: Congressional Quarterly.

Primack, Richard B. 1993. *Essentials of Conservation Biology.* Sunderland, MA: Sinauer Associates.

Public Land Law Review Commission. 1970. *One Third of the Nation's Land.* Washington, D.C.: Government Printing Office.

Putnam, Robert D. 1995a. Bowling alone: America's declining social capital. *Journal of Democracy* 6 (1):65–78.

————. 1995b. Tuning in, tuning out: the strange disappearance of social capital in America. *PS: Political Science and Politics* 28 (4):664–683.

————. 1996. The strange disappearance of civic America. *The American Prospect* 24 (Winter):34–48.

Quarles, Steven P. 1996. The failure of federal land planning. In *Testimony before the U.S. Congress, House of Representatives, Committee on Resources, Subcommittee on National Parks, Forests and Lands.* Washington, D.C.

Quine, W. 1962. Paradox. *Scientific American* 206:84–96.

Rapaport, Anatol. 1967. Escape from paradox. *Scientific American* (July):50–56.

Reeves, G. H., D. L. Bottom, and M. H. Brookes. 1992. *Ethical Questions for Resource Managers.* Portland, OR: USDA Forest Service Pacific Northwest Research Station.

Reich, Robert B. 1985. Public administration and public deliberation: an interpretive essay. *The Yale Law Journal* 94:1617–1641.

————. 1988. *The Power of Public Ideas.* Cambridge, MA: Harvard University Press.

————. 1997. The unfinished agenda. Paper read at the Council on Excellence in Government, January 9, at Washington, D.C.

Reidel, Carl, and Jean Richardson. 1992. A public/private cooperative paradigm for federal land management. In *Multiple Use and Sustained Yield: Changing Management for Federal Land Management (the Proceedings and Summary of a Workshop Convened on March 5 and 6, 1992),* edited by Library of Congress Congressional Research Service, 145–168. Washington, D.C.: Government Printing Office.

Reisner, Mark. 1986. *Cadillac Desert: The American West and its Disappearing Water.* New York, NY: Viking.

Richardson, Sherri, and George Stankey. 1996. Privatizing forest land in New Zealand: for the U.S.? *Forestry Research West (a publication of the USDA Forest Service Pacific Northwest Research Station)* (August):10–12.

Rivlin, Alice. 1993. Values, institutions and sustainable forestry. In *Defining Sustainable Forestry,* edited by Gregory H. Aplet, Nels Johnson, Jeffrey T. Olson, and V. Alaric Sample, 255–259. Washington, D.C.: Island Press.

Roberts, Paul. 1997. The federal chain-saw massacre. *Harper's Magazine* 294 (June):37–51.

Robertson, F. Dale. 1992. Ecosystem management of the national forests and grasslands, June 4 Memo to Regional Foresters and Station Directors. Washington, D.C.: USDA Forest Service.

Rocco, Christopher. 1994. Between modernity and postmodernity: reading 'Dialectic of Enlightenment' against the grain. *Political Theory* 221:71–97.

Rodman, J. 1977. The liberation of nature. *Inquiry* 20 (1):83–145.

————. 1980. Paradigm change in political science. *American Behavioral Scientist* 24 (1):49–78.

Rohlf, Daniel J. 1994. Six biological reasons why the Endangered Species Act doesn't work—and what to do about it. In *Environmental Policy and Biodiversity,* edited by R. Edward Grumbine, 181–200. Washington, D.C.: Island Press.

Rosenau, Pauline. 1992. *Post-Modernism and the Social Sciences.* Princeton, NJ: Princeton University Press.

Rosenbaum, Walter A. 1995. *Environmental Politics and Policy.* 3rd ed. Washington, D.C.: Congressional Quarterly Press.

Rousseau, Jean-Jacques. 1987. *The Basic Political Writings*, edited by Donald A. Cress. Indianapolis, IN: Hackett Publishing Company.

Rylander, Jason C. 1996. Accounting for nature: a look at attempts to fashion a 'green GDP.' *Renewable Resources Journal* 14 (2):8–13.

Sagoff, Mark. 1995. Carrying capacity and ecological economics. *BioScience* 45 (9):610–621.

Sale, Kirkpatrick. 1990. Schism in environmentalism. In *American Environmentalism: Readings in Conservation History*, edited by Roderick Frazier Nash, 285–293. New York, NY: McGraw-Hill.

Salwasser, Hal. 1994. Ecosystem management: can it sustain diversity and productivity? *Journal of Forestry* 92 (8):6–10.

Salwasser, Hal, Douglas W. MacCleery, and Thomas A. Snellgrove. 1993. An ecosystem perspective on sustainable forestry and new directions for the U.S. National Forest System. In *Defining Sustainable Forestry*, edited by G. H. Aplet, N. Johnson, T. Olson, and V. A. Sample, 44–89. Washington, D.C.: Island Press.

Sample, V. Alaric. 1994. Budget reform and integrated resource management. *Resource Hotline (newsletter of American Forests)*, February 11.

Sample, V. Alaric, Anthony S. Cheng, Maia J. Enzer, and Margaret A. Moote. 1995. *Building Partnerships for Ecosystem Management on Mixed Ownership Landscapes: Regional Perspectives.* Washington, D.C.: American Forests Forest Policy Center.

Sample, V. Alaric, Nels Johnson, Gregory H. Aplet, and Jeffery T. Olson. 1993. Introduction. In *Defining Sustainable Forestry*, edited by Gregory H. Aplet, Nels Johnson, Jeffery T. Olson, and V. Alaric Sample, 3–10. Washington, D.C.: Island Press.

Sandel, Michael J. 1996. *Democracy's Discontent: America in Search of a Public Philosophy.* Cambridge, MA: Belknap Press of Harvard University Press.

Sax, Joseph L. 1993. Property rights and the economy of nature: Understanding Lucas v. South Carolina Coastal Council. *Stanford Law Review* 45 (5):1433–1455.

Schiff, Ashley. 1962. *Fire and Water: Scientific Heresy in the U.S. Forest Service.* Cambridge, MA: Harvard University Press.

Schlager, Daniel B., and Wayne A. Friemund. 1994. Institutional and legal barriers to ecosystem management (unpublished manuscript). Portland, OR: USDA Forest Service Pacific Northwest Research Station.

Schneider, Anne Larason, and Helen Ingram. 1997. *Policy Design for Democracy.* Lawrence, KS: University Press of Kansas.

Sedjo, Roger A. 1996. Toward an operational approach to public forest management. *Journal of Forestry* 94 (8):24–27.

Senge, P. M. 1990. *The Fifth Discipline: The Art & Practice of Learning Organization.* New York, NY: Doubleday/Currency.

Seymour, Frances J. 1994. Are successful community-based conservation projects designed or discovered? In *Natural Connections: Perspectives in Community-Based Conservation*, edited by David Western and R. Michael Wright, 472–496. Washington, D.C.: Island Press.

Shands, William E., Anne Black, and James W. Giltmier. 1993. *From New Perspectives to Ecosystem Management: The Report of an Assessment of New Perspectives.* Milford, PA: Grey Towers Press.

Shannon, Daniel. 1996. Report blasts NAFTA environmental legacy along U.S.–Mexico border. *Environmental Science and Technology* 30 (3):115A.

Shannon, Margaret A. 1990a. Building public decisions: learning through planning (an evaluation of the NFMA forest planning process). In *Forest Service Planning: Accommodating Uses, Producing Outputs, and Sustaining Ecosystems*, Vol. II: Contract Papers, 227–338. Washington, D.C.: Office of Technology Assessment.

———. 1990b. Building trust: the formation of a social contract. In *Community and Forestry*, edited by Robert G. Lee, Donald R. Field, and William R. Burch Jr., 229–240. Boulder, CO: Westview Press.

———. 1990c. Public participation in the RPA process. In *Forest Service Planning: Setting Strategic Direction Under RPA*, Vol. II: Contractor Documents, 278–357. Washington, D.C.: Office of Technology Assessment.

———. 1992a. Community governance: an enduring institution of democracy. In *Multiple Use and Sustained Yield: Changing Philosophies for Federal Land Management (the Proceedings and Summary of a Workshop Convened on March 5 and 6, 1992)*, edited by Library of Congress Congressional Research Service, 219–246. Washington, D.C.: Government Printing Office.

———. 1992b. Foresters as strategic thinkers, facilitators, and citizens: a call to social integration and migration. *Journal of Forestry* 90 (10):24–27.

Shannon, Margaret A., and Alexios R. Antypas. 1996. Civic science is democracy in action. *Northwest Science* 70 (1):66–69.

———. 1997. Open institutions: uncertainty and ambiguity in 21st century forestry. In *Creating a Forestry for the 21st Century: The Science of Ecosystem Management*, edited by Kathryn Kohm and Jerry F. Franklin, 437–445. Washington, D.C.: Island Press.

Shannon, M. A., and C. Anderson. 1994. Institutional strategies for landscape management. In *Forest Landscape Management Project—Progress Report*, edited by Andrew B. Carey and Catherine Elliot, 143–174. Olympia, WA: Washington State Department of Natural Resources.

Shearman, Richard. 1990. The meaning and ethics of sustainability. *Environmental Management* 14 (1):1–8.

Shepard, W. Bruce. 1990. Seeing the forest for the trees: 'new perspectives' in the Forest Service. *Renewable Resources Journal* 8 (2):8–11.

Simon, Julian. 1981. *The Ultimate Resource*. Princeton, NJ: Princeton University Press.

———. 1990. *Population Matters: Resources, Environment, and Immigration*. New Brunswick, NJ: Transaction Publishers.

Sirianni, Carmen, and Lewis Friedland. 1995. Social capital and civic innovation: learning and capacity building from the 1960s to the 1990s. Paper read at the American Sociological Association Annual Meeting, August 20, 1995, at Washington, D.C.

Sirmon, Jeff, William E. Shands, and Chris Liggett. 1993. Communities of interests and open decisionmaking. *Journal of Forestry* 91 (7):17–21.

Slocombe, D. Scott. 1993a. Environmental planning, ecosystem science, and ecosystem approaches for integrating environment and development. *Environmental Management* 17 (3):289–303.

———. 1993b. Implementing ecosystem-based management: development of theory, practice, and research for planning and managing a region. *BioScience* 43 (9):612–622.

Smith, E. Lamar. 1979. An evaluation of the range condition concept. *Rangelands* I (2):52–54.

Smith, Greg. Community-arianism: Community and Communitarianism—Concepts and Contexts. (World Wide Web http://www.btwebworld.com/communities/greg/gsum.html.)

Smith, Wm. Randolph. 1993. Antitrust and ecosystem management: no good deed goes unpunished. Paper read at American Forests Forest Policy Center Symposium on Ecosystem Management, at New Haven, CT.

Smyth, Arthur V. 1995. Foresters and the land. *Journal of Forestry* 93 (9):22–25.

Social Science Research Group. 1994. *Principles of Sustainability.* Seattle, WA: University of Washington College of Forest Resources Institute for Resources in Society.

Society of American Foresters. 1993. *Task Force Report on Sustaining Long-Term Forest Health and Productivity.* Bethesda, MD: Society of American Foresters.

Souder, Jon A., and Sally K. Fairfax. 1996. *State Trust Lands: History, Management, and Sustainable Use.* Lawrence, KS: University Press of Kansas.

Soulé, Michael E. 1985. What is conservation biology? *BioScience* 35 (11):727–734.

———. 1986. *Conservation Biology: The Science of Scarcity and Diversity.* Sunderland, MA: Sinauer Associates.

Stankey, George H. 1994. Ecosystem management: how to institutionalize inspiration? Paper read at the Institutional Problem Analysis Workshop, October 20–22, at Stevenson, WA.

Stanley, Manfred. 1983. The mystery of the commons: on the indispensability of civic rhetoric. *Social Research* 50 (4):851–883.

———. 1990. The rhetoric of the commons: forum discourse in politics and society. In *The Rhetorical Turn,* edited by Herbert W. Simons, 238–257. Chicago, IL: University of Chicago Press.

Stanley, Thomas R. Jr. 1995. Ecosystem management and the arrogance of humanism. *Conservation Biology* 9 (2):255–262.

Steering Committee of the 75th Anniversary Symposium. 1994. National parks for the 21st century: the Vail Agenda. In *America's National Park System: The Critical Documents,* edited by Lary M. Dilsaver, 434–445. Lanham, MD: Rowman and Littlefield Publishers.

Steffen, Lloyd J. 1992. In defense of dominion. *Environmental Ethics* 14:63–80.

Stegner, Wallace. 1987. *The American West as Living Space.* Ann Arbor, MI: The University of Michigan Press.

Stelzer, Irwin M., and Howard P. Kitt. 1986. *Selected Antitrust Cases.* Homewood, IL: Richard D. Irwin, Inc.

Stone, Christopher D. 1972. *Should Trees Have Standing? Toward Legal Rights for Natural Objects.* Los Altos, CA: William Kaufmann.

Stone, Deborah A. 1988. *Policy Paradox and Political Reason.* New York, NY: HarperCollins.

Stroup, Richard L., and John A. Baden. 1983. *Natural Resources: Bureaucratic Myths and Environmental Management.* San Francisco, CA: Pacific Institute for Public Policy Research.

Swanson, Fred V., and Dean Berg. 1991. The ecological roots of new approaches to forestry. *Forest Perspectives* I (3):6–8.

Tamez, Sonia. 1995. The urban forest ecosystem and cultural values: the Greenlink example. In *Inside Urban Ecosystems: Proceedings of the 7th National Urban Forest Conference, New York,*

New York, edited by Cheryl Kollin and Michael Barratt, 74–76. Washington, D.C.: American Forests.

Tarrow, Sidney. 1996. Making social science work across space and time: a critical reflection on Robert Putnam's *Making Democracy Work. American Political Science Review* 90 (2):389–397.

Teixeira, Ruy A. 1992. *The Disappearing American Voter.* Washington, D.C.: Brooking Institute.

Thomas, Jack Ward. 1995. The instability of stability. Paper read at the Landscapes and Communities in Asia and the PNW Conference, October 16, at Missoula, MT.

Thomas, R. L., J. R. Vallentyne, K. Ogilvie, and J. D. Kingham. 1988. The ecosystems approach: a strategy for the management of renewable resources in the Great Lakes Basin. In *Perspectives on Ecosystem Management for the Great Lakes: A Reader*, edited by Lynton K. Caldwell, 31–57. Albany, NY: State University of New York Press.

Tipple, Terence J., and J. Douglas Wellman. 1989. Life in the fishbowl: public participation rewrites public foresters' job descriptions. *Journal of Forestry* 87 (3):24–30.

Tribe, Laurence H.. 1973. The limits of instrumental rationality. *Southern California Law Review* 46:617–670.

Twight, Ben W., Fremont J. Lyden, and E. Thomas Tuchmann. 1990. Constituency bias in a federal career system? a study of district rangers of the U.S. Forest Service. *Administration and Society* 22 (3):358–389.

U.S. Department of the Interior Bureau of Land Management. 1987. *Fish and Wildlife 2000: A Plan for the Future.* Washington, D.C.: Bureau of Land Management.

———. 1991. *Riparian-Wetland Initiative for the 1990s.* Washington, D.C.: Bureau of Land Management.

———. 1994. *Ecosystem Management in the BLM: From Concept to Commitment.* BLM/SC/GI-94/005+1736. Washington, D.C.: Bureau of Land Management.

———. 1946. *The Colorado River: A Comprehensive Report on the Development of the Water Resources of the Colorado River Basin for Irrigation, Power Production, and Other Beneficial Uses in Arizona, California, Colorado, Nevada, New Mexico, Utah, and Wyoming.* Washington, D.C.: U.S. Department of the Interior.

Vogel, David. 1997. International trade and environmental regulation. In *Environmental Policy in the 1990s: Reform or Reaction?*, edited by Norman J. Vig and Michael E. Kraft, 345–364. Washington, D.C.: Congressional Quarterly Press.

Volkman, J. M., and K. N. Lee. 1994. The owl and the Minerva: ecosystem lessons from the Columbia. *Journal of Forestry* 92 (4):48–52.

Walker, Samuel. 1993. The communitarian cop-out. *National Civic Review* (Summer):246–254.

Wallace, Mary G., Hanna J. Cortner, and Sabrina Burke. 1996. Taming nature: the Enlightenment's legacy for the future? *Journal of Forestry* 94 (11):39–44.

Wallace, Mary G., Hanna J. Cortner, Sabrina Burke, and Margaret A. Moote. 1996. Moving toward ecosystem management: examining a change in philosophy for natural resource management. *Journal of Political Ecology* 3. (World Wide Web http://www.library.arizona.edu/ej/jpe/vol3~1.htm.)

Wallinger, Scott. 1995. A commitment to the future: AF&PA's Sustainable Forestry Initiative. *Journal of Forestry* 93 (1):16–19.

Ward, Veronica. 1996. Sovereignty and ecosystem management: clash of concepts and boundaries. Paper read at the International Studies Association, at San Diego, CA.

Wear, David N., Monica G. Turner, and Richard O. Flamm. 1996. Ecosystem management with multiple owners: landscape dynamics in a Southern Appalachian watershed. *Ecological Applications* 6 (4):1173–1188.

Webster, Henry H., and Daniel E. Chappelle. 1997. The curious state of forestry in the United States. *Renewable Resources Journal* 15 (1):6–8.

Weeks, W. William. 1997. *Beyond the Ark: Tools for an Ecosystem Approach to Conservation.* Washington, D.C.: Island Press.

Weiss, Edith Brown. 1990. Our rights and obligations to future generations for the environment. *American Journal of International Law* 84 (1): 198–207.

Wenger, Karl F. 1997. What is ecosystem management? *Journal of Forestry* 95 (4):44.

Western, David, and R. Michael Wright, eds. 1994. *Natural Connections: Perspectives in Community-Based Conservation.* Washington, D.C.: Island Press.

Westoby, Mark, Brian Walker, and Immanuel Noy-Mier. 1989. Opportunistic management for rangelands not at equilibrium. *Journal of Range Management* 42 (4):266–274.

Wheat, Andrew. 1996. Troubled NAFTA waters. *Multinational Monitor* 17 (4):23–25.

White, Alan T., Lynne Zeitlin Hale, Yves Renard, and Lafcadio Cortesi. 1994. Lessons to be learned from experience. In *Collaborative and Community-Based Management of Coral Reefs: Lessons from Experience*, edited by Alan T. White, Lynne Zeitlin Hale, Yves Renard, and Lafcadio Cortesi, 107–121. West Hartford, CT: Kumarian Press.

White, Lynne. 1967. The historical roots of our ecological crisis. *Science* 155:1203–1207.

White, Richard. 1991. *It's Your Misfortune and None of My Own: A New History of the American West.* Norman, OK: University of Oklahoma.

Wilkinson, Charles F. 1992. *Crossing the Next Meridian: Land, Water, and the Future of the West.* Washington, D.C.: Island Press.

Wilson, James Q. 1997. *American Government: Brief Version.* 4th ed. Boston, MA: Houghton Mifflin.

Wilson, Woodrow. 1887. The study of administration. *Political Science Quarterly* 2 (2):197–222.

Wolf, Robert E. 1992. The concept of multiple use: the evolution of the idea within the Forest Service and the enactment of the Multiple-Use/Sustained-Yield Act of 1960. In *Forest Service Planning: Accommodating Uses, Producing Outputs, and Sustaining Ecosystems*, Vol. II: Contract Papers, 1–84. Washington, D.C.: Office of Technology Assessment.

Wolfe, Linnie Marsh. 1945. *Son of the Wilderness: The Life of John Muir.* Madison, WI: University of Wisconsin Press.

Wondolleck, Julia M. 1985. The importance of process in resolving environmental disputes. *Environmental Impact Assessment Review* 5:341–356.

Wondolleck, Julia M. 1988a. *Public Lands Conflict and Resolution: Managing National Forest Disputes.* New York: Plenum Press.

———. 1988b. Resolving forest management planning disputes: obstacles and opportunities. *Resolve* 20:1, 7–12.

Wood, Christopher A. 1994. Ecosystem management: achieving the new land ethic. *Renewable Resources Journal* 12 (1):6–12.

World Commission on Environment and Development. 1987. *Our Common Future.* New York, NY: Oxford University Press.

Worster, Donald. 1992. *Rivers of Empire: Water, Aridity, and the Growth of the American West.* New York, NY: Oxford University Press.

Wright, R. Michael. 1994. Recommendations. In *Natural Connections: Perspectives in Community-Based Conservation,* edited by David Western and R. Michael Wright, 524–535. Washington, D.C.: Island Press.

Yaffee, Steven Lewis. 1994. *The Wisdom of the Spotted Owl: Policy Lessons for a New Century.* Washington, D.C.: Island Press.

———. 1996. Ecosystem management in practice: the importance of human institutions. *Ecological Applications* 6 (3):724–727.

Yaffee, Steven L., Ali F. Phillips, Irene C. Frentz, Paul W. Hardy, Susanne M. Maleki, and Barbara E. Thorpe. 1996. *Ecosystem Management in the United States: An Assessment of Current Experience.* Washington, D.C.: Island Press.

Yaffee, Steven L., and Julia M. Wondolleck. 1997. Building bridges across agency boundaries. In *Creating a Forestry for the 21st Century,* edited by Kathryn A. Kohm and Jerry F. Franklin, 381–396. Washington, D.C.: Island Press.

Yankelovich, Daniel. 1991. *Coming to Public Judgment: Making Democracy Work in a Complex World.* Syracuse, NY: Syracuse University Press.

About the Authors

Hanna J. Cortner is a professor in the School of Renewable Natural Resources, the University of Arizona, Tucson, Arizona, where she teaches and does research in the area of natural resource policy and administration. She is also past director of the university's Water Resources Research Center. She graduated with a B.A. in political science from the University of Washington and a M.A. and Ph.D. in government from the University of Arizona. She has lived in the West all of her life, except for the times she held visiting appointments with the USDA Forest Service's Policy Analysis Staff in Washington, D.C. and the U.S. Army Corps of Engineers' Institute for Water Resources in Fort Belvoir, Virginia. In the mid-1980s, she also briefly worked as the executive assistant to an elected county official. She has written extensively in the areas of forest and water policy, and for the past several years has been examining the institutional–political aspects of ecosystems management.

Margaret A. (Ann) Moote is a senior research specialist at the Udall Center for Studies in Public Policy, University of Arizona, where she divides her time between academic research and facilitating community-based conservation efforts. Ann holds degrees in physical geography and renewable natural resource studies from McGill University and the University of Arizona, respectively. Her research interests include public participation in natural resource management, community-based conservation, environmental conflict resolution, and cooperative land management. She is author of the *Partnership Handbook*, an on-line resource and guidebook for community-based conservation groups, and coauthor of several articles on natural resource policy.

Index